THE ACCIDENTAL PRIME MINISTER

THE ACCIDENTAL PRIME MINISTER

THE MAKING AND UNMAKING OF
MANMOHAN SINGH

SANJAYA BARU

PENGUIN
VIKING

VIKING
Published by the Penguin Group
Penguin Books India Pvt. Ltd, 7th Floor, Infinity Tower C, DLF Cyber City,
Gurgaon 122 002, Haryana, India
Penguin Group (USA) Inc., 375 Hudson Street, New York, New York 10014, USA
Penguin Group (Canada), 90 Eglinton Avenue East, Suite 700, Toronto, Ontario,
M4P 2Y3, Canada (a division of Pearson Penguin Canada Inc.)
Penguin Books Ltd, 80 Strand, London WC2R 0RL, England
Penguin Ireland, 25 St Stephen's Green, Dublin 2, Ireland (a division of Penguin Books
Ltd)
Penguin Group (Australia), 707 Collins Street, Melbourne, Victoria 3008, Australia
(a division of Pearson Australia Group Pty Ltd)
Penguin Group (NZ), 67 Apollo Drive, Rosedale, Auckland 0632, New Zealand
(a division of Pearson New Zealand Ltd)
Penguin Group (South Africa) (Pty) Ltd, Block D, Rosebank Office Park, 181 Jan
Smuts Avenue, Parktown North, Johannesburg 2193, South Africa

Penguin Books Ltd, Registered Offices: 80 Strand, London WC2R 0RL, England

First published in Viking by Penguin Books India 2014

Copyright © Sanjaya Baru 2014

All rights reserved

10 9 8 7 6 5 4 3

The views and opinions expressed in this book are the author's own and the facts are
as reported by him which have been verifi ed to the extent possible, and the publishers
are not in any way liable for the same.

ISBN 9780670086740

Typeset in Bembo by R. Ajith Kumar, New Delhi
Printed at Replika Press Pvt. Ltd, India

In memory of my mentors
H.Y. Sharada Prasad
and
K. Subrahmanyam

Contents

Introduction

The Book I Chose to Write

None of my predecessors in the Prime Minister's Office (PMO) has ever written a full account of his time there. Editors, some far more distinguished than I, who served various prime ministers as media advisers, such as Kuldip Nayar, B.G. Verghese, Prem Shankar Jha and H.K. Dua, did not do so, nor did officials who performed those duties, such as G. Parthasarathy, Ram Mohan Rao and P.V.R.K. Prasad. Parts of Nayar's and Verghese's memoirs do, of course, cover that period of their careers, and Prasad has written a series of columns in the Telugu press on his tenure in South Block, but no one has devoted an entire book to his years at the PMO, reflecting on his boss's personality and policies.

This reticence is peculiar to India. In both the United States and Britain, several press secretaries to Presidents and prime ministers respectively, have written freely about their jobs and their bosses. In India, my most distinguished and longest-serving predecessor, H.Y. Sharada Prasad, set a very different tone. An unfailingly discreet and low-profile man, he was Indira Gandhi's information adviser, speech-writer and confidant for almost all her sixteen years as prime minister, yet had to be coaxed, over several years, before he agreed to write a few newspaper columns about his time at the PMO.

I first met the legendary Sharada Prasad in 1981 when he was at the height of his career, serving an all-powerful Indira Gandhi who had been re-elected prime minister in 1980 with a landslide vote after being rejected in the General Elections of 1977. I was visiting Delhi

a few weeks after my marriage and my wife, Rama, was keen that I
should meet family friend 'Shourie mama', as she had addressed him
since her childhood, and his wife, Kamalamma. I met Kamalamma
at their home near Delhi's verdant Lodi Gardens, but Sharada Prasad
himself was hard to meet, simply because he was never home. Finally,
we met in his office.

One could then still enter the PMO through its main gate facing
Rashtrapati Bhavan and walk up the grand staircase, instead of
entering, as visitors now do, by a modest and inelegant side entrance.
So I climbed those stairs, and met him in the same room that I would
come to occupy more than two decades later. It was four times larger
than the editor's room in the various newspaper offices in which I had
worked, and faced the imposing west wing of North Block, home of
the ministry of finance.

I spent a few minutes with Sharada Prasad, noting how humble
and low profile a man he appeared in this imperial setting. Since I
was, for him, Rama's husband and nothing more, the conversation,
naturally, centred around Rama and her parents. I was too overawed by
my surroundings to say much. I met him again only after I moved to
Delhi to join the *Economic Times* (*ET*) in 1990, when he came home
for our daughter's first birthday party. In 1993, after I moved from *ET*
to the *Times of India*, I invited him to write a column for the paper.
He declined, saying he did not feel like commenting on contemporary
issues. Undeterred, I asked him, repeatedly, to write about his time in
the PMO, but he always had the same cryptic reply: 'I do not know
everything that happened in the PMO. Not only do I not know all
sides of the truth, I do not even know how many sides the truth has.'

Finally, in the late 1990s, he began writing a column for the *Asian
Age* about his time with Indira Gandhi. He then put these columns
together into a collection titled *The Book That I Won't Be Writing and
Other Essays*. 'Putting it all down,' wrote Sharada Prasad, commenting
on why those once in power write memoirs, 'is a substitute for the
authority they once commanded by virtue of their position but now
miss.' He then went on to explain why he resisted this temptation.
'Suppose you have no urge to project yourself or play the justifier of

God's ways to man or man's ways to other men . . . Suppose you feel that what you know might not be the whole truth in the *Rashomon*-like ambivalence of events. Then you will come to the same conclusion as I have, and not write the book that friends expect.'

His words left their mark on me. I never planned to write a book about my eventful time in the PMO as Dr Manmohan Singh's media adviser from 2004 to 2008. That is why I never kept a diary, though I did make notes on key events during my tenure. Right up to the end of 2012, I was clear in my mind that I would not write a book about that phase in my life, despite being coaxed by friends in the media and pursued by friends in the publishing world.

Chiki Sarkar and Kamini Mahadevan of Penguin Books India made me change my mind. I yielded to their persuasions largely because of my own sense of profound sadness as I watched Manmohan Singh being unfairly treated as an object of public ridicule during his second term as prime minister. As I told *Caravan* magazine when it did a cover story on Dr Singh in 2011, it is natural for a political leader to be either admired or hated, but a politician should never become an object of ridicule. Dr Singh's descent was disturbingly steep. When I left the PMO in 2008, television news channels were serenading him with the popular refrain from a Hindi movie song, 'Singh is king'. Four years later, a newsmagazine punned on that very refrain to deliver a bleak verdict on the prime minister: 'Singh is Sin'king'.

He did not deserve this fate. He has many faults, and I have not hesitated to record them in this book. However, he remains not just a good man but, in the final analysis, also a good prime minister. This is especially true of his first term in office. He is, even at his worst, a cut above the competition, be it from within the ruling Congress party, or would-be prime ministers in other parties. No Congress leader—and I include here the party's leader Sonia Gandhi and its 'heir apparent' Rahul Gandhi—can match his unique combination of personal integrity, administrative experience, international stature and political appeal across a wide swathe of public opinion. These qualities were strikingly evident during the first term of the Congress-led United Progressive Alliance, from 2004 to 2009 (UPA-1), with Dr Singh at its helm. However, as bad news, largely a series of financial scandals, tumbled out of the UPA's second term from 2009 (UPA-2), and the media became hostile, his many talents began to recede from public view. Sadly, his own office became ineffective and lost control over the political narrative.

As Dr Singh's public image plummeted, the fallout was hard to contain. Finance Minister Pranab Mukherjee, later to become President of India, put it pithily to me in 2011, when I ran into him in the corridors of Parliament and he invited me into his room for tea. 'As long as the prime minister's image is good,' he said to me, 'so, too, the image of the government and the country. When the image of the PM suffers, the government's image, and the country's, also suffers.'

As Dr Singh battled a series of political problems during UPA-2, I, on account of having worked closely with him in the past, found myself being questioned by journalists, politicians, diplomats, business leaders, friends and complete strangers in airport lounges. Why, I was asked, was UPA-1 more successful than UPA-2? Why had the PM's image taken such a beating? What is the nature of the relationship between the Congress party president, Sonia Gandhi, and Manmohan Singh, the man she anointed as prime minister in 2004? What do you think his legacy will be? Why did you quit the PMO?

This book does not bother to address the last question. My reasons for quitting the PMO in August 2008 were mainly personal. Dr Singh, my family and close friends were well aware of them, and I did not see why I owed anyone else an explanation. When asked for one, my stock response has always been to quote M.S. Swaminathan, the agricultural scientist. Swaminathan recounted to me that he told Prime Minister Indira Gandhi, when she asked him why he wanted to quit as her adviser after doing such good work, 'Madam, it is best to leave when everyone asks you *why* rather than *when!*'

This book does, however, try to address the other four questions based on my knowledge of events and personalities from my time in the PMO in UPA-1. I have not ventured to speculate on UPA-2 beyond my limited knowledge of what happened during Dr Singh's second term in office. I will argue, in the coming chapters, that the Manmohan

Singh of UPA-1 was not the 'puppet PM' that he came to be seen as in UPA-2. He was certainly an 'accidental prime minister', as he readily confessed, to all and sundry, but that did not prevent him from occupying the country's most important chair with both dignity and great competence. With regard to the relationship between Manmohan Singh and Sonia Gandhi, I do not claim deep knowledge of how the two dealt with each other in closed-door meetings; my account is based only on what I saw and came to reliably know. However, I hope this book will help readers understand, at least in part, the complex relationship between the PM and the party president. After all, the complexity of this relationship lies at the root of both Dr Singh's success, and failure, as prime minister. His ability to manage this relationship better than any other Congress party politician has done, or could have done, laid the foundation for his two terms in office. He is the only Indian prime minister not from the Nehru–Gandhi family to have served this long. On the other hand, the public perception that he accomplished this feat through unquestioning submissiveness lies at the heart of the image problem that has come to haunt Dr Singh.

Questions about Dr Singh's legacy are often asked by people who take a short-term view of his image and record. As Dr Singh himself said at his national press conference in January 2014, history will no doubt be kinder to him than contemporary commentators have been. When the story of his life and achievements is fully told, he will be judged more fairly than now. His journey from a modest home in the dusty, desolate village of Gah, lacking both electricity and water supply, to the high tables at Cambridge and Oxford, his academic achievements and his record of public and national service, make for a truly uplifting story.

I once said to him that his life story was comparable to Barack Obama's and his professional achievements greater than Obama's. Obama made history by becoming America's first black President. Dr Singh, too, made history by becoming India's first prime minister from a minority community. Before he became the PM, he had held every important position in economic policymaking in India. Obama had scored, however, in securing a popular mandate for his rule that

Dr Singh never chose to secure for himself. That made all the difference to how their individual achievements were perceived by their own peoples.

Dr Singh, too, could have secured that popular mandate, in 2009. There is no doubt he was the architect of the UPA's electoral victory that year. Alas, he chose not to use the confidence and trust reposed in him by the people of India to assert himself within the Congress party and take control of his prime ministership. That unfortunate decision proved to be the fatal flaw that weakened his authority in UPA-2. In UPA-1 he was 'in office' and exercised some authority but he was not 'in power'. In UPA-2 he could have been in power as well.

All told, Dr Singh had a powerful story to tell about his achievements as prime minister, but he invariably shied away from telling it. He held me back when I sought to project him during my time as his media adviser, saying, 'I want my work to speak for me.' Perhaps Dr Singh was nervous about projecting himself because he thought that was the undoing of P.V. Narasimha Rao, the prime minister who, in 1991, brought Dr Singh into politics by making him his finance minister. Rao, whom Dr Singh described, in a heartfelt tribute at the time of his death in 2004, as his 'mentor' and the man from whom he had learnt whatever he knew about politics, came to be viewed with hostility by the Gandhi family and those close to it, and has been relegated to an insignificant place in the party's official memory.

Despite Dr Singh's discouragement, I did publicize his work and project his personality. Indeed, I saw it as an integral part of my job. In the process, I often burnt my fingers, as the reader will learn, earning the ire of Gandhi family loyalists who treated any effort to promote the prime minister as an affront to the family.

This book does not claim to be an exhaustive account of all that happened during UPA-1. What it does offer is a sense of what it was like to be at the heart of the hopeful and heady enterprise that was UPA-1 as the PM's 'eyes and ears,' and as a loyalist who wanted him to succeed. I have combined personal, admittedly subjective, accounts of what I regard as important events with an analysis, hopefully objective, of policies and issues. While the notes I kept have come in handy, much of what I have written is based on memory, refurbished by the newspaper archives I used to get my dates and facts right. I have also spoken to a few key players of that period—who will remain anonymous—to refresh my memory and I thank them for their time. All the quotations in the book are substantially correct but some may not be verbatim.

During my time at the PMO, I rarely had the occasion, or indeed the need, to look at government files, much less confidential files. Rather than seek access to files, I demanded access to the PM, to hear his views directly on any given issue. During my initial weeks in the PMO, its bureaucrats tried to restrict my access to the PM, but Dr Singh intervened and ensured his doors were always open to me. I was able to put to good use a *Los Angeles Times* obituary to Pierre Salinger, a distinguished American journalist and press secretary to US President John Kennedy, that my research officer, Vijay Kumar, downloaded for me in October 2004. Salinger, it seems, confronted similar problems of access to information in the White House that my immediate staff knew I was facing at that time in the PMO. The obituary quoted him as having told Kennedy, 'A press secretary has to be involved in the inner discussions so he knows what can be said and what cannot be said to the public.'

When I put this argument to Dr Singh, he accepted its logic, as Kennedy had done in his time, and gave me unrestricted access to himself, at work and at home. I would not, however, be allowed to sit in on Cabinet meetings or the weekly meeting of the Congress core group. Even so, I was undoubtedly privileged in the level of access I enjoyed to the prime minister.

Direct contact with Dr Singh helped me do my job efficiently since it enabled me to feed a hungry media something or the other all the time. It also gave me invaluable insight both into the PM's thinking and into the kind of advice he was getting. On the flip side, free access to the PM also placed an enormous responsibility on me since I was often required to sift the information I got and decide what I would send out as statements to the media, what I would spin as stories for journalists, and what I had to keep to myself. I would consult colleagues, especially the prime minister's private secretaries, who had a good idea of what should and should not be shared with the media.

While giving me the freedom to use my discretion in deciding what to tell the media, Dr Singh did, from time to time, tell me to keep some matters strictly confidential. Sometimes, he would explicitly instruct me to not share a piece of information with others, even in the PMO. On occasion, Dr Singh would also ask me to meet people on his behalf, and carry messages to them, or draft confidential letters for him, and, on each such occasion, instruct me to not mention this to anyone. I have respected that understanding to this day. This book does not contain any material that I promised Dr Singh I would not share with anyone else. Moreover, nothing mentioned here contravenes the provisions of the Official Secrets Act, since I have avoided any reference to official information that was made available to me in the discharge of my duties. For these reasons, the book will have some information gaps, especially in the chapters dealing with policy.

Finally, I have not shared the contents of this book with Dr Singh prior to its publication. Indeed, he may not approve of many of my observations in these pages and may even disapprove of my decision to write this book. That places on me even greater responsibility to ensure that this book is an honest account of my time with the PM, offering my view of what I saw and believed had happened. Never forgetting Sharada Prasad's caution that those once in government and now retired 'know that things did not always go right even in their heyday, but they want us to believe they would have, if only their counsel had been accepted by the political masters', I have consciously tried to purge myself of pride or prejudice while telling a story that I believe needs to be told.

1

The Call from PMO

'Call the doctor!'

Financial Express editorial
19 May 2004

It was approaching midnight on an early May night in 2004. J.N. Dixit and I were in the studios of the BBC on the top floor of the AIFACS building on Rafi Marg in New Delhi, discussing how the result of the General Elections, now in its final stages, would impact Indian foreign and economic policy. The election campaign had come alive in its last stages, after having begun with the widespread assumption that the National Democratic Alliance (NDA) government, led by Prime Minister Atal Bihari Vajpayee, would be returned to office. Vajpayee had advanced the election dates by six months in the hope of riding a wave of optimism about India's economic prospects captured by the 'India Shining' campaign mounted by his Bharatiya Janata Party (BJP), the leading party in the alliance. However, reports of suicides by cotton farmers in Andhra Pradesh and Maharashtra had tarnished the NDA's image and it now appeared that its battle with the principal Opposition party, the Indian National Congress, would be closely fought.

Dixit, known by the nickname Mani, was a former foreign secretary, and an outstanding one at that. After his retirement, he had joined the Congress party and guided party president Sonia Gandhi through the foreign policy debates of the early years of the new millennium. Until Mani Dixit joined her, Sonia Gandhi's principal adviser on foreign policy had been K. Natwar Singh, a diplomat who had worked closely with Indira Gandhi and then joined the Congress party. Natwar was a quintessential Nehruvian and his thinking was shaped by the Cold War and India's policy of non-alignment. Mani Dixit's views, on the other hand, were shaped by the end of the Cold War and India's increased engagement with developed economies. As foreign secretary during the Congress government headed by Narasimha Rao in the early 1990s, he had crafted India's response to the end of the Cold War and the collapse of its ally, the Soviet Union, authoring radical departures such as Rao's 'Look East Policy' and his openings to South Korea and Israel.

In 2003 Mani Dixit had been authorized by Sonia Gandhi to draft an alternative view on foreign and national security policy and had put together a discussion group that included, among others, Manmohan Singh, then leader of the Congress party in the Rajya Sabha, the Upper House of Parliament, N.N.Vohra, a retired defence secretary, K. Subrahmanyam, who was until his death in 2011 India's leading thinker on strategic affairs, and myself. I was then chief editor of the *Financial Express* (*FE*). We would meet in the private dining room of the India International Centre, the club favoured by Delhi's policy elite.

Since Mani had been given this new political task, I assumed he would play an important role if the Congress came to power in Delhi. I was therefore surprised to hear him ask the anchor at the BBC studio that night to wind up the discussion since he had to leave Delhi in the morning to spend the summer in the hills. The elections would soon be over and some expected the Congress party to form a government. Would you not prefer to remain in Delhi and see if they need you in the new government, I asked Mani curiously.

He laughed the question off. He pointed out that even if the Congress did come to power, Natwar Singh would be in the government, not him, and went on to ask, 'You think we will win?' I echoed the popular view around Delhi that the result would be narrow but Prime Minister Vajpayee was likely to return to office. He agreed with me.

As we walked out of the studio I said to him cheerily, 'You go to the hills, I am off to DC.'

Neither of us could have imagined on that May night that within a month we would be colleagues in the PMO.

It became clear, just a day later, that Sonia Gandhi had got enough seats to form a new coalition government led by the Congress party. Shortly before I flew to Washington DC to speak at a conference organized by the historian Sunil Khilnani, I typed out an editorial comment that appeared on 15 May with the title 'Thoughts on a Government'. It was typical of the editorials that editors like to write, advising politicians what they should do. My advice to the victorious Congress President Sonia Gandhi was simple—'. . . invite Dr Manmohan Singh to take charge as the Prime Minister' and make herself 'the chairperson of the Congress and allies coordination committee that would oversee the functioning of the government'.

My suggestion that Dr Singh be made PM was not a new idea. I had floated it five years earlier, almost to the date, on 25 May 1999, in a column in the *Times of India*. This was shortly after Sonia Gandhi's failed attempt to form a Congress-led coalition government after the fall of a BJP-led government. She had famously and, as it turned out, erroneously announced, 'We have 272 (MPs), and we hope to get more.' Provocatively titled 'Perils of Sonia Gandhi as PM', my column advised Sonia to resist the temptation of claiming the job and, instead, name Manmohan Singh as PM, were Congress to form a government.

Reading my 2004 editorial, journalist friends who had scoffed at me in 1999 for coming up with a wild idea were amused that I had not given up my 'campaign', as some saw it, to make Manmohan Singh prime minister. I was, however, looking at the issue from Sonia's point of view. She needed to bury the controversy over her Italian birth and retain control of the Congress party till her son or daughter was old enough to take charge. She required, therefore, a reliable, trustworthy and capable head of government. A political leader would always nurse political ambitions and perhaps seek to marginalize the Gandhi family. Hadn't Narasimha Rao, low profile though he was before he became PM, tried to strike out on his own once he assumed office? By this argument, senior Congress leaders and possible prime ministerial aspirants like Arjun Singh and Pranab Mukherjee were pretty much ruled out. Among the safer choices, few had the experience for the job. A.K. Antony, a Congress leader from Kerala whom Sonia Gandhi reportedly liked, did not, for example. So, I surmised, Dr Singh stood the best chance.

On the day I arrived in DC, 15 May, news reports suggested that Sonia Gandhi was in two minds on whether or not to head the government that was now likely to be formed. Sycophantic as ever, the rank and file of the party demanded that she become prime minister. On the other hand, BJP leader Sushma Swaraj, who had campaigned vociferously against an Italian-origin prime minister, was dramatically threatening to shave her head if Sonia did so.

Over the next two days, the subject of government formation in India dominated coffee- and lunch-break conversations at the conference I was attending. On 18 May, the last day of the conference, I shared the dais with Khilnani and Montek Singh Ahluwalia, an economist who had worked with Rajiv Gandhi and had been secretary in the finance ministry when Dr Singh was finance minister, and was now with the International Monetary Fund (IMF) in Washington DC.

Montek spoke first. Shortly after he began speaking, I received an SMS message on my mobile phone from my colleague Rohit Bansal, resident editor of the Delhi edition of the *Financial Express*. It announced, 'Sonia says she will not be PM!' I thought to myself: Step one, she will not be PM. Step two, she will make Dr Singh the PM.

When my turn came, I gave my audience the breaking news. I then said mischievously that if Sonia named Manmohan Singh as PM, they may have just heard the future principal secretary to the Indian prime minister speak. I was referring, of course, to Montek. Not surprisingly, Montek was mobbed as soon as the session got over. Later that day, Sonia announced that Dr Singh would head a coalition government. The next day, I met Montek and his economist wife, Isher, for lunch at the IMF headquarters. They were excited about the news from Delhi. All we talked about over lunch was what a Manmohan Singh prime ministership would mean for the country.

While Isher had been Dr Singh's student at the Delhi School of Economics, Montek's association with Dr Singh dated back to the late 1970s when he returned to India after a stint at the World Bank to join the ministry of finance as an economic adviser. Dr Singh was at the time a secretary in the ministry of finance and had encouraged Montek to join the government. The two worked together again in 1992–96 when Dr Singh, by then finance minister in the Rao government, re-inducted Montek into the ministry. None of us spoke about what role Montek expected to play—it was too early to engage in that kind of speculation. I did ask, though, if he had spoken to Dr Singh and he said he had called and wished him.

As we ordered dessert, I asked Montek if he would quit his IMF job and move to India. 'Of course!' Isher replied for him, instantly.

———

I returned home just in time for the new government's swearing-in ceremony at Rashtrapati Bhavan. It was the first I had witnessed. Dr Singh appeared nervous and hesitant as he took his oath of office. There was a celebratory air about the place with Congress party leaders present in strength, happy as they were returning to power after six years. Few had, in fact, expected to win the elections and many had been sceptical about the Congress's ability to stitch together a coalition. Dr Singh's family, including his daughters and grandchildren, were present but kept a low profile. As soon as the ceremony ended, I tried to walk up to Dr Singh and congratulate him but, unsurprisingly, he was surrounded by an eager throng of Congress party leaders, among them ministers clearly seeking good portfolios (they had not yet been allocated), and journalists. I managed to make eye contact and greet him with folded hands. He smiled.

Moving away from the crowd milling around the new PM, I wandered around the hall, looking for news. Soon enough, I ran into Prithviraj Chavan, a Congress party politician from Maharashtra whom I had known for close to a decade. We were both regulars at the weekly lunch discussion group, the Saturday Group, at the India International

Centre. Prithvi had just been sworn in as minister of state (MoS) and
I asked if he knew what his new portfolio would be. Looking very
pleased with himself, he told me that the PM had confided in him
that he would be MoS finance. That was front-page news. So who,
I quickly followed up, would be the new finance minister? Prithvi
leaned closer to almost whisper into my ear, 'PM will retain finance.'
I had my headline.

I sat up late into the night waiting for portfolios to be announced
but by the time we went to press there was no official word. Finally,
we ran the news that Dr Singh would retain the finance portfolio and
that Chavan would be named MoS finance.

The morning our story appeared, I had a call from P. Chidambaram,
a senior Congress party leader who had served as finance minister in
a short-lived coalition government formed in 1996. At that time, he
had belonged to a party that had broken away from the Congress, and
had returned to its fold shortly before the 2004 elections. Some years
earlier he became a weekly columnist in my newspaper and remained
one till he returned to government in May 2004.

'Is your report accurate?' he asked me. I assured him that I had heard
it 'from the horse's mouth'.

'You mean the PM?' he asked at once. No, the MoS, I said. 'If the PM
keeps finance, what will they give me?' Chidambaram wondered aloud.

I was amused and surprised to hear that question from the usually self-
confident Chidambaram. There was already speculation in the media
that he would be given charge of commerce or telecommunications,
and I mentioned that to him.

He retorted angrily, 'Mr Editor, I have been finance minister before!
Do you think I will accept anything less than a senior Cabinet position?'

The finance minister sits, along with the PM, the external affairs,
defence and home ministers, on Raisina Hill. These are the leading
occupants of Delhi's North and South Blocks. They are all members
of the Cabinet Committee on Security (CCS), a body that has seen its
clout grow in an era of national security and nuclear power.

So I asked Chidambaram what he would do if he was not on the Hill.

'I will sit in the backbenches!' he declared.

'Good,' I told him, pulling his leg, 'you can then continue your weekly column with *FE*.'

By the time the portfolios were announced that evening, the sands had shifted. Chidambaram was named finance minister. Prithviraj was named MoS in the PMO. I called Prithvi to find out what happened. He told me that the PM had been advised against keeping finance, a heavy portfolio, since his hands would be full managing the government and the coalition. But Prithvi was far from disappointed. Instead of MoS finance under Dr Singh, he was now MoS in the PMO. He had entered the government's sanctum sanctorum.

While Prithvi clearly owed his portfolio, if not his ministerial berth, to Dr Singh, this was not the case with most of the new council of ministers. The Congress's allies in UPA-1 nominated their own ministers and bargained for their portfolios with Sonia, not with Dr Singh. The bargaining process reflected the political reality on the ground. No matter how prominent a political leader was, he was not likely to get the portfolio he or his supporters wished for, if his party did not have the numbers in the Lok Sabha, the Lower House of Parliament. Thus Sharad Pawar, who had been defence minister in Narasimha Rao's Cabinet, could not climb Raisina Hill. Since his party, the Nationalist Congress Party (NCP), had only nine seats in the new Parliament, he had to be content with agriculture. On the other hand, Dravida Munnetra Kazhagam (DMK), a political party that won all the sixteen seats it had contested in Tamil Nadu, made sure it got key economic ministries with, to use a popular phrase, 'rent-seeking' opportunities.

As for senior Congress leaders, they owed their Cabinet posts almost entirely to Sonia Gandhi, who did, however, consult Dr Singh and close aides before finalizing the names. When the council of ministers was reshuffled during the term of UPA-I, Dr Singh did have more of a say but even so, few of its members ever behaved as if they owed their ministerial positions to the PM. With time, even the loyalties of Prithviraj Chavan, handpicked by Dr Singh to serve in his own office, became divided as he made sure he was on the right side of his party's leader. Prithvi was Dr Singh's protégé but he knew that his political career depended on demonstrating loyalty to Sonia and Rahul.

Dr Singh, far more politically astute than his detractors believed him to be, would have been well aware of the limits to prime ministerial authority under such a dispensation. Prime ministers in earlier coalitions had also had to share their power to nominate ministers with leaders of coalition parties. While his predecessor Atal Bihari Vajpayee had been able to assert himself quite strongly in the NDA coalition, partly because of his standing as a popular leader of his own party, Dr Singh took his cue from the more circumscribed role that H.D. Deve Gowda and I.K. Gujral enjoyed as heads of the United Front coalition in the mid-1990s. He was also, perhaps, more accepting than another prime minister might have been of his limited power over his own partymen because he saw himself as an 'accidental prime minister', by which he meant that he was not the natural choice for the job. After all, had Sonia Gandhi not been born an Italian she would have kept the job for herself. The fact of her alien status had made it necessary for her to choose another leader and Dr Singh was the man she chose.

Manmohan Singh had not expected to become PM. At best, it can be said that he had hoped this opportunity might one day come his way. People have often asked me whether I thought Dr Singh was ambitious. My sense is that 'ambition' is too strong a word to describe how he felt about his destiny. I would rather say he had faith in his own abilities, and all the pride, albeit never openly expressed, of a self-made man. Even while he modestly called himself an 'accidental prime minister' he did not doubt that he could do the job, and do it better than the other senior leaders around Sonia.

He had, over the previous eight years, made clear his commitment to active politics. A technocrat when Narasimha Rao inducted him into his government in 1991, he did not return to that predictable world after Rao was defeated at the hustings in 1996 and later abandoned by the Congress party. Dr Singh remained a party loyalist and as leader of the Opposition in the Rajya Sabha participated actively in the party's political programmes. He came to play the role of a 'second in command' even if he was not explicitly named as such. When Sonia failed to garner enough support to form a coalition government under her own leadership in 1999 and Dr Singh was asked to contest a Lok

Sabha elections a few months later, he may have seen this as a signal that he was being groomed for a larger political role. Even though he lost that election, he did emerge as Sonia's right-hand man in the years between 1999 and 2004. It was Manmohan Singh, not Arjun Singh or Pranab Mukherjee, who was by her side when she met foreign heads of government. Therefore, while he neither planned nor schemed to become prime minister, Dr Singh was not taken by complete surprise when he got the job.

This was, however, the first time ever that the Congress party would be running a coalition government in Delhi. The tough task of managing a fourteen-party coalition was made trickier by the fact that the Congress was to be in office with the support, from the 'outside', of the Left Front, a group of Left parties that had been unwavering critics of Dr Singh's policies as finance minister. Some in the Left were prepared to join the government. It was rumoured that Sitaram Yechury, a member of the politburo of the Communist Party of India-Marxist [CPI(M)], a leading constituent of the Left Front, had even voiced the hope of becoming minister for railways in a Left-supported and Congress-led coalition. Another member of the front, the Communist Party of India (CPI), was willing to join the government. After all, the CPI had been a part of coalition governments at the Centre in the past, namely those led by H.D. Deve Gowda and I.K. Gujral in the 1990s, and the party's senior leader Indrajit Gupta had even served as India's first communist home minister. However, the leadership of the CPI(M) vetoed the idea of the Left joining the government.

On 24 May, the new ministers took charge of their ministries. The formation and agenda of the new government was front-page news every day. One morning, the media reported that a little-known civil servant, T.K.A. Nair, a member of the Indian Administrative Service (IAS), belonging to the Punjab cadre, had been named to the most important administrative post in the PMO, that of principal secretary to the PM.

This surprised me. I had thought the job was Montek's. But, knowing the relationship between Montek and Dr Singh, I assumed a bigger job was in the works for him, should he return from Washington.

That weekend I took a week's holiday and flew to Hyderabad with my daughter, Tanvika, to celebrate my fiftieth birthday with my parents. My wife, Rama, had gone to Canada to take up a research fellowship. On Friday, 28 May, the day I turned fifty, we were in the dining room of my parents' home when my mobile phone rang.

'Is it Mr Sanjay Baru?' asked an unmistakably sarkari voice from Delhi. 'Principal secretary to PM, Mr Nair, will speak to you.'

Nair came on the line and introduced himself. 'Mr Baru, we have never met. I am principal secretary to the PM. The PM would like to meet you. Can you come this evening?'

I informed him that I was in Hyderabad and would only return after the weekend. He said he would get back to me and called a few minutes later to schedule an appointment for Monday morning.

That evening, when I was at a family party, I received another call from Delhi. The caller was N.N. Vohra, a distinguished former civil servant who had served as home and defence secretary and had been Prime Minister Inder Gujral's principal secretary. I got to know Vohra intimately when he was director of the India International Centre in the late 1990s and I was the convenor of the centre's economic affairs group. We had also both been members of the National Security Advisory Board (NSAB) from 1998 to 2001, and had, moreover, travelled together to many foreign capitals, notably Tokyo, as part of a delegation sent by the Vajpayee government to persuade Japan to end the economic sanctions imposed on India after the nuclear tests. Vohra had regaled us with jokes and humorous anecdotes from his varied career in the civil and intelligence services. During long walks in Tokyo, we discovered we had similar views on many issues and despite the several years that separated us, became good friends. Our most recent association had been as members of Mani Dixit's foreign policy group.

'Sanjaya,' said Vohra, 'you are meeting the PM on Monday? He will ask you to join his office. He asked me what I thought of you. I told him you were a good fellow!'

Vohra laughed in his characteristic nasal tone. 'He said he was planning to appoint you as his information adviser. I told him he had made a wise choice.'

I thanked Vohra for his vote of confidence and returned to join the partying, feeling my excitement rising at what lay ahead. My professional life had been full of twists and turns. At the age of thirty-six, I had given up the staid world of a university campus in Hyderabad where I had taught economics, and entered the rough and tumble of journalism at a time of sweeping economic and political change in India and the world. Later, I had also ventured into the esoteric field of strategic policy as a member of India's NSAB. Now, I would be making yet another turn and, to tell the truth, I was ready for it. Working in a PMO headed by Manmohan Singh, whom I had come to respect as a professional and a human being, was an opportunity not to be missed. However, while I discreetly shared Vohra's news with my parents, I did not mention it to anyone else. That day, I was more than happy to celebrate turning fifty with family and friends for whom Delhi was a distant durbar.

2

Getting to Know Dr Singh

'Sometimes in life it is wise to be foolish.'

Raul Prebisch to Manmohan Singh, 1969

I first met Manmohan Singh in early 1991 at his office in the University Grants Commission (UGC), across the road from my own office at Times House, on New Delhi's Bahadur Shah Zafar Marg. The *Economic Times*, where I was then associate editor, was to celebrate its thirtieth anniversary in March 1991. I was put in charge of producing a special supplement for the occasion. We decided that it would carry interviews with economists who had shaped policy during those thirty years. We picked K.N. Raj, the doyen of the Delhi School of Economics, consulted by both Jawaharlal Nehru and Indira Gandhi; P.R. Brahmananda, who created a rival group dubbed the Bombay School of Economics; and Manmohan Singh, a disciple of Raj at the Delhi School, but one who had served the Indian government in important policymaking capacities for two-thirds of the period that was our focus.

His career had been brilliant by any reckoning. After studying economics at Punjab University, Manmohan Singh went on to secure an honours degree in economics from Cambridge University, followed a few years later by a doctoral degree from Oxford University. He then taught economics at his alma mater, Punjab University. Sometime in the early 1960s, his neighbour in Amritsar, the writer Mulk Raj Anand, took him to Delhi and introduced him to Nehru, who invited the talented young economist to join his government. Dr Singh could not do so at the time, since he was serving out a contract with his college, which had funded his studies abroad.

In 1966, Dr Singh, who had written his doctoral thesis on India's export trends and prospects, joined the United Nations Conference on Trade and Development (UNCTAD) in Geneva. However, three years later, India beckoned and Dr Singh came home to join the faculty of the Delhi School of Economics at K.N. Raj's invitation. The Delhi School had acquired global prominence under Raj, and Dr Singh became part of an enormously talented faculty that included Amartya Sen, Jagdish Bhagwati and Sukhamoy Chakravarti. Taken aback by his promising colleague's decision, the head of UNCTAD, Raul Prebisch, advised Manmohan Singh to stay back and not return home. Manmohan explained to Prebisch that the Delhi School appointment was a prestigious one and that he would not like to turn down an invitation from Professor Raj.

'You are being foolish,' Prebisch admonished Manmohan, but then added thoughtfully, 'Sometimes in life it is wise to be foolish.'

It was a line I heard Dr Singh repeat many years later in his modest office in the prime minister's official residence on New Delhi's Race Course Road, a small room that could accommodate just a table and two chairs but overlooked a lovely lawn where peacocks strutted around. Faced with a veritable avalanche of advice urging him to drop the idea of pursuing the civil nuclear energy cooperation agreement with the United States, including from many of his closest aides—advice that he did not finally take—Dr Singh said to me with a smile, 'It is time, again, to be foolish.'

However, at our first meeting that afternoon in February 1991, I had no sense of what, if anything, was remarkable about Manmohan Singh. I was in awe of K.N. Raj, who had been my teacher, and I saw Dr Singh as just another student of his who had spent most of his life in the government. True, he had held a series of important positions, including chief economic adviser to the Government of India, economic affairs secretary in the Union finance ministry, governor of the Reserve Bank of India, deputy chairman of the Planning Commission and secretary general of the South Commission, and had just demitted office as an adviser to Prime Minister Chandra Shekhar. But I was not brought up to be overawed by authority.

I was also less than reverential because the world in which I grew up overlapped with his. Both my father, whose term as finance and planning secretary of Andhra Pradesh coincided with Dr Singh's stint as secretary in the ministry of finance in Delhi, and my father-in-law, who had been in the Planning Commission, knew Dr Singh well. Indeed, my father and Dr Singh had several close friends in common, most importantly, K.N. Raj, the economist; Amrik Singh, the educationist; and Mohit Sen, the communist.

When I walked across Bahadur Shah Zafar Marg and into the UGC office that day, I expected to meet an officious and self-important bureaucrat, another VIP belonging to the Delhi 'durbar'. However, the first thing that struck me when I came face-to-face with Manmohan Singh was his gentle politeness. He greeted me warmly, got up from his chair and suggested we sit on a sofa, and offered me a cup of tea. I switched on my tape recorder and began asking my questions. A few minutes into the interview, the tape recorder stopped working. Feeling a little rattled, I tried shaking it, took the batteries out and put them back in, but nothing helped. Dr Singh was patient, but gently warned me that he had a meeting to go to and was travelling over the next few days. He suggested we try finishing the interview.

While I was contemplating writing down his answers in longhand, it occurred to me that it would take very little time to summon Mr Anand, the stenotypist from *ET*, who duly arrived and wrote down Dr Singh's replies in shorthand. At the end of the interview, Dr Singh suggested I show him the typed draft before it went into print. Since Dr Singh was travelling, I managed to show him a draft only a week later. This he promptly returned with several changes made with a ballpoint pen, in a handwriting that was neat, legible and compact. Requesting Mr Anand to incorporate his changes and forward the file to my colleague who was handling the production of the special pages, I left Delhi on work.

Early in the morning of 5 March the *ET* special edition arrived at my doorstep. But even before I could open it, the phone rang. It was Manmohan Singh on the line. His tone was even, but his displeasure was sharply evident. 'You did not make all the corrections I asked you to,' he said. 'I had added an entire paragraph that I do not find published. It was an important point I was making. This is highly irresponsible. I didn't expect you to be so careless.'

He put the phone down even as I kept saying, 'Sorry, Sir, I haven't seen the paper yet.'

That was the first of the two admonishments I have received from Dr Singh. The second was to come sixteen long years later, when he chastised me for crediting him with an important decision that the Congress party was eager to claim was Rahul Gandhi's idea.

The mistake turned out to be the kind of embarrassing mix-up that does occasionally happen in newspapers. While Mr Anand had done his job properly, the person making the page had accidentally downloaded and placed on the page, the earlier, uncorrected version of the interview. I was curious, now, to discover the contents of that additional paragraph that Dr Singh had scribbled on to the draft, and had been so upset to find missing in the printed version. It turned out to be about his recent visit to South Korea and the important lessons India ought to learn from South Korea's model of development. He had pointed out that South Korea had invested in education and had an open economy, and India ought to do the same.

It was only years later that I fully understood why Dr Singh had been so upset at this omission. He was signalling the relevance of his own views, views that he had articulated decades ago in his doctoral thesis, on the importance of foreign trade and greater openness to the world economy in India's own development. No Indian policymaker had till then held South Korea up as a role model. In fact, in the mid-1980s, Professor Raj had had a high-profile spat with Bela Balassa, the Hungarian economist at the World Bank, in which he disparaged the so-called lessons to be learnt from the East Asian growth experience which Balassa was advocating. Indian-trained economists like myself were taught to pooh-pooh the relevance of the Korean experience for India on the grounds that the strategies followed by small-sized economies that had tied their fortunes to American power were not relevant for a large, independent nation like India. In February 1991, weeks before he was unexpectedly summoned to become India's finance minister, Dr Singh was once again drawing attention to his own views about trade and development.

Indeed, Dr Singh was always more open-minded than his critics have painted him to be. Contrary to the mischievous remarks of some of them that he had been converted to economic liberalization after becoming finance minister, the fact is that he had always been an advocate of trade liberalization and a critic of export pessimism. (This is the now-discredited theory that India had little to supply to the world economy and therefore ought to reduce its demands on it.) As he told me in this March 1991 interview:

> I was a critic of the export pessimism of the fifties, although I must say that there was some change in thinking after the foreign exchange crisis in 1957. If you recall, it was the Second Plan which made the assumption relating to exports not being an option. At the time, textiles and engineering goods were the leading industries and we must remember that in 1945 India was a leading textiles exporter. But we lost ground because we failed to modernize.
>
> On the other hand, countries like South Korea which came to the field only in the fifties were able to modernize and emerge as leading textiles exporters. We missed the sixties boom in trade because we believed that there was no scope for labour-intensive techniques in the world market. We failed to recognize the scope for technological change and to evolve a trade policy suited to that purpose. There is inadequate recognition in our country that on a per capita basis, India is not well endowed with natural resources and that we have to be a major trading nation to fill this gap.

Clearly, Dr Singh wanted, through these comments and those accidentally omitted from the published interview, to bring his views to bear on the ongoing debate in India at the time on issues like trade liberalization and industrial policy. In fact, he had been moved out of the PMO where he had been an adviser to Prime Minister Chandra Shekhar, because the PM's more left-wing advisers were unhappy with the kind of policy advice that Dr Singh was offering the PM. Sitting in the UGC, he was now keen on giving a clearer public expression to these views. And I had botched it!

That was the last I heard from Dr Singh till June 1991, when he became India's finance minister. Narasimha Rao took charge as the Congress party leader after Rajiv Gandhi's assassination in May 1991, in the midst of an election and a balance of payments crisis. He needed a finance minister who enjoyed international credibility and could negotiate a loan with the IMF. Rao's first choice was I.G. Patel, a former secretary in the ministry of finance who had just returned to India after a stint as director of the London School of Economics. A critic of many of Indira Gandhi's policies, Patel had called for a 'bonfire of controls' in an influential essay written in the 1980s. However, Patel chose not to return to public office and went into retirement in his home town, Vadodara. Dr Singh's name was then suggested to Narasimha Rao by P.C. Alexander, who had been principal secretary to Prime Minister Rajiv Gandhi. Alexander had called Dr Singh and informed him that he was to become the finance minister. However, Dr Singh either did not take the offer seriously or wanted to hear it directly from the PM. So he just stayed at home until he was summoned by Narasimha Rao at short notice to the swearing-in ceremony at Rashtrapati Bhavan.

On the day Dr Singh assumed charge, I called his home and left a message congratulating him. That night the phone rang just as I had finished dinner. 'Sanjaya, this is Manmohan,' the new finance minister said. 'I received your good wishes. Thank you. We will meet after I have settled down.' I was relieved that he had either forgotten the *ET* special-edition fiasco or was now ready to forgive me for that lapse. It clearly helped that a finance minister handling a crisis needed to be on good terms with an economic journalist.

For six months after that I enjoyed a cordial equation with him. Those were exciting and heady days for an economic journalist in India. It all began with the two-step rupee devaluation on 1 July and

3 July, dubbed by Dr Singh and the Reserve Bank's deputy governor
C. Rangarajan as 'hop, skip and jump'. Major policy announcements
followed, including the end of India's infamous 'Licence Permit Raj',
as its web of bureaucratic controls was popularly described, and an
across-the-board reduction of import tariffs.

Dr Singh's first budget speech on 24 July 1991 concluded with the
now-famous quotation from Victor Hugo: 'No power on Earth can
stop an idea whose time has come.' He went on to say: 'I suggest to
this august House that the emergence of India as a major economic
power in the world happens to be one such idea. Let the whole world
hear it loud and clear. India is now wide awake. We shall prevail. We
shall overcome.'

At *ET*, we were generally supportive of the government's
initiatives, though some of us remained sceptical of the likely impact
on growth and welfare of the economic liberalization measures. I also
knew, from my conversations with the then chief economic adviser
to the Union government, Deepak Nayyar, a former colleague from
our time together in the mid–1980s on the faculty of economics
at the Jawaharlal Nehru University (JNU), that there were internal
differences within the finance ministry on what ought to be done.
Even on a matter such as exchange-rate policy there were divisions,
with C. Rangarajan and Y. Venugopal Reddy, then a joint secretary
in the Union finance ministry, opting for more graduated changes in
the exchange-rate regime, while others, like Montek, were votaries
of the 'big bang' approach.

These differences found their reflection in the wider public space.
There was a lively debate, for instance, in the press on the merits of
'gradual' reform versus 'big bang' reform. My columns reflected the
views of the gradualists and, therefore, attracted those who agreed
with me. One such person was Charles Clift, a junior diplomat in
the British High Commission in Delhi. Charles had done his PhD
in economics from Sussex University and his doctoral supervisor was
Biplab Dasgupta, a Marxist economist who later returned to India to
become a CPI(M) member of Parliament. (He died in 2005.) Charles
told me that every document and letter sent by the Indian finance

ministry to the IMF was circulated among all IMF directors and the British had a policy of sending the papers dealing with a programme country to their diplomatic outpost in that country.

This meant that every letter Dr Singh wrote to the IMF's managing director Michel Camdessus found its way back to Delhi, to the British High Commission. Given his loyalty to Biplab, who as a CPI(M) member would have been only too happy to have the finance minister's dealings with the IMF subjected to public scrutiny, Charles had no qualms about handing over some of those documents to me. It helped that Biplab had once mentioned to him that I, as a former member of the Communist Party of India (Marxist) during my days at the University of Hyderabad, was a 'fellow traveller'. Thanks to Charles's generosity, I was able to write some interesting news reports and columns.

On the eve of Dr Singh's second budget in February 1992, the *Indian Express* published some of Dr Singh's letters to the IMF, suggesting that India's 'budget secrets' had been leaked to the Fund. I called Charles and asked if he had all the documents cited in the *Express* report. He promptly handed them over to me. The *Economic Times* was, therefore, able to quickly take the story forward, and Dr Singh had no choice but to table all the documents in Parliament on 26 February, shortly before he presented his budget.

On the morning of the 29th, the day of the budget presentation, *ET* carried a front-page piece by me titled 'Loan Terms: How Many Steps Beyond the Fund?' My analysis, based on the documents supplied by Charles, highlighted the government's commitment to the IMF and argued that the government's sovereignty was compromised since the IMF's staff was already privy to budgetary policy.

I reported that Dr Singh had already assured the IMF and the World Bank that India would, among other policy measures, decontrol the price of steel, till then fixed by the government. This was a decision awaiting Cabinet approval. When Dr Singh stood up to read his budget speech in Parliament, the CPM leader Somnath Chatterjee waved a copy of *ET*. He charged the finance minister with 'leaking' the budget and sought to move a privilege motion against the government. Dr Singh was not amused.

Rising to present his budget to Parliament, Dr Singh was constrained
to respond to these charges. Stating that as a founder-member of the
IMF and the World Bank India had a right to borrow from them,
Dr Singh explained that, 'As lenders, they (the IMF and the World Bank)
are required to satisfy themselves about our capacity to repay loans
and this is where conditionality comes into the picture. All borrowing
countries hold discussions with these institutions on the viability of
the programmes for which assistance is sought. We have also held
such discussions.' However, he assured Parliament, 'The conditions we
have accepted reflect no more than the implementation of the reform
programme as outlined in my letters of intent sent to the IMF and the
World Bank, and are wholly consistent with our national interests. The
bulk of the reform programme is based on the election manifesto of
our party. There is no question of the government ever compromising
our national interests, not to speak of our sovereignty.'

He refused to meet me after that. During the months that followed,
I continued to write on the government's economic policies but his
doors remained closed to me. My access in the finance ministry was
restricted to joint secretaries like Y.V. Reddy, Valluri Narayan and
Duvvuri Subbarao, all from Hyderabad, and Deepak Nayyar. When
Deepak exited the ministry later that year I did a full-page analysis in
ET on the intellectual differences within the government, especially
between Deepak and Montek, with the title 'The Importance of
Dissent'. I was told Dr Singh had been irritated by my piece, and had
quipped to someone that the ministry of finance was not a 'debating
society'.

In early 1993, shortly after I had moved from *ET* to the *Times of
India* as its business and economics editor, Dileep Padgaonkar, the paper's
editor, asked me to seek an appointment with the finance minister and
interview him for the paper. I confessed to Dileep that I was unlikely to
secure an appointment from Dr Singh. He offered to make the call and
managed to get him to agree to a meeting. When Dileep mentioned,
during the phone conversation, that I would be accompanying him
and we would like to interview him for the *Times*, Dr Singh fell silent.
He then told Dileep that he could not trust me to report his views

accurately and recalled the '*ET* at 30' special-supplement fiasco. It was only after Dileep assured him that he would read the interview before it went to press that he agreed to meet us.

When we arrived the next day at Dr Singh's North Block office, I tried to hide behind Dileep and be as unobtrusive as possible. To my surprise, Dr Singh walked up to me, placed his hand on my shoulder and with his signature smile, asked how I was. Dileep was visibly relieved to see that his business and economics editor was now on good terms with the finance minister, and the interview went off smoothly. Years later, while working for Dr Singh, I discovered that misleadingly friendly smile was especially reserved for his critics and opponents. Leaders of the Left Front, editors who had been critical of him in their columns and colleagues in the Congress party known for planting stories against the PM in the media were all greeted with that disarming smile.

The very next day, I received a call from the finance minister's office inviting me to dinner that night. I found myself at an intimate gathering in the private dining room of a five-star hotel. Around the small table at which I was seated, next to Dr Singh, were only four other guests, the then commerce minister P. Chidambaram, Montek and Isher, and the chairperson of the *Hindustan Times* (*HT*), Shobhana Bhartia. I knew, as we sat down, that I had been rehabilitated.

As a journalist, I had heard stories of how Indira Gandhi would suddenly win over a detractor with a smile or a special gesture. As a communist in my youth, I had also read stories of how Stalin had invited a colleague home for dinner before he was sent off to Siberia or just shot dead. Dr Singh was certainly not a Stalin, nor was he an Indira, but I felt he may well have learnt a lesson or two about winning friends and disarming critics from her.

Later, when I came to work with him closely, I saw how much Dr Singh had imbibed from watching the prime ministers he had worked for. While he did play favourites by meeting journalists and others who were nice to him and refusing to give appointments to those he did not like, he would floor critics, every now and then, with impeccable courtesy. He also learnt to value differences of opinion among his advisers. As PM, he would listen to all opinions, only rarely disagreeing with anyone in meetings, so as not to discourage free expression, and then doing what he felt was needed to be done. An important lesson he seemed to have learnt from his predecessors was to never reveal his mind on a policy issue till it was absolutely necessary to do so.

That dinner was a turning point in our relationship. By then I had tempered my own views and had become more appreciative of his policies. He too had understood the need to build bridges to his critics. While Narasimha Rao stood like a rock behind him and offered unstinted political backing for his policies in public, he would privately urge his finance minister to be more accommodating of the Congress party's political concerns, and Dr Singh was clearly learning to soften his stance.

Even as he learnt the political ropes, he found it hard to handle vociferous public attacks. In August 1991 and March 1992 Dr Singh had offered to resign, the first time when the government was accused of favouring a bank with dubious credentials and the second time when some of his Cabinet colleagues, led by Arjun Singh, attacked his policies. As a staunch Gandhi family loyalist and a prime ministerial aspirant, Arjun Singh was inimical to Rao, as he later would be to Dr Singh, when he became PM. Both times, Narasimha Rao backed Dr Singh to the hilt and told him that he should not take such attacks personally because they were, in fact, directed against the PM. However, in December 1993, when Dr Singh offered to resign a third time, after a parliamentary committee criticized the finance ministry's handling of a stock market and banking sector scam, Rao was annoyed. He had had enough of Dr Singh's resignation dramas.

Narasimha Rao's aide P.V.R.K. Prasad, an IAS officer from Andhra Pradesh and a relative of mine, who also doubled up as the PM's press secretary, gave me a blow-by-blow account of the drama around that resignation episode. Prasad told me that Rao did not want to reach out directly to Dr Singh to get him to withdraw his resignation. But he was wary of moves being made by both Pranab Mukherjee and Chidambaram to become finance minister in case Dr Singh quit. According to Prasad, Narasimha Rao told him that since Dr Singh was not a politician he had to be handled differently. 'I cannot send a politician to persuade him,' Narasimha Rao told Prasad. 'Even if I send one, he will not relent.' Prasad was then deputed to win over Dr Singh.

Prasad had been P.V.'s personal secretary when the latter was chief minister of Andhra Pradesh in 1971. He had run errands for Rao, handling many tricky issues, and the PM trusted him. Prasad had to meet Dr Singh several times to persuade him to withdraw his resignation. Finally, recalls Prasad, he went to Dr Singh's home and had a long conversation with him, in the presence of his wife, Gursharan Kaur. Prasad thinks it was a nudge from her that finally persuaded Dr Singh to go meet Rao and sort out the matter, ending the resignation drama. I had reported most of this in the *Times of India*. Dr Singh was aware of my proximity to Rao and Prasad, and also knew that the prime minister often asked my father to draft his speeches. These factors may have also prompted Dr Singh to be warmer with me, and over time, to trust me.

In 1995, I had the opportunity to discover other facets of the finance minister's personality. I covered the annual meetings of the IMF and the World Bank at Madrid, an event that was more special than usual that year because the Fund and the Bank were also celebrating their fiftieth anniversary. Dr Singh, who led the Indian delegation, was in his element. By then he was a celebrated finance minister who had won several international awards. I noted his popularity among fellow finance ministers and watched many of them engage him in lengthy conversations. When he addressed the Fund–Bank meetings he spoke with confidence and authority and was heard with respect. His views prevailed in discussions on development assistance and proposals for opening new lines of credit for developing economies.

Despite his growing confidence in addressing international gatherings, he was careful, I discovered, when it came to handling issues that could get him into trouble at home. The Sindhi Association of Spain had decided to host a reception one evening in honour of the Indian finance minister, to which I was also invited. On the day of the reception, I ran into Prakash Hinduja at the venue of the Fund–Bank meetings. He was engaged in a serious conversation with the finance minister of Iran, a country with which the businessman and his family had strong connections. Hinduja recognized me and invited me to a party that evening in honour of Dr Singh that he said he was hosting. I told him I was already committed to attending an event hosted by the Sindhi Association. 'Same thing,' he said blithely. 'We are the Sindhi Association!'

I casually mentioned this encounter to Dr Singh when I ran into him later that afternoon. He became worried, called the Indian ambassador for advice on whether or not he should go to the dinner and finally went only after being assured that it was indeed the Sindhi Association that was hosting the event and the Hindujas would not be playing host. Dr Singh was squeamish about associating with the Hinduja brothers, rich Sindhi businessmen based in Europe who were accused at the time of being middlemen in the Bofors gun deal, the cause of a long-running political scandal. Ironically, years later, when Dr Singh was negotiating the nuclear deal with the US and had to keep a line open to Iran while reaching out to US senators and Congressmen, it was the Hinduja brothers, legally cleared by now of the Bofors charges, who played a key role in winning support for India both in Washington DC and Tehran.

———

After the Congress's defeat in the General Elections of 1996, Dr Singh, still a member of the Rajya Sabha, became involved in the activities of the Rajiv Gandhi Foundation (RGF), a developmental organization set up by the Gandhi family. Abid Hussain, a retired civil servant from Hyderabad, who had served as India's ambassador to the United States, took charge of the RGF and involved me in the academic activities of its sister organization, the Rajiv Gandhi Institute for Contemporary Studies. This kept me in continued contact with Dr Singh, whom I often met at lectures, seminars and lunches that Hussain hosted. Now that he was no longer finance minister, he had more time on his hands, especially when Parliament was not in session. Our interactions became more conversational, and I even turned to him for advice that

I knew would always be sound. When I decided to take a sabbatical from journalism in 1997, Dr Singh advised me to join the Research and Information System for Non-aligned and Other Developing Countries (RIS), of which he was then chairman. It was again on his advice that I moved from the RIS to the Indian Council for Research on International Economic Relations, where Isher Ahluwalia had just taken over as the institute's director.

It was Dr Singh who encouraged me to study India's relations with East and Southeast Asian economies, a subject that had remained close to his heart over the years, and I wrote a paper on the importance of trade with ASEAN (Association of South East Asian Nations) countries for India. When Dr Singh became chairman of the governing council of the India Habitat Centre (IHC) in 1997, he drew me into the IHC's activities. As a result, a plum assignment fell into my lap. I joined a team that included climate-change scientist R.K. Pachauri and others, that tasted the food prepared by applicants for catering licences at the IHC's various restaurants.

In 1999, when the Congress party picked Dr Singh as the candidate for the south Delhi Lok Sabha constituency, I joined the Friends of Manmohan group set up by Isher Ahluwalia, G.S. Bhalla and other academics to campaign door to door for him. My daughter and I would walk around our neighbourhood distributing pamphlets. Sadly, Dr Singh lost that election by close to 30,000 votes to the BJP's Vijay Kumar Malhotra, a considerably less distinguished political personality. His views on the massacre of some 3000 Sikhs in Delhi by Congress party activists and goons after Indira Gandhi's assassination in 1984 became a subject of controversy. While he condemned the killings unequivocally, the fact that he blamed both the Congress and the Rashtriya Swayamsevak Sangh (RSS) for them did not go down well with either. Nor was this argument appreciated by Sikh voters.

Delhi's Sikh community had, in fact, been grateful to the RSS for protecting Sikh families from the wrath of mobs attacking them, often led by local Congressmen. Their anger was reserved wholly for the Congress. The Congress, on the other hand, was also upset with Dr Singh's stance because it had pretended all along that the killing of Sikhs after Indira's assassination was a spontaneous expression of popular anger rather than an organized pogrom. In attempting to take a principled position on the massacre without frontally attacking his own party, Dr Singh ended up satisfying nobody.

But Dr Singh's family and close friends were convinced that his defeat was in part due to internal sabotage and blamed the local leaders of the Congress party for doing little to get him elected. Perhaps some Congressmen had already suspected by then that Sonia was grooming Dr Singh as a future head of government and hoped to nip this plan in the bud. In any event, the campaign, run mainly by his friends, did not succeed, and the race was lost. Dr Singh was never to contest another Lok Sabha election, preferring to enter Parliament through a less turbulent route, the Rajya Sabha. The Delhi defeat left a scar on the family's memory. While Dr Singh never discussed this with me, his family members did, on several occasions, refer to this episode as an experience that left them with the bitter taste of betrayal.

———

Despite the fact that I got to know Dr Singh well over the years, he continued to remain an enigma. A man of few words, he almost never engaged in conversation of a private or intimate nature. While he found it easier to 'talk shop'—policy or current affairs—he was rarely animated. When I began to work for him, I would often see him sitting quietly, even awkwardly, with visitors and betraying very little emotion. He had no gift for small talk. When obliged to interact with relatives during a visit to Kolkata or Amritsar, or with old friends in Geneva, it seemed Dr Singh did not quite know what to say to them, and it was left to Mrs Kaur to keep the conversation going. Amusingly, even with fellow economists who were his friends, like Jagdish Bhagwati or I.G. Patel, he would be happy to let them do most of the talking.

In a moment of frankness, Dr Singh narrated a typical tale of his diffidence to Mark Tully, the legendary BBC correspondent in India. When Tully interviewed him for *Cam*, the Cambridge University alumni magazine, Dr Singh told him that as a student at St John's

College he would get up early in the morning before his fellow students to finish bathing because he felt shy about going into the common bathing rooms with his turban off and his hair tied up. Since hot water was not available at that hour, Dr Singh chose to bathe in cold water, justifying this to his friends on health grounds, as a way of fighting the common cold.

His shyness, however, often made him appear lacking in warmth and emotion. Successful politicians are Janus-faced. They know when to be withdrawn and cold, and when to be warm and expressive. The wilier among them make the switch between these two personas in a flash. Dr Singh was not capable of such swift transformations. He may well have learnt the art of disarming his critics, but he could never create the illusion of intimacy that journalists crave in their interactions with the powerful. Worse, he seemed to find it hard to be genuinely expressive. I always wondered how much of this 'shyness' was a defence mechanism acquired during a difficult childhood when, after his mother's death, he had to live with an uncle's family because his father was rarely at home. Since his uncle and aunt had their own children to take care of, the young Manmohan was left to his own devices. Dr Singh had happy memories of his student and teaching life in Amritsar but I noticed that he rarely spoke about his childhood in Gah.

Working with him in the PMO, I discovered his introverted nature extended to his family as well. His daughters would say that they did not know their father's mind on many issues because he kept his work and family life in two separate, largely watertight, compartments and rarely gave expression to his thoughts, his desires or frustrations when at home. As Mrs Kaur once put it to me, 'He swallows everything, doesn't spit anything out.'

At work, he spoke even less than at home. His public silences, for which the media would often chastise him, were only an extension of his private ones. In formal meetings with visiting heads of government, he had a prepared brief that he often memorized like a good student and followed. In Cabinet and official meetings, he became notorious for his silences. He would mostly listen and then say a few words, if he wished to offer a view. Mostly, however, his style was to allow everyone to have their say and then take a decision on file, rather than stating his own views explicitly. He was happy if he could provoke his interlocutors into talking so that he could himself sit back and listen. But he would ask questions, and those questions sometimes revealed his mind.

Over time, as he became bolder as PM, he devised a new strategy. If he agreed with the views of a person in a meeting, he would give that person more time to speak, while cutting short those whose views he did not share. Sometimes, he would ask a person to speak, knowing full well what his views were and that these were not shared by many around the table. That was a signal to others to fall in line. While he adopted all these strategies, he himself rarely spoke in an assertive manner. Over time, his silences and his overt shyness seemed to be more strategy than the habits they had probably been, to begin with.

When I entered the PMO, I was aware of Manmohan Singh's shyness and knew that in order to be a successful media adviser communicating on his behalf to the media, I would have to improvise. It would be easy to be his 'eyes and ears', which is what he wanted me to be when I joined the PMO. The tough part would be to be his 'voice'.

3

Manmohan's PMO

'I want you to be my eyes and ears.
Tell me what you think I should know,
without fear or favour.'

Manmohan Singh, 30 May 2004

I went to meet Dr Singh on Monday at the prime minister's sprawling official residence, 7 Race Course Road—7 RCR as it is popularly called—at the edge of Lutyens' Delhi and bordering diplomatic enclave. After Rajiv Gandhi's assassination, the security around the PM's official residence has become so elaborate that entering it is quite an ordeal. The Special Protection Group (SPG), an elite security unit protecting the PM, which was created in 1985 after Indira Gandhi's assassination, allows in only such visitors whose names have been provided to them by the personal secretary to the PM. After driving through the first gate of the outer compound, visitors alight near the second gate. Only ministers, authorized officials and foreign dignitaries are allowed to drive through the second gate, and get into SPG vehicles that will take them a couple of hundred yards down the road to the PMO. Those less privileged must first walk into a visitors' room, deposit their mobile phones and be screened by security. Only then are they ferried by the SPG in its fleet of Maruti cars to the Prime Minister's Office.

Having done the ride, I was ushered straight in to meet Dr Singh.

He was in the chair on the right side of the room on which PMs usually sit when they meet visitors, and welcomed me with a smile. I walked up and sat on a chair placed to his left.

'I was not prepared for this role,' he confessed. 'This is a new experience and it will not be easy. We are a minority government. The Left has only agreed to support us from the outside. The Congress party has never run a coalition government. I will have to make a success of it. I need a press secretary. I know you, so I would be happy if you agreed to work here. I know it will mean a financial loss for you, but you will have to view this as an opportunity to serve the nation.'

I told him Vohra had already briefed me about his impending offer and, without further ado, accepted his invitation to work for him. Our conversation turned to matters of rank and nomenclature. I pointed out that two persons had handled the media in the PMO of the previous prime minister, Atal Bihari Vajpayee, and both were called 'officer on special duty'—OSD in bureaucratic parlance. However, when other editors had taken up the same assignment in the past, they had been called information advisers to the PM. I would prefer to be called media adviser, I said, explaining that with the advent of news television the word 'media' had replaced 'press', and 'information' sounded archaic. He agreed.

Finally I asked him what he expected of me. He reflected for a moment, then said, 'Sitting here, I know I will be isolated from the outside world. I want you to be my eyes and ears. Tell me what you think I should know, without fear or favour.'

Those words remained embedded in my mind and every time I hesitated to convey an inconvenient truth or an embarrassing tale over those four years with him, I would recall them and feel emboldened. Even after leaving the PMO, I used the privilege bestowed on me by those words to tell him, impartially, what I felt he ought to know.

I told Dr Singh that Sharada Prasad, Indira Gandhi's widely respected information adviser, was a family friend and that I would meet him and seek his guidance. He agreed. 'Yes, Sharada is a good man. You should keep in touch with him and take his advice.'

Anxious to get his team in place quickly, he insisted I join immediately since the new Parliament was scheduled to convene that week. I agreed to begin work two days later.

Strangely, on a day when my life took a new turn, Rama was in distant Canada and Tanvika in Hyderabad. I had no one at home to go to. So I first called my parents to give them the news, and then Shekhar Gupta, CEO of the Express group, to which the *Financial Express* belonged. Shekhar was attending a conference in Istanbul and was understandably dismayed at the prospect of my immediate exit. Yet he graciously said he would keep my chair at *FE* vacant since it was unlikely this new coalition experiment with the Left would work.

'It is a thankless job, boss!' he warned me. 'This government will not last its term. You will be unemployed in a year's time.'

Shekhar stuck to his promise of keeping the editor's chair warm for me for nearly six months, before deciding that the Manmohan Singh government would last longer than many had imagined and that he needed a full-time editor to run the paper.

By Monday evening, the orders were issued and the news was splashed across TV screens. My life changed instantly and my mobile phone never ceased to ring.

A day after joining the PMO, I called on H.Y. Sharada Prasad to seek his blessings and advice. A compact, personable man, Sharada Prasad exuded sagacity. His tiny apartment was filled with books and memorabilia from his years in public life. Rare photographs of Gandhiji and Nehru adorned the walls. He spoke softly, choosing his words with deliberation and care.

'So what room have they given you?' he asked keenly, as any veteran of the PMO would, knowing how much perceptions about an official's proximity to the PM, and hence his power and influence, were shaped by what room he had been given.

I said I would be sitting in the very room that he had sat in, when I met him for the first time in 1981. However, since that room was being refurbished, I would temporarily occupy the corner room next to the Cabinet room, near the prime minister's office on the first floor.

'Ah!' he exclaimed. 'That is a historic room. The first office room of the first prime minister of free India!'

Jawaharlal Nehru spent his first few days in office sitting in that small room adjacent to the Cabinet room because the room that he was to occupy as PM was being used by Sir Girija Shankar Bajpai, secretary general of the ministry of external affairs (MEA). It took a few days for Bajpai to move to a new room and for the room to be refurbished for India's first prime minister.

'In my time I met the editors of the major dailies regularly,' Sharada Prasad said to me. 'But in those days there were only five editors who mattered. The editors of the *Statesman,* the *Times of India, The Hindu,* the *Indian Express* and *Hindustan Times.* These days you have too many newspapers, and television too. But try and keep in touch with those who matter. Make sure the PM meets them informally once in a while. Make sure the PM compliments an editor and a columnist whenever something worth complimenting is written. Reach out to the Indian-language media. Every morning give the PM a list of major headlines. Make sure you have some role in speech-writing. The civil servants will not like it. But as an editor you have writing skills that the PM would benefit from. Use them.'

I asked him if the PM should address a press conference.

'Of course, but not right now,' he said. 'In the next month, let him meet editors and publishers in small groups. These should be off-the-record conversations. They should get to know him, he should get to know them. After a couple of months, organize a press conference. Make sure you conduct it. And make sure you have thought of the headlines you want the next day. Never organize a media interaction without deciding what headline you want to come out of it!'

In the following weeks, I faithfully followed each of these instructions. I arranged a series of breakfast meetings with important editors, publishers and TV anchors. As an early riser, Dr Singh would schedule his breakfast meetings for half past eight. Being late to bed and late to rise, editors and TV anchors would protest, but turn up on time. When I invited a group of publishers, the only ones to arrive late were Shobhana Bhartia of *Hindustan Times* because, as she told me, she took a long time drying her hair, and Indu Jain, chairperson of the *Times of India*, because she had to finish her morning puja.

Whenever the PM visited a state capital, I would arrange an interaction with the local media. This became an important institution of communication for the PM. It helped break the monopoly of the largely English-language Delhi media over access to him. Editors and correspondents from the Indian-language media got an opportunity to interact with Dr Singh and make their own assessment of a man few of them had ever known. Between 2004 and 2008, Dr Singh addressed a press conference, open to all media, in every single state capital he visited, including Port Blair, the capital of the Andaman and Nicobar Islands. This investment of time in befriending regional media, including the Urdu-language media, proved invaluable during the national debate on the India–US civil nuclear agreement, and whenever the PM came under attack from Delhi's media. I did incur the wrath of New Delhi's prima donnas every now and then for adopting this inclusive policy, especially if I opted to give the editor of a regional media group exclusive time with Dr Singh on board the PM's aircraft on one of his foreign trips, ignoring the requests of a New Delhi editor.

As I entered into my new role, my last courtesy call was to the home of P.V. Narasimha Rao. During his tenure as PM, there were only two Hyderabadi editors in Delhi, A.M. Khusro at the *Financial Express* and myself, and he knew us both. I had kept in touch with Rao even after he had retired from active politics. On this latest visit, I found him all alone and reading a book, when his long-serving assistant, Khandekar, ushered me in. Over tea and biscuits, I gave Rao an account of the call from the PMO and my meeting with Dr Singh, and the words of advice from Sharada Prasad.

Rao found it significant that Dr Singh had not opted for a political journalist or a government official as his media adviser but had chosen an economic journalist like myself. 'Of course, he knows Vithal,' he added, referring to my father, and suggested Dr Singh's choice may have also been shaped by that fact.

'Good,' he said, as he sipped his tea. 'Manmohan needs your help.'

Dr Singh's three key aides in the PMO happened to be, by mere happenstance, Malayalees and all Nairs to boot: J.N. 'Mani' Dixit, the new national security adviser (NSA), T.K.A. Nair, the prime minister's principal secretary, and M.K. Narayanan, the special adviser for internal security.

The power and importance of the principal secretary to the PM has always been dependent on the latter's political clout, apart from the officer's own standing within the civil service. As the bureaucratic link between the PM and senior ministers and secretaries to government, the principal secretary commands authority and influences policy. Most principal secretaries have been extremely capable men, well regarded by their peers and respected by their subordinates, like P.N. Haksar in Indira Gandhi's PMO, P.C. Alexander in Rajiv's, A.N. Varma in Narasimha Rao's, Satish Chandran in Gowda's, N.N. Vohra in Gujral's and Brajesh Mishra in Vajpayee's. However, every now and then, a nondescript official of limited talent has also adorned that job.

The national security adviser is an institution created during Vajpayee's first term, after India declared herself a nuclear weapons power and a National Security Council (NSC) was established. The NSA is the executive head of the council and, within the PMO, typically deals with the ministries of defence and external affairs, the service chiefs and intelligence agencies and the Department of Atomic Energy (DAE). Since Manmohan Singh's PMO also included a special adviser, a novelty created to accommodate Narayanan, part of the NSA's turf, namely the area of internal security, was hived off to him.

Mani Dixit was, without doubt, the dominant personality among the three. His stature ensured that T.K.A. Nair was not quite the 'principal' secretary that many of his predecessors had been. Of course, Nair's immediate predecessor, the larger-than-life Brajesh Mishra, was more than just a principal secretary. I once jokingly remarked to Dr Singh that in Vajpayee's time the principal secretary functioned as if he were the PM, while in his case, it was being said that the PM functioned like a principal secretary. This was a comment on Dr Singh's attention to detail, his involvement in the nitty-gritty of administration, his chairing of long and tedious meetings with officials, which Vajpayee rarely did. He ignored the remark, knowing well that it was also a taunt, drawing attention to the fact that Sonia was the political boss.

Nair was not Dr Singh's first choice for the all-important post of principal secretary. He had hoped to induct N.N. Vohra, who had given me the news of my job. Not only was he a fellow refugee from west Punjab, now Pakistan, but both had taught in Punjab University and Vohra also went to Oxford, though some years after Dr Singh. Vohra even cancelled a scheduled visit to London to be able to join the PMO. Sonia Gandhi had another retired IAS officer, a Tamilian whose name I am not at liberty to disclose, in mind for the job. He had worked with Rajiv Gandhi and was regarded as a capable and honest official. However, he declined Sonia's invitation to rejoin government on a matter of principle—he had promised his father that he would never seek a government job after retirement.

With these two distinguished officers ruled out, Dr Singh turned to Nair, a retired IAS officer who had worked briefly as secretary to the PM in Gujral's PMO and had also served as Punjab's chief secretary, the top bureaucrat in the state. Nair's name was strongly backed by a friend of Dr Singh's family, Rashpal Malhotra, chairman of the Chandigarh-based Centre for Research on Rural and Industrial Development (CRRID). Dr Singh himself was the chairman of the CRRID and Nair a member of its governing board. Apart from his stint in the Gujral PMO, Nair had neither held the rank of secretary in any of the powerful ministries on Raisina Hill—home, finance and defence—nor in any key economic ministry. He had only done so in the less powerful ministries of rural development and environment and forests. In short, he was a bureaucratic lightweight.

Always impeccably attired, Nair, small-built and short, lacked the presence of a Brajesh Mishra, whose striking demeanour commanded attention. He rarely gave expression to a clear or bold opinion on file, always signing off with a 'please discuss' and preferring to give oral instructions to junior officials such as joint secretaries and deputy secretaries. They would then be required to put those instructions on file as their own advice. It was classic bureaucratic risk aversion aimed at never getting into any controversy or trouble. Nair depended a great deal on Pulok Chatterjee, a joint secretary who had worked with both Rajiv Gandhi and Sonia, for advice on important policy decisions.

Pulok, like Nair, suffered from the handicap that his own service had never regarded him as one of its bright sparks. A serving IAS officer, he had never worked in any important ministry. He was inducted into Rajiv's PMO as a deputy secretary after having served as a district official in Amethi, his constituency in Uttar Pradesh, where he had caught Rajiv's eye. After Rajiv's death, he chose to work for the Rajiv Gandhi Foundation where he did some worthwhile social development work. But this meant that he was not just outside government but completely identified with the Gandhi family. When Pulok returned to government, it was to work on the personal staff of Sonia Gandhi when she was leader of the Opposition in the Lok Sabha.

Pulok, who was inducted into the Manmohan Singh PMO at the behest of Sonia Gandhi, had regular, almost daily, meetings with Sonia at which he was said to brief her on the key policy issues of the day and seek her instructions on important files to be cleared by the PM. Indeed, Pulok was the single most important point of regular contact between the PM and Sonia. He was also the PMO's main point of contact with the National Advisory Council (NAC), a high-profile advisory body chaired by Sonia Gandhi, with social activists as members. It was sometimes dubbed the Shadow Cabinet.

When not at these meetings, the affable, pipe-smoking, and understated Pulok remained mostly confined to his room in South Block, rarely travelling outside Delhi. During my time in the PMO, the only occasion on which I found him keen on accompanying the PM was when Dr Singh went to Cuba. With leftist leanings, Pulok was never too enthusiastic about Dr Singh's focus on improving relations with the US. Whenever Dr Singh and Sonia had to speak from the same platform, Pulok and I would exchange their draft speeches so that they remained in step in their public utterances. While I always wrote these speeches for the PM, Pulok was largely a messenger carrying Sonia's speeches to me, since her speeches were mostly written by Congress party politicians or her close associates. Pulok was in charge of monitoring the implementation of the UPA's National Common Minimum Programme (NCMP)—the joint key objectives of the coalition government. This enabled him to seek regular information from all ministries on what they were doing. Pulok would duly produce elaborate charts that listed the promises—more than a hundred— enshrined in the NCMP, assign responsibility for their implementation to various ministries and report back to the PMO on the status of their implementation.

Apart from teaming up with Pulok, Nair also sought to make himself politically relevant to the PM by projecting himself as the PM's link with the Left. He had been a member of the CPI(M)'s Students Federation of India (SFI) during his college days in Kerala. He revived these ties by becoming close to the senior CPI(M) leader Harkishan Singh Surjeet, who hailed from Punjab, Nair's parent state in the IAS. Proximity to Surjeet served Nair well, earning him a place in Gujral's PMO. Apart from being fellow Punjabis, Gujral and Surjeet were close friends. During his second stint in the PMO, Nair was able to use his association with Surjeet and with CPI(M) leaders from Kerala, especially S.R. Pillai, a member of the CPI(M) politburo, to help Dr Singh manage the Left.

Even with its combined strength, I felt that the Nair–Pulok duo was not a patch on the magisterial Brajesh Mishra who ran Vajpayee's PMO with great aplomb. Even though he was a diplomat by training, Mishra, the son of a former Congress chief minister of Madhya Pradesh, had politics in his genes and knew exactly what stratagems to adopt to strengthen the authority of the PM in a coalition government. His other great qualification, one that both Nair and Pulok lacked, was that he was a risk-taker. On critical occasions, Mishra was willing to push the envelope and take things forward on behalf of the PM. He established that reputation by taking the decision, along with Vajpayee, to conduct nuclear tests in May 1998 and declare India a nuclear weapons state. Mishra's stature consolidated and expanded Vajpayee's

clout within the government. Though he had belonged to the Indian
Foreign Service (IFS), he was widely respected by the rival IAS. In the
Manmohan PMO, on the other hand, Nair's risk-averse personality
only compounded Dr Singh's careful approach and contributed to a
further dilution of the PM's authority.

The third Malayalee, M.K. Narayanan, claimed that he was offered
the post of national security adviser by Sonia Gandhi, but had instead
proposed Mani Dixit's name for the job because he had to tend to his
ailing mother, who lived in Chennai. He claimed it was he who drove
to Mani's home in Gurgaon to tell him he was being offered the job,
and to urge him to take it. Mani, on the other hand, believed Sonia
may have pushed for Narayanan but Dr Singh wanted him in the job
and that Narayanan was inducted as a special adviser as a compromise.

I tended to believe Mani's version. It was clear to me that
Dr Singh shared a bond with him that was never there between him
and Narayanan. It seemed plausible that the latter had been inducted
as the third leg of PMO leadership as a concession to Sonia. MK,
or Mike, as his contemporaries called him, was the intelligence
czar who had headed the Intelligence Bureau (IB), India's internal
intelligence agency, under both Rajiv Gandhi and Narasimha Rao.
He earned his spurs by playing a role in the unseating of the first-ever
democratically elected communist party government in the world,
E.M.S. Namboodiripad's ministry in Kerala, way back in 1957. He
was director, IB, when Rajiv was assassinated. Narayanan's favourite
line was, 'I have a file on you.' He used it, humorously, with ministers,
officials, journalists and others he met, leaving them, however, with
the uneasy feeling that he wasn't really joking. Indeed, Narayanan
himself gave currency to the tales that circulated about his proclivity
to snoop on everyone. He seemed to derive great pleasure in letting
me know that he kept a tab on the credit-card spending of influential
editors. On long flights in the PM's aircraft, he would regale us with
stories about how various prime ministers had summoned him for
information on their colleagues.

If those stories were true, Dr Singh was clearly the exception to
that rule. He not only resisted this temptation to spy on his colleagues,

but gave up even the opportunity to be offered such information by declining to take a daily briefing from the intelligence chiefs. He was the first prime minister not to do so. The chiefs of both the IB and the Research and Analysis Wing (R&AW) were told to report to the NSA instead. I didn't think the intelligence chiefs would deliver their best if they reported to an intermediary instead of the prime minister himself, and repeatedly implored him to take a direct daily briefing from them. Every now and then he would, but the NSA became their effective boss in the UPA PMO.

Narayanan, when he succeeded Dixit as NSA, used this power to its limits, and not without controversy—he was accused by R&AW officers of being partial to the IB. But his control over the system also derived from his professional competence and the respect he commanded even from junior officers for his non-hierarchical style of functioning. He would deal directly with them, not bothering about rank and protocol and focusing on getting the job done. My nickname for him, while talking to friends, was 'Ed', for J. Edgar Hoover, the powerful boss of the FBI of whom even US presidents were wary. Dr Singh too was wary of Narayanan's reputation and would, on occasion, warn me to be cautious while carrying out sensitive assignments for him that he did not want anyone to know about.

Mani Dixit entered the NSA's office as if he were destined for the job. Of the three seniormost officers in the PMO, he was clearly the PM's favourite. The two shared a common worldview, acquired during their respective stints in Narasimha Rao's government. More recently, as fellow members of the Congress party, Dr Singh and he had worked together to draft a foreign policy paper for the party for the new 'post-Cold War world'. Mani was both an 'ideas man' and a boss who expected delivery from subordinates. During the Kargil war, Brajesh Mishra constituted a multidisciplinary advisory group from among the members of the NSAB that was tasked to offer 'big picture' strategic advice to a government preoccupied with managing the daily tactics of winning a war. As a member of that group, along with K. Subrahmanyam, N.N. Vohra and a couple of others, I saw Mani's strategic brilliance at first hand.

Mani was, without doubt, one of India's finest diplomats and strategists. Subrahmanyam, India's pre-eminent strategic affairs guru, once said to me that he was probably the best foreign secretary in post-Nehruvian India. He made his mark early, and was chosen by Indira Gandhi for the challenging assignment of setting up the Indian mission in a newly liberated Bangladesh when he was just thirty-five years old. As Dr Singh's NSA, Mani swiftly picked up every issue that Mishra had been dealing with and sought to take it forward—dialogue with the US, dubbed the Next Steps in Strategic Partnership (NSSP), with Pervez Musharraf on Pakistan and the border talks with China.

By the time Dr Singh went to New York in September 2004, Mani's progress on several foreign policy fronts enabled Dr Singh to have very good meetings with President George Bush and President Musharraf as well as a series of bilateral meetings with Blair, Koizumi, Mbeki, Lula and others. But Mani's assertive personality meant that, while he was admired and feared by his younger colleagues in the foreign service, he often rubbed both the new foreign minister, K. Natwar Singh, and Narayanan the wrong way.

The tension between the NSA and the foreign minister was inherent in the arrangement. Even in the United States, ego and policy clashes between the NSA and the secretary of state are part of the national capital's folklore. In India, prime ministers have always sought to remain in charge of foreign policy but foreign ministers have had greater control over day-to-day management of policy. The institutional powers of the NSA, and the fact that both Mishra and Dixit were from the foreign service and knew its ins and outs, meant that the PMO had begun to chip away at even day-to-day management, including postings. The tension this generated between Jaswant Singh and Brajesh Mishra was well known and I began to see it rising between Natwar and Dixit. The ego clash was greater for the fact that Natwar had been Mani's senior in the foreign service.

Between Narayanan and Mani, there was both a clash of personalities and sharp differences of opinion. Mani was a pragmatist and a realist, Narayanan a hawk whose aggression was both a product of his years in intelligence and a means, it appeared to me, of asserting his authority over the foreign service. In India's bureaucratic pecking order, officers of the Indian Police Service (IPS), are regarded as lesser mortals by the high-flyers of the foreign service, the IFS, and the real wielders of power, the IAS.

Mani and Narayanan, just two years apart in age, would often explode into angry arguments in the presence of the PM. On one occasion, Narayanan shouted at Mani: 'You are a diplomat who knows a lot about the world but knows nothing about India.' Mani countered by asking Narayanan what he thought he knew about the country, considering he had never done 'a good police officer's job'. This was a reference to the fact that Narayanan, while belonging to the IPS, had spent most of his career in the IB and had never done any important 'field' job. These outbursts were partly a reflection of a turf war between the two, with Narayanan seeking greater control over the intelligence agencies than Mani wanted him to have.

Dr Singh would sit through such altercations with a worried look. But on one occasion, it got a bit too much for even a man as patient as him. While Mani and Narayanan were arguing vociferously in his presence, each accusing the other of overstepping his bounds, Dr Singh at first kept quiet, then got up abruptly, looking visibly irritated. That was a signal that the meeting was over and we could all leave. Nair, Mani and MK trooped out, while I walked with the PM to the ante-chamber where he read his files and letters.

He seemed disturbed by this sharp exchange in his presence, so I tried to cheer him up. I pointed out that it was good that different points of view were being aired. This would allow the PM to decide which view to take. I also reminded Dr Singh that when there were such differences between Montek and Deepak Nayyar in the ministry of finance, Dr Singh had chosen to ease Deepak out on the grounds that there was no time for intellectual arguments in the ministry in the midst of a balance of payments crisis. But there was no crisis at hand now and a new team was taking charge, so let 'a thousand ideas bloom and a hundred views contend', I suggested, paraphrasing Mao Zedong.

I also reminded him that even Indira Gandhi and Nehru had around them officials and colleagues who disagreed bitterly with one another.

After hearing me out, he smiled and said, 'I am not sure they all shouted at each other!'

———

I had a lesson in the PMO's internal dynamics on day one in the new job. The first piece of paper that landed in the in-tray on my desk was a newspaper clipping marked for my attention by Nair, with his handwritten comment, 'Quite interesting indeed!!!' It was a report in a local tabloid with the headline 'Musical Chambers at PMO', and referred to the battle for rooms in South Block.

The principal secretary's room was located at the other end of the corridor from the PM's room. Brajesh Mishra, the room's occupant during Vajpayee's term, had doubled up as principal secretary to the PM and India's first NSA. The Manmohan Singh PMO had a problem. Now that the two posts had been separated, where would Nair, as the new principal secretary, sit and where would Mani Dixit, the new NSA, have his office? To add to the complications, a new special adviser (SA), Narayanan, had also to be accommodated. A third room of equal importance had to be identified for him.

The news report suggested that Nair, Mani and the new minister of state in the PMO, Prithviraj Chavan, were all eyeing the corner room and that Nair had won the first round. He was now the proud occupant of Brajesh Mishra's room. I found it amusing that Nair should choose to mark that news item to me with his comment and the three exclamation marks. As it happened, he did inherit Mishra's room, with Mani seated in what used to be the room of the secretary in the PMO and Narayanan given a room of similar size down the corridor.

This was not, of course, the kind of problem that some had anticipated when they criticized Dr Singh's decision to give the jobs of principal secretary and NSA to two different people, and not vest them in a single individual, as Vajpayee had done. Dr Singh had taken this decision on the advice of K. Subrahmanyam, who had championed the creation of the office of the NSA. The process of appointing an NSA had begun immediately after the nuclear tests in 1998, when a committee set up by Vajpayee on revamping India's national security management to meet the needs of the times, had recommended a National Security Council with a dedicated secretariat, a Strategic Policy Group and an NSAB. The NSC Secretariat (NSCS) would be headed by an NSA.

Subrahmanyam, who had been consulted by this committee before it wrote its report, imagined that the NSC would be something like the Planning Commission, a group of experts heading various sections, and that the NSA would be a full-time functionary, like the deputy chairman of the Planning Commission. Since the Planning Commission sits at a distance from the PMO, in Yojana Bhavan, he imagined the NSA and the NSCS would similarly be located outside the PMO.

However, while accepting the substance of the committee's report, Vajpayee chose to name his principal secretary, Brajesh Mishra, as NSA. The NSCS was placed in the charge of a deputy NSA whose office was located outside the PMO, in the nearby Sardar Patel Bhavan. Subrahmanyam did not like the idea of Brajesh Mishra keeping both positions. He felt that since the principal secretary, to the PM would be under 24x7 pressure to address day-to-day challenges, the urgent task of improving India's national security management would end up being neglected.

Many years later, after watching the experience of UPA-1, Subrahmanyam apparently developed second thoughts about the wisdom of separating the two positions. At a private dinner after the First K. Subrahmanyam Memorial Lecture, in January 2012, Mishra told a few friends, including the current NSA, Shivshankar Menon, and myself, that Subrahmanyam had told him that he erred in recommending the separation of the offices of the NSA and principal secretary to the PM, because he realized the PM could not take a holistic and politically informed view of national security with his two key aides functioning in non-intersecting silos.

In June 2004, however, Dr Singh not just accepted Subrahmanyam's advice to separate the posts of principal secretary and the NSA, but went a step further, by dividing up the NSA's beat, with foreign affairs, defence and nuclear strategy allotted to Mani Dixit and internal security to Narayanan. However, instead of then asking the NSA and SA to sit in Sardar Patel Bhavan, home of the NSCS, he chose to locate them within the premises of the PMO.

For the first few weeks of its existence, the Manmohan Singh PMO just did not get along. The NSA wanted all files relating to the external affairs, home and defence ministries to go through him to the PM. This would, for the first time, seriously abridge the principal secretary's role in decision-making and, more vitally, appointments pertaining to these ministries. Narayanan, even though he lived in Chennai and flew down to Delhi for a few days every week, then got into the act and demanded that he should be looking at files pertaining to the home ministry and the internal security agencies.

The media got wind of this internal turf war, with a senior journalist being briefed by Brajesh Mishra, who in turn had heard of it from his subordinates who were still in the PMO and were in touch with him. It was then decided that an office order would be issued clarifying the individual responsibilities of Nair, Dixit and Narayanan. This was then made public.

Matters did not rest there. Over the next few weeks, media reports appeared suggesting there was a problem of turf between the PM's advisers and his senior Cabinet ministers, the ministers for external affairs and home, Natwar Singh and Shivraj Patil. They had sought a clarification from the PM about what role Mani and Narayanan would play and whether they would interfere in the work of the home and external affairs ministries.

One day, Natwar Singh, the foreign minister, called me to his room in South Block and unburdened himself of his grievances against Mani Dixit. As he narrated his long list of complaints, he grew angrier and angrier. Natwar's major complaint was that Mani was interfering far too much in the affairs of the foreign affairs ministry. Natwar and Mani were both retired diplomats, but with very different views. They were, understandably, in competition with each other to influence foreign policy. Indeed, Mani was an effective buffer between a reform-minded PM and the MEA's conservative establishment, just as Brajesh Mishra had been similarly used by Vajpayee.

Even as the PM attempted to sort out this conflict, newspaper reports appeared, drawing attention to the developing conflict between Home Minister Shivraj Patil and Narayanan. They even dragged the PM into the controversy by suggesting that these turf issues had come up because of prime ministerial activism, that is, the PM, through his advisers, was trying to encroach on ministerial turf. Dr Singh wanted this denied and asked me to draft a public clarification to clear the air. My draft read:

> There have been some speculative and tendentious reports in the media in the recent past suggesting that the Prime Minister has taken direct charge of matters relating to Jammu and Kashmir, the North-Eastern States and the Naxalite-affected regions of the country. These reports are not accurate. All matters pertaining to internal security are directly dealt with by the Ministry of Home Affairs in the Government of India and by the relevant State governments. There is no change in the extant situation.

The PM asked me to show this to each of the three concerned—Nair, Mani and Narayanan. All of them agreed that this was an acceptable formulation. I went back to the PM with their three signatures on the draft. He smiled as he read the text and, returning the file to me, asked: 'So what will you call it? Press release or joint statement?'

———

My own position within this structure was formally defined by my rank. I had insisted with Dr Singh that I should be given the rank of secretary to government. Dr Singh had readily agreed, but Nair had baulked at the thought. At fifty he thought I was too young to be secretary to government, having himself been promoted to that rank in his late fifties, like most civil servants. He advised me to accept the rank of additional secretary, a step below, so as to not become a victim of bureaucratic jealousy, as he put it. Dr Singh opted for a compromise, urging me to join as additional secretary and assuring me that I would be promoted within the year. I did get promoted a year later and discovered that the only major perk that I was now entitled to was an executive suite at a hotel while travelling with the PM. However, as the son of a civil servant I knew that rank is all in government. It determines seating at meetings, it decides the car in which you travel in a prime ministerial cavalcade; more importantly, it shapes how you are perceived and how much influence others assume you command. I had pushed for a high rank so that I could be a more effective media adviser. It was no bad thing that apart from the big three, all of whom had the rank of a minister of state, all other officials in the PMO, including Pulok, were below me in official rank. Nair feared this would cause resentment but I rarely felt any from my IAS colleagues. The more protocol-conscious IFS diplomats, however, played their little games.

An amusing early episode featuring some of my protocol- and seniority-obsessed colleagues was played out at the Council on Foreign Relations (CFR) in New York in September 2004. Dr Singh had been invited to deliver a lecture at the CFR. When we arrived at the venue both Montek and Mani were whisked into a special room where Dr Singh was to have lunch with the high-profile CFR leadership before delivering his lecture. Since I, along with Montek and Mani, had been closely involved in writing it, I had assumed I would be part of the lunch group. However, I was told that I should sit outside along with other PMO officials. Even before I could protest, the economist Jagdish Bhagwati, a senior CFR fellow and an invitee to the lunch, spotted me and waved. He walked up to me, gave me a warm hug and inquired about my in-laws and Rama, whom he had known for years. He then held my hand and walked me into the room. At the entrance to the room, two foreign service gatekeepers reminded me that I was not on the PMO's list for the luncheon, upon which Bhagwati told them I was his guest. Protocol had been worsted by family ties.

Ultimately, more than my rank, it was my proximity to Dr Singh that finally defined my access and influence in the PMO. My equations with the three senior officials in the PMO were also affected by the fact that in the process of resolving their differences, Dr Singh had come to assign me the role of a referee.

I had a good equation with Mani from our time together in the NSAB in 1999–2000 and our travels abroad as part of India's 'track 2' diplomacy. He quit the NSAB in 2000, but we remained in touch and met regularly after he drafted me into his effort at writing an alternative foreign policy vision for the Congress party. I enjoyed his company, and we were both fond of good Scotch and cigars.

But within the PMO, Mani's imperious style inevitably came into conflict with my own more freewheeling and irreverent style of functioning. Our first disagreement was on who could travel with the PM on his official plane. Seeing the name of *Times of India* journalist Siddharth Varadarajan, who later served as editor of *The Hindu*, on the media list, Mani sent me a note informing me that Siddharth was not an Indian national but an American citizen and, as a foreign national, was not entitled to travel on the PM's plane. I was aware of Siddharth's citizenship, since this matter had come up when I had hired him as an assistant editor at the *Times of India*. I chose not to make an issue of it then and Samir Jain, vice chairman of Bennett, Coleman and Co. Ltd, the publishers of the *Times of India*, who took particular interest in the hiring of editorial writers, did not object either. Now the matter had surfaced again.

I wrote on the file that since Siddharth had recently accompanied External Affairs Minister Natwar Singh on a foreign trip in an official aircraft, the PMO need not make an issue of his citizenship. The file went to the PM with my observation and returned with his signature. I was told that in officialese a signature with no instructions meant the PM had approved the recommendation on the file. Mani was miffed. He returned the file to me with a caustic reference to my signature on the file being in red ink, which I had used without thinking. His note said, 'Only service chiefs are allowed to sign in red ink!'

I won that round but some irritants remained. What really bothered Mani was that I would often brief the media on the PM's views on foreign affairs. Mani wanted all such briefings routed through and approved by him. One day, he issued an office order stating that all interaction between the media adviser and the media on issues pertaining to foreign affairs and national security, and all press statements on those subjects, should be authorized by the NSA. I was livid.

I drove down to 7 RCR with Mani's order in my hand, barged into the PM's room unannounced, showed him the order and asked if it had his approval. Dr Singh was surprised to see the order and said he had not authorized it. I remonstrated that I was as much an 'adviser' to the PM as Mani was.

'He is your national security adviser and I am your media adviser. We are both "your advisers". I see no reason why I should seek anyone's approval for what I do, apart from yours.'

After the PM calmed me down, I explained to him that as the only non-civil servant in the PM's team, I often felt alone and isolated because I had no internal peer group and a gap of more than a decade separated me from my three senior colleagues. The loneliness sometimes got to me and I was not enjoying this job. So if he still wanted me to remain in the PMO, it was important that everyone there understood that I reported only to the PM and to no one else. I told him that I viewed it as my duty to brief the media directly on the PM's thinking on ongoing events. In the age of 24x7 television, such responses would often have to be immediate. Putting up files and notes and securing approval for a statement to the media was no longer possible. As the PM's media adviser, I would, I emphasized, also have to function as his 'spokesman', offering quotes to the media on his behalf.

I assured him that on important matters I would seek his approval for any statement I was about to make, but I saw no reason why I should seek any other official's approval. The PM told me my understanding was correct and that he would sort out the matter with Mani. Late that night, Mani called.

'I say, Sanjaya,' he said in his usual gruff tone, 'I am sorry, I made a mistake. PM told me you were upset about some silly note I issued. Tear it up. Come and smoke a cigar with me tomorrow.'

The next day we met over coffee and a cigar in his room. I remarked that I was surprised he smoked in the office since there were instructions that smoking was not permitted in the PMO.

'I have always smoked in my office. What are all these silly instructions? You and I can afford to ignore such orders,' he said loftily, puffing away at his cigar. He then gifted me a box of cigars and a copy of a book written by his mother, Ratnamayi Devi, who had had a profound influence on him. I became truly fond of Mani after that.

———

While the PM's core team was in place on the day Parliament opened, 2 June 2004, the government got off to a rough start. Dr Singh was neither allowed to introduce his council of ministers nor make any statement in the House. The BJP had recovered neither from the shock of its defeat nor from the surprising ease with which the Congress had stitched together a coalition and found a credible prime minister to head it. Unhappy with the situation in Parliament, Dr Singh settled down to tying up the loose ends of government formation. On my second day in office, I was summoned by the PM to his room in South Block.

'I have to name a new Planning Commission,' he said. 'Can you draw up a list of names?'

Over the next two days, I prepared a list. One afternoon a meeting was called at which Nair and Pulok were also present. I had my list and Nair arrived with his. As we read out names, Dr Singh would indicate his preference. Nair was asked to secure the consent of those selected, bar one. The one I was asked to sound out was Anu Aga, chairperson of Thermax. Her husband, Rohinton Aga, had been a contemporary of Dr Singh at college in England and she had distinguished herself as a corporate leader when she took charge of the family company after his death. When I called Anu, who was then in London, she asked for a day to consult her family. She called back the next day and accepted Dr Singh's invitation to join the Planning Commission.

But when I went back to him with her acceptance, the PM looked sheepish and informed me that he had already agreed to appoint Syeda Hameed, a Muslim writer and social activist, and so, I was told, there was no place left for Anu. Clearly, the 'gender' and 'minority' boxes had been filled up with Syeda's appointment. I was left with the embarrassing task of explaining away the confusion to Anu. What I obviously could not say to her was that the political benefits of rewarding a Muslim may well have trumped those of appointing a Parsi! To my dismay, even Dr Singh seemed to take this embarrassment lightly. For those who had served a lifetime in government, such slips seemed to be par for the course. Ironically, while it was Manmohan Singh who had been initially keen to find a niche for Anu, it was Sonia who finally provided one, by inducting her into her NAC in UPA-2.

Even as the process of making these appointments was going on, I was summoned by the PM one afternoon and asked if I had any suggestions for who should be named deputy chairman of the Planning Commission. I suggested Montek, who was still with the IMF in Washington DC but was willing to return if asked to do so.

'The party has some politicians in mind,' he said. He then mentioned the names that had been suggested to him—Digvijaya Singh, S.M. Krishna and Veerappa Moily. All former chief ministers, I thought to myself, and all without a seat in Parliament. So, naturally, the three would covet a job like this one with all the perks of a Cabinet rank and without the necessity of being a member of Parliament. These were good names, I said to him diplomatically, but repeated that if he was thinking of a job for Montek, this would be a good one. As deputy chairman Montek would be able to act as a bridge between the PM and other ministers as well as chief ministers, with whom Dr Singh needed a trustworthy link. Vajpayee had excellent relations with chief ministers across the country whereas Dr Singh knew very few on a personal level. A deputy chairman who was a politician, I reasoned, like the three suggested to him, might have good relations with chief ministers, but might not be a reliable bridge with them.

The days when the Planning Commission was composed entirely of subject experts were long gone. Various political and social quotas had now to be filled. North, south, scheduled caste, woman, minority. In the era of coalitions, every constituent political party wanted to name a member. For the PM, himself a former deputy chairman, the Planning Commission had become the place where he could park a trusted aide.

Now that he knew exactly where I stood on the deputy chairmanship of the Planning Commission, Dr Singh summoned Nair and Pulok.

When the two arrived, he first asked them for their advice. Nair kept quiet. Pulok said, 'The party has suggested Mr Moily.' I assumed 'the party' in this case meant Sonia. Dr Singh then turned to me. On cue, I offered my rationale for suggesting Montek's name. At this point, Nair piped up to say the Left Front might object.

I knew I was meant to make a good case for Montek's induction, and so I did. The Planning Commission, I pointed out, was a prime ministerial creation. Nehru had formed the institution through an administrative order to be able to guide long-term economic policy, partly because he had lost control of the ministry of finance to his critics. How could anyone object to the PM naming a person of his choice? If the PM could not name his own deputy chairman, what authority would he have while naming heads of other institutions? The 'party' might have good political reasons for seeking one person or another to be appointed, but the PM should name whomever he wanted to. The Planning Commission, after all, was the only institution directly under his charge, apart from the PMO.

The PM remained silent and there was no further discussion. That afternoon, Montek was in South Block. He had stopped off in Delhi for a few days en route to Beijing. I later learnt that he had a meeting that morning with Finance Minister P. Chidambaram who had invited him to return to his old job as finance secretary. Clearly, Chidambaram did not know that the PM was mulling other plans for Montek. I briefed Montek about the discussions in the PMO. 'Barkis is willin',' he quipped, quoting the famous line from *David Copperfield* to confirm his interest in the job. When I told him that the Left seemed to be blocking his entry, he replied that he would speak to Prabhat Patnaik, his contemporary from college and now a leading Left intellectual.

Late that evening, I found the PM still in South Block. In the few days I had been there, I would usually see him leave around 7 p.m. for RCR. Intrigued by the fact that he was in his office well beyond that hour, I came out of my room to see what was happening, found the door of the visitors' room open and CPI(M) leader Sitaram Yechury waiting there. He had escorted his party boss Harkishan Singh Surjeet, the general secretary of the CPI(M), to South Block. The PM and

Surjeet were closeted inside Dr Singh's room. I chatted for a while with Yechury, whom I knew as Sita from our schooldays in Hyderabad and learnt from him that the opposition to Montek's name was not the handiwork of the Left but of economist Arjun Sengupta. Arjun (now deceased) had been a member of the Planning Commission during Narasimha Rao's time and had been an economic adviser in the Indira Gandhi PMO in the early 1980s. Then close to Pranab Mukherjee, he had been leveraging his connections with the Left to become deputy chairman. When Surjeet and Sita left, I went to see the PM to find out what had transpired, but by then he was already on his way out.

The first thing I did the next morning was to go across to RCR and ask him why Surjeet had come to call on him. He merely said, 'Montek will be deputy chairman.' But his smile, exuding both mischief and triumph, gave the game away. One wily Sardar had secured the support of another wily Sardar to get a third one on board.

The episode gave me some interesting insights into Dr Singh's ways. Clearly, he had made up his mind to give Montek the job well before he staged that internal debate within the PMO. Before he could get Surjeet to support his plan, he needed arguments to be made to fob off the party hopefuls and the likes of Arjun Sengupta. I had been drafted to make them. It was a role I would be called upon to play on many occasions.

On 16 June, Montek's appointment was announced. On the 18th *The Hindu* quoted anonymous 'Left leaders' expressing their disapproval of his appointment. I heard subsequently that the CPI(M)'s Prakash Karat was furious with Surjeet for giving Dr Singh the go-ahead. This was an early pointer to the differences between Surjeet and Karat. To ease the situation, the Left was then approached for a name to be included in the Commission and they suggested Abhijit Sen, a professor at JNU.

———

About six months into UPA-1, early on the morning of 3 January 2005, Mani Dixit died of a massive heart attack. His sudden death

shocked and saddened Dr Singh. It also put at risk the foreign policy
agenda. Dr Singh knew that Mani was capable of taking on the more
conservative elements in the Indian foreign policy establishment.
With him gone, the danger of Dr Singh's foreign policy falling prey
to Congress party and South Block conservatives was real. Dr Singh
realized that he would now have to personally handle things that he
could have trusted Mani with.

On the morning of Mani's death, the PM was to go to Ahmedabad
to address the Indian Science Congress. He first went to Mani's house,
met his wife, Anu, and their family, and drove straight to the airport.
He sat shell-shocked, all alone, in his cabin and looked drawn and tired
through the day. He issued instructions that Mani should be given a
ceremonial funeral at the Delhi cantonment. As the NSA he was, after
all, technically the head of the newly emerging nuclear command and
the service chiefs reported to him. As soon as he returned to Delhi
that evening, the PM issued orders naming the deputy NSA, Satish
Chandra, a career diplomat, as acting NSA.

Soon after, the succession struggle began. The foreign service
officers in the PMO, Vikram Doraiswamy and Sujata Mehta, seemed
keen on regularizing Chandra's appointment as NSA. I viewed this
as motivated by foreign service loyalty. Dr Singh was clearly not keen
on this option but he did not name anyone else either for a full three
weeks. *Hindustan Times* reported that three names were being considered
for the job, including India's former high commissioner to Pakistan,
Satinder Lambah, the Indian ambassador in Washington DC, Ronen
Sen, and of course, the PMO's very own M.K. Narayanan.

The Indian Foreign Service had clearly come to view the NSA's job
as its turf. Both Brajesh and Mani belonged to this service. Thus, the
media was effectively deployed by this lobby to debunk MK's claim.
Vir Sanghvi wrote a column in *HT* dubbing Narayanan a 'flat-footed
policeman' and pushing the idea that the NSA ought to be from the
foreign service. As the days went by, the media became curious about
what was going on in decision-making circles and began floating
various names.

One day, I asked Dr Singh if he had made up his mind about

what to do. He told me he hadn't, and added, 'Will you please ask Subrahmanyam what he thinks I should do?'

That evening I drove to Subrahmanyam's DDA flat in Vasant Kunj. We went over the pros and cons of various names being mentioned in the media. He was not sure if Satish Chandra would be the right man for the job but had high regard for both Satinder Lambah and Ronen Sen. 'In any case,' he said to me, 'the NSA should be someone that the PM implicitly trusts.' At the end of a long evening, with Mrs Subrahmanyam plying us with tea, he suggested three options.

Option One: Use this opportunity to implement the original idea of moving the NSA out of the PMO. In this case, the NSA's role would have to be redefined more in line with the role played by the deputy chairman of the Planning Commission. This would mean the NSA need not be an IAS or IFS or even IPS officer. He could be from the services, or from a scientific organization or even from a think tank.

'If Sukhamoy [the economist] could be deputy chairman of the Planning Commission, why cannot someone like Roddam Narasimha [the scientist] or Raja Mohan [the international relations expert] be the NSA?'

This was truly an out-of-the-box solution. The problem, I told him, was that this would not fly with Dr Singh, who would regard it as too radical an option.

Option Two would be to simply appoint Narayanan as the NSA and retain Satish Chandra as deputy NSA, placing him in charge of the day-to-day functioning of the NSC. Option Three was to stay with the status quo, retaining Narayanan as adviser for internal security and appointing another NSA. For Option Three he had two names for NSA—Ronen Sen and S.K. Lambah.

As I was leaving his flat, Subrahmanyam called me back and said, 'I suggest you tell MK [referring to Narayanan] that this is what I am suggesting to PM. Tell PM that he should take MK into confidence on whatever he plans to do. After all, if PM opts for the first or third option, the new NSA will have to work as part of a team that will include MK.'

The next morning I met the PM and briefed him. He agreed that

Narayanan should be spoken to, and said, 'You tell him. See what he says.'

I walked down the corridor to Narayanan's room and reported to him what had happened, that the PM had sought Subrahmanyam's advice through me and that Subrahmanyam had suggested three options, and so on.

Narayanan heard me out patiently and with no expression on his face. At the end he asked, 'So what has PM decided?'

I told him the PM had not decided anything. He just mumbled 'Okay' and I went back to my room.

For several days thereafter there was no further news. The occasional journalist would call me to find out if there was any update on naming a full-time NSA, in place of Satish Chandra's part-time role, and I would have nothing to offer. One day, Narayanan called me and asked if I knew what was happening. I mentioned to him that there was a news report that Ronen might be coming to Delhi on a visit. Narayanan burst out.

'I say! The PM should be made aware that if I am not appointed, I will quit.'

He then narrated the story of how Sonia Gandhi had first offered the position to him and that it was he who had suggested Mani's name to the PM because of his personal obligation to be in Chennai with his ailing mother. He said he had found a solution to this problem and he was now ready to move his home to Delhi and so expected to be named NSA.

I delivered this message to the PM. Dr Singh responded instantly, saying, 'Yes, it will be Narayanan. I have decided.'

I asked him why then he had not yet conveyed this to Narayanan. Why was he holding back? If the decision has been taken, why not inform all concerned and make the announcement?

Dr Singh looked up and asked, 'What is the hurry?'

I was flummoxed. I had no real answer. But I managed to come up with one.

'Today is the 25th, tomorrow is Republic Day. If you appoint him today he can go to the Republic Day parade and to the Rashtrapati Bhavan reception as the new NSA. You will make him happy. Otherwise, at Rashtrapati Bhavan everyone will ask what is happening about the

NSA's appointment and this will irritate him. Why do you want to irritate him? If you have anyway decided to give him the job, do it today.'

He picked up the phone and asked his PS to get Nair on the line. That evening Narayanan's appointment was announced. Next morning, as I made my way to my designated seat at the Republic Day parade on Rajpath, I could see many service officers lift a hand smartly to salute the new NSA. Narayanan was in his steel-grey bandhgala. Smart, bright and happy. He took every salute given to him, then walked across the carpet and busily shook hands with several Cabinet ministers.

I was never sure if Dr Singh's final decision to appoint Narayanan was his alone or jointly taken with Sonia or was in fact Sonia's. An incident three days later made me believe that Narayanan himself may have felt he owed his job to Sonia. At the Beating Retreat ceremony at Vijay Chowk on Rajpath, I found myself seated just behind Narayanan. He suddenly stood up and walked straight to the very front where Sonia Gandhi sat. Standing in front of her, in full view of the Cabinet, senior officials and diplomats, and the thousands gathered around Vijay Chowk, he chose to publicly display, it seemed, his gratitude to her. Bending forward a bit, he brought his hands together and did a respectful namaste!

Narayanan's appointment did not alter Nair's status. While Mani's intellectual and administrative prowess gave him a stature that Nair never had, Narayanan's long record as the Congress party's favourite intelligence czar and his impressive control over the IB ensured that he too stood taller than the principal secretary. If Mani was the cynosure of all eyes within the IFS, Narayanan enjoyed the same kind of reverence within the IPS. Nair never had that stature within the IAS. He sought to build a constituency for himself both by burnishing his leftist credentials and by reaching out to fellow Malayalees within the civil service. The one field in which he enjoyed some professional standing was within the public sector, from his time as secretary of the public enterprises selection board. He was a strong advocate of the public sector and remained loyal to the cause of strengthening state-owned enterprises. Apart from using his equation with Pulok to bolster his position, Nair also benefitted from having the assistance of some very competent joint secretaries in the PMO: Sanjay Mitra, an IAS officer of the West Bengal cadre, who had served as Jyoti Basu's secretary; R. Gopalakrishnan, who had served as Digvijaya Singh's secretary in the chief minister's office in Madhya Pradesh and was also related to the Kerala communist leader, the late E.M.S. Namboodiripad; and Vini Mahajan, from the Punjab cadre, like Nair. They were all very capable officers and constituted the administrative bulwark of the PMO.

A key member of Manmohan's team in UPA-1 was his private secretary, B.V.R. Subrahmanyam or Subbu, as we called him. Narayanan paid Subbu and me the highest compliment a Malayalee possibly could when he once said to us, 'I always thought Tamil Brahmins were the cleverest chaps, but you Telugu Brahmins have proved to be cleverer!' Subbu was a 1987-batch officer of the IAS, originally from the Madhya Pradesh cadre, and then assigned to Chhattisgarh. As a highly talented officer with good academic credentials and a keen understanding of politics, he proved an invaluable asset for Dr Singh in UPA-1. Subbu's personal interest in astrology meant that he became the resident PMO expert for fixing dates and times for the PM's important engagements.

While Subbu's astrological guidance never determined the PM's dates of travel or the timing of his major official appointments, he did manage to convince Dr Singh to adhere to his advice on 'auspicious' dates and times when it came to certain personal decisions like the date of an operation or the filing of his nomination for re-election to the Rajya Sabha and the family's moving into 3 RCR, the private, residential part of the official residence, after its renovation.

However, it was the PM, never much of a believer in astrology, who had the last laugh. In 2007, when his government appeared particularly wobbly with the CPI(M) issuing its first threat to withdraw support to it, some political reporters from the Hindi media informed me that BJP leader L.K. Advani was offering prayers and conducting a havan to ensure the ouster of the Singh government. I reported this story to the PM. He burst out laughing, something he rarely did. 'He will never succeed,' he said emphatically, 'if his priests are going by my official date of birth!'

Dr Singh's date and time of birth in the village of Gah was never recorded. With his mother dead and his father away at the time, Dr Singh was admitted to school by his grandmother who gave whatever date came to her mind. That date, 26 September, has since become his official birth date. Hindu astrology, however, is based on the time and date of birth, which also determines the birth star of an individual. At the time of offering prayers in a temple or conducting an auspicious ceremony like a wedding or a havan, Hindu priests ask the person concerned for his birth star and subsequent incantations refer to it.

Clearly, Advani's prayers for Dr Singh's ouster went unheeded because the basic data used was incorrect! However, in a political environment where astrology was not irrelevant, Dr Singh was no doubt fortunate to have on his staff a religiously orthodox and learned person like Subbu, who knew his Vedas, Shastras and astrology well. Very quickly Subbu and I became a team and worked in tandem.

The PM's second PS, Vikram Doraiswamy, from the foreign service, was a bright and energetic officer, but a stickler for protocol, like most diplomats. Subbu and he were an effective pair and played an important role in ensuring that the Manmohan PMO worked efficiently and smoothly. While Vikram had the good fortune of having to deal with the talented Mani Dixit, Subbu had to compensate on many occasions for the foibles and shortcomings of Nair. Subbu left the PMO around the same time that I did, but Dr Singh continued to be well served by the very competent and reliable successors, Jaideep Sarkar and Indu Chaturvedi.

Officials come and go but the one person who has remained by Dr Singh's side through his entire tenure is Muralidharan, Dr Singh's 'Man Friday' and his personal assistant. Dr Singh inherited Murali from Murali's previous boss, the Kerala MP M.M. Jacob, when he became leader of the Opposition in the Rajya Sabha. Murali was a member of the Congress party in Kerala and had a good understanding of the way the party functioned. Murali was never far away from the PM, in the office and at home. In the best tradition of Malayalee personal assistants, who form a formidable network across sarkari Delhi, he was a remarkably effective, efficient and loyal assistant, who knew when to get everyone out of a room to ensure the PM ate his lunch, took his insulin shot or got some rest. Murali never misused his access and extended unquestioned loyalty to Dr Singh. He was a good judge of the PM's moods and was able to lighten the boss's burden whenever he felt Dr Singh was tired or angry. Murali remained my direct link to the PM long after I left the PMO.

The prime ministerial compound that went by the name 7 RCR actually contained five addresses, 1, 3, 5, 7 and 9 RCR. While 1 was a helipad and 9 was the home of the SPG, 3, 5 and 7 RCR were more or less identical bungalows with the large lawns common to all ministerial homes in Lutyens' Delhi. All the three bungalows were linked through a path that cut through the walls separating one from the other. All movement within this enclosed space was closely monitored by the SPG. Dr Singh's family members and Sonia Gandhi, also an SPG protectee, were exempted from the security drill of alighting near 9 RCR and being driven by the SPG to the other bungalows. They had the privilege of driving straight in in their SPG-protected vehicles, as did heads of government calling upon the prime minister.

It was 7 RCR that housed the PMO, with a small set of half a dozen officers staffing his personal section, responsible for all the appointments and correspondence of the PM. 7 RCR was also the venue for meeting official visitors, including foreign dignitaries. During Vajpayee's time a conference room, Panchavati, had also been constructed. Next door, at 5 RCR, there was a small reception room for secretarial staff whom the PM could summon at odd hours from his home. 3 RCR was where the prime minister and his family lived.

Returning to government after eight years in the Opposition benches, Dr Singh took his job seriously. He rose early and, after a morning walk, exercise and a light breakfast, usually walked down from 3 RCR to 7 RCR between quarter to nine and nine o'clock.

For those who had worked in the Vajpayee PMO, this was all very new. Vajpayee had slowed down towards the end of his term and his working day would begin late and end early. Dr Singh worked from nine in the morning to nine in the evening, with an hour's siesta after lunch.

Meals were frugal, mostly vegetarian, with some fish occasionally, and chapatti rather than paratha, with Mrs Kaur strictly monitoring what the PM ate, and when. At 7 RCR, the staff had inherited a snacks menu from Vajpayee's time that included samosas and kachoris. When the news reached Mrs Kaur that Dr Singh had been biting into a samosa or two during meetings, she had the samosa replaced by the healthier dhokla. Dr Singh's standard energy source at work was tea with Marie biscuits. Before Dr Singh's very first breakfast meeting with editors, Vikram Doraiswamy asked the PM what he should order for breakfast and was told 'the usual'. Having worked in the Vajpayee PMO where 'the usual' was a sumptuous meal, Vikram ordered a full English breakfast with cereal, fruits and eggs as well as a hearty south Indian breakfast of idli, dosa and upma. The editors had barely tucked into their first course of a three-course breakfast when Dr Singh finished his fruit and toast and ordered tea. I had to nudge my friends from the media to continue eating and not feel restrained by Dr Singh's frugality.

A PM working from South Block was also a new routine in the PMO. Vajpayee worked mostly from 7 RCR. Dr Singh, on the other hand, normally worked in the morning in South Block, went home for lunch at half past one and returned either to 7 RCR or South Block by four, and worked till dinnertime. At South Block, the prime minister's large, high-ceilinged room had windows to the south that always remained closed and a private anteroom with a door behind the PM's chair, covered by a wooden panel. Though an unpretentiously furnished room, with just a bare table and sofas for visitors, its teak walls would have heard the voice of every PM this country has had. His working space at 7 RCR, in the prime ministerial compound, was used only from Rajiv Gandhi's time. It was less grand than his office at South Block, but with lawns and peacocks to gaze at, had a prettier view.

Dr Singh followed the routine that he set for himself day after day, and year after year. He never took a vacation, apart from a few snatched hours between meetings and the departure of his plane, when he was abroad. He would use that time to be with family or just read a book. Once, in May 2006, he was scheduled to go to Goa to inaugurate the new campus of the Birla Institute of Technology and Sciences. It was a Saturday and the plan was for him to land in Goa in the morning, and return to Delhi by evening. I suggested to his daughter, Daman, that we spend Saturday night in Goa and return on Sunday evening. She didn't think her father would agree. What would justify an extra day in Goa when there was no work? I decided to try my luck and suggested the plan to him.

'Why?' he asked me. I said this would allow his entourage to spend Saturday night and Sunday morning on the beach.

'And do what?' he asked, vetoing the idea.

The media loved writing about Dr Singh's frugal lifestyle and long working days, comparing them with Vajpayee's more leisurely style of functioning, and I was happy to feed them such stories. But Dr Singh's 'early to rise and late to sleep' schedule had its pluses and minuses. On the plus side, his habit of tuning in to the BBC early in the morning helped the Government of India respond with alacrity to the tsunami in December 2004. Long before any disaster management, national security or intelligence agency woke up to alert government agencies, the PM was up and heard the news of the tsunami. On that morning, our phone first rang with a call from Rama's father in Chennai, who had gone to the beach for his early morning walk and returned after finding the water level to be unusually high. Immediately after that came the call from Subbu, prompted by Dr Singh who had heard the news on the BBC and was contacting one official after another. Woken up by the PM, Cabinet Secretary B.K. Chaturvedi then summoned a meeting of the crisis management team.

If that was the upside of Dr Singh's long waking hours, the downside—for his media adviser—would be the occasional late night call when I was either at a party or sleeping. On one occasion, he called to tell me, 'TV says Madhu Dandavate has passed away,' referring to a veteran, retired socialist politician, and then added, 'Please issue a condolence message right away.'

4

Managing the Coalition

'I do not know if he is an overrated economist,
but I know he is an underrated politician!'

Digvijaya Singh on NDTV, 2012

A couple of years before Sonia Gandhi took charge of the Congress, the communist ideologue Mohit Sen wrote a persuasive column in the *Times of India* underlining the historic role Sonia would be called upon to play and urging her to do so. The first woman president of the Indian National Congress, he argued, was also a European woman, Annie Besant. The party, he stressed, should once again be led by another. When Mohit's column landed on my table—I was then the editorial page editor of the *Times of India*—I was amused and surprised. Mohit was an 'uncle', a close friend of my father from their time together in Hyderabad, and the person from whom I received my first lessons in Marxism. I called Mohit and told him that his suggestion that Sonia should take charge of the Congress was an outlandish idea. As the political party of India's freedom struggle, surely it had to have a future independent of the Nehru–Gandhi family? How could he suggest that Sonia become the party's president merely because she was Rajiv's widow? I told him people would laugh at him for his political naivete and suggested the column be junked. He was most offended and threatened to go elsewhere if I refused to publish his piece. Finally, I agreed to use it because of my affection and regard for him.

Mohit's column was the first credible public call for Sonia's induction into public life. Mohit had already drawn close to Sonia and he later also warmed towards Dr Singh. He had been a critic of Dr Singh's economic policies in the early 1990s, but within the next decade came around to accepting the view that Dr Singh would make a good PM, though he saw nothing wrong in Sonia herself taking up that post. It was Dr Singh who released Mohit's autobiography at the India International Centre. When Mohit died in 2003, Sonia's condolence message referred to him as a 'father figure' in her life. After Mohit's death, Dr Singh took on that role. Perhaps he was not precisely a 'father figure' to Sonia, but there was certainly something avuncular about his relationship with her.

I assumed that Mohit, as an Indira loyalist, had a special regard for her heirs. But his opinion that Sonia should enter politics was also based on his conviction that without a Nehru–Gandhi family member at the top, the Congress party would splinter and wither away. This view was also encouraged by members of the Delhi durbar—a 'power elite', to use sociologist C. Wright Mill's term, comprising civil servants, diplomats, editors, intellectuals and business leaders who had worked with or been close to the regimes of Nehru, Indira and Rajiv. Some of them inhabited the many trusts and institutions that the Nehru–Gandhi family controlled. They had all profited in one way or another, over the years, from their loyalty to the Congress's 'first family'.

In opposition to this view was the one held by a Congressman like Narasimha Rao who, while ironically titling his semi-autobiographical book *The Insider*, believed he was an 'outsider' among Delhi's Nehru–Gandhi 'power elite'. Rao believed that a political organization that was more than a century old, the party of India's freedom movement, inspired and led by a Gandhi, a mahatma who was no relative of these Gandhis, ought to imagine for itself a life beyond the Nehru–Gandhi family. Many small regional parties might have become feudal, even despotic, 'family-led' parties, but how could a grand old political organization like the Indian National Congress link its future only to the fortunes of one political family? This view had few takers among family loyalists, who took charge of the party after the unceremonious ouster of Sitaram Kesari, the man Narasimha Rao chose as his successor and who in turn placed the party's crown in Sonia's hands.

When Sonia Gandhi decided to join active politics and take charge of the Congress party, becoming its president in 1998, few thought through how her elevation would affect the relationship between the party and a future Congress government. While her loyalists argued there was nothing to resolve here, since she would become prime minister, her detractors in the party said they were willing to accept her as party president but not as a future PM because of her Italian origin. It was this issue that led Sharad Pawar and others to exit the party in 1999 and form the NCP.

It was against this background that the arrangement that came into place in 2004 would be viewed and tested. Would Sonia really remain only party president and leave the government for Dr Singh to handle? Having led the Congress back to power, especially in the face of scepticism about her abilities to win an election and the open revolt of party warlords like Pawar, would she rest content allowing someone else to wield that power? What should Dr Singh's strategy be? Should he assume that while Sonia was the leader of the Congress, he was the head of a coalition government, with non-Congress constituents, including a rebel like Pawar, and carve out his own political space and retain administrative control of government? Or should he be running every day to 10 Janpath, Sonia's residence-cum-office, to take her instructions? Some chief ministers had done that with their party bosses. Jyoti Basu, in his early days as chief minister (CM) of West Bengal, had a daily meeting with his party boss Pramode Dasgupta at the party headquarters. Manohar Joshi, the Shiv Sena CM of Maharashtra, did the same with his party supremo Bal Thackeray.

Handling the delicate equation with Sonia was Dr Singh's first and biggest political challenge. How a CM is perceived at the state level is different from the way a PM is perceived at the national and international levels. The prime minister is a national leader and the international face of a country. He negotiates with other heads of government and must be seen to be his own man. Moreover, Dr Singh was PM because the UPA coalition as a whole was willing to accept him. In 1999 Mulayam Singh Yadav had refused to support Sonia when she claimed she had the numbers to form a government. So I, at any rate, saw my job as one of establishing Dr Singh's credibility as PM, while ensuring that the relationship with Sonia and the party was on an even keel.

The first tricky situation presented itself in early August 2004. The PM's SPG asked me if I would participate in the dress rehearsal for Dr Singh's first Independence Day address from the ramparts of the Red Fort. This involved travelling in the PM's motorcade from RCR to Red Fort, stopping to place imaginary wreaths at Mahatma Gandhi's memorial at Rajghat and the memorials of members of the Nehru–Gandhi family, and then spending forty minutes on the ramparts of the fort, from where the PM would address the nation, before returning to RCR.

As I walked around the ramparts, accompanied by a defence ministry official, I curiously examined the name cards placed on chairs set out for guests at the event. The first seat in the first row, adjacent to the podium from where the PM would speak, was reserved for Mrs Kaur. After that, the seating was in accordance with the defence ministry's protocol and order of precedence, as issued in the *Gazette of India,* which meant senior Cabinet ministers, leader of the Opposition, chief justice of the Supreme Court and other holders of high office. Sonia Gandhi's name was nowhere to be found in the front row. When I asked the official where Sonia would be seated, he looked at the protocol list in his hand and pointed to a chair in the middle of the fourth or fifth row. She was to be seated next to Najma Heptullah, former Congresswoman and deputy chairperson of the Rajya Sabha, who had crossed floors and joined the BJP!

I was aghast. Such an arrangement would embarrass the PM and, I imagined, make Sonia livid. I then recalled noticing that Sonia was always seated in the front row at Rashtrapati Bhavan events, perhaps on the first seat along the aisle. I immediately called Muthu Kumar, an official in the PMO's media department, and asked him to check with the President's secretariat how it managed to seat Sonia in the front row when her status as an MP, albeit one who was also chairperson of the NAC with Cabinet rank, merited only a fourth- or fifth-row chair.

Muthu discovered that Rashtrapati Bhavan had made a minor alteration in the seating procedure during President Shankar Dayal Sharma's time. Sharma, India's President from 1992 to 1997, had authorized that the spouse of a former prime minister would get the same protocol status as a former PM. The reasoning was that if a former PM had been accompanied by his spouse at a Rashtrapati Bhavan event, the two would have been seated together. This issue had not arisen for previous prime ministers because Nehru, Indira, Morarji Desai and Narasimha Rao had all been pre-deceased by their spouses and the spouses of other deceased PMs were clearly not in the habit of attending state functions. Sonia was the first widowed spouse of a PM in public life.

This episode drew early attention to the purely protocol dimension of Sonia's new status vis-à-vis the PM. While Sonia did have Cabinet rank as chairperson of the NAC, which was set up on 4 June 2004 shortly after UPA-1 assumed power, and was 'entitled to the same salary, pay, allowances and other facilities to which a member of the Union Council of Ministers is entitled', she had to be given a rank that put her next only to the PM and his wife and not further down the order of precedence.

While the protocol issues raised by Sonia's status were new to the party president–prime minister equation, the relationship problem itself was neither new nor peculiar to India. Defining the relationship between party president (or general secretary in the case of communist parties) and the head of government has bedevilled many regimes around the world for a long time. In non-democratic systems like the erstwhile Soviet Union and contemporary China the protocol and division of real power between the communist party general secretary and the head of government is a complex issue. In democracies, it becomes even more complicated when the popularly elected head of government is different from the leader of the party in power.

In India the problem raised its head on day one. As the first post-Independence Congress party president, Acharya Kripalani demanded that he be taken into confidence on the policies of the government headed by Prime Minister Jawaharlal Nehru. Nehru rejected this demand, taking the view that while the party could be briefed on broad policy issues, it would not be possible for ministers sworn to secrecy and holding constitutional office to share the contents of government files with the party president. Nehru invited Kripalani to join the government as a minister without portfolio and secure this entitlement, drawing a sharp distinction between party and government. Ministers, he argued, functioned under a constitutional oath and were subject to the Official Secrets Act. No minister, not even the prime minister, could show a file to someone outside the government, not even to the Congress president.

Kripalani did not accept Nehru's view or his invitation to join the government, and quit as Congress president. Nehru then took over the party presidency in 1950, combining the two posts for the first time, and continued in this manner until 1954, when U.N. Dhebar became party president. While Indira Gandhi, who had served as party president in 1959, managed a working relationship with Congress presidents during her tenure as PM, including Kamaraj, Jagjivan Ram and Shankar Dayal Sharma, she took over as party president after her defeat in 1977 and retained that post when she returned to office as PM in 1980. Rajiv Gandhi followed suit, keeping the Congress presidency till his death in 1991.

Keeping control over both the party and the government was viewed as the best way for a prime minister to ensure political support for his policy initiatives, especially and increasingly so in the Congress party where political loyalty was based on personal advancement and enrichment rather than a commitment to a shared ideology.

On Rajiv's death, Narasimha Rao took over as Congress president and he, too, retained the post after he was elected prime minister in 1991. However, Rao was challenged at the All India Congress Committee (AICC) session at Tirupati in 1992 by a group led by Arjun

Singh and N.D. Tiwari that demanded a separation of roles. Rao had to then fight hard to get re-elected president and retain his control over the Congress Working Committee, the executive committee of the party. Once he was elected, he kept the post till after his defeat in the 1996 General Elections. He was then succeeded by Sitaram Kesari who yielded power to Sonia in March 1998. It was an early mark of Sonia's regard for and trust in Dr Singh that when she took charge as the party's leader in the Lok Sabha, she nominated Dr Singh as the party's leader in the Rajya Sabha.

———

Apart from the weekly meeting of the Congress 'core group', initially comprising Sonia, the PM, Arjun Singh, A.K. Antony, Pranab Mukherjee and Sonia's political secretary Ahmed Patel, and messages exchanged through two intermediaries, Pulok and Patel, or occasional telephone conversations, there was not much other regular contact between Dr Singh and Sonia in the early years of UPA-1. The core group met regularly at 7 RCR. Sonia would arrive first and get her exclusive ten minutes with Dr Singh. That was when the two spoke to each other in private. Once their one-to-one conversation was over, the others would be invited in. Dr Singh rarely spoke in the core-group meetings. He would hear what others had to say and take his decisions after having another word with Sonia.

There was also very little social contact between the families of the two leaders. Mrs Kaur and Sonia met rarely, except at official functions and banquets. Rarely, too, did Dr Singh's daughters or Sonia's children join the Congress president and the prime minister at social gatherings. On the odd occasion, Sonia would call on Dr Singh to discuss family matters. There were, after all, few family elders available to give her advice on things that may have bothered her in her personal life. While she was very close to her mother, her father had passed away. Rajiv's friends, like Satish Sharma, Sam Pitroda and Suman Dubey, were all her age. I was aware that on at least one occasion she came to see Dr Singh to discuss her concerns about Rahul's personal plans.

Following that conversation, Dr Singh invited Rahul for lunch and the two spent time together.

In private, Sonia often addressed Dr Singh as Manmohan, which, given her Western background, suggested she felt closer and more familial in her relationship with him than with other senior leaders of his generation. Dr Singh, for his part, always referred to her as Soniaji or Mrs Gandhi and treated her with old-fashioned courtesy. At the annual UPA anniversary function at 7 RCR he always made it a point to stand up on the dais when Sonia stood up to walk to the podium and deliver her speech, a practice that other Congressmen did not follow. Culturally, it is a Western gesture for a man to stand up when a woman does and women are not expected to reciprocate, so Sonia naturally did not. But Delhi's political journalists, who were always watching the two like hawks at public events for evidence that the PM was more deferential to her than he needed to be, would draw my attention to the leaders' 'body language' with wicked smiles.

When Sonia turned sixty, Dr Singh sent her a personal letter praising her courage and fortitude. She had been widowed at a young age, and had to bring up her children in the very difficult social and security context of Delhi. And, she had allowed herself to be persuaded to take on the mantle of party presidency by Congressmen who feared the party would disintegrate without her at the helm. Recounting these facts, Dr Singh praised her for her courage and her poise in the face of such adversity and for the energy and wisdom with which she had led the Congress party back to power.

Sonia and Dr Singh's warm personal equation was also evident in the little gestures he made to show his concern for her welfare, like always calling her to check how she was whenever she took ill.

I had no reason to doubt that Dr Singh and Sonia implicitly trusted each other. Reports appearing in the media about differences between the two were often planted by disgruntled Congressmen and mischievous journalists, some of whom would then point a finger in my direction. That did not mean the two had no differences on policy issues. But any such differences between them would have been aired only in their private meetings and the PM almost never allowed any of this to trickle into the public realm.

The PM never questioned Sonia's right, as party president, to influence portfolio allocations though, over time, he became quite forthcoming in giving his opinions, and she did accept his advice. While I knew it was not realistic to argue that Dr Singh should have full control over ministerial appointments, I felt he needed to assert himself at least in the allocation of portfolios to junior ministers and would press him when I got the chance. In 2005, for example, when he asked me whether I thought Jairam Ramesh should be inducted into government, I replied that Jairam ought to be more demonstrative of his loyalty to the PM if he wanted a berth in the ministry. I was taken aback when, a few days later, Montek took me aside at a Christmas party at journalist T.N. Ninan's house and asked me why I was opposing Jairam's induction. I clarified to Montek that I was not against it, and had only said to the PM that at least younger Congress MPs should feel they owed their ministerial berths to the PM rather than just to Sonia. I am not aware of what transpired after that, but in the following month, January 2006, Jairam did get inducted as a minister of state in the commerce ministry. I was not surprised to learn that Jairam later called on Sonia's friend Suman Dubey and thanked him for the job.

Politics is about power and patronage, and ministerial positions are won not just on the basis of competence but also in recognition of a politician's political clout or loyalty to the leader. For Congress MPs, the leader to please was always Sonia. They did not see loyalty to the PM as a political necessity, nor did Dr Singh seek loyalty in the way in which Sonia and her aides sought it. That Jairam's loyalty was only with Sonia became clearer within weeks of his becoming a minister when he chose to embarrass the PM by leaking a letter that Sonia had written to Dr Singh cautioning him against pursuing an initiative he valued a lot—the free trade agreement (FTA) with member countries of the ASEAN.

Dr Singh viewed the India-ASEAN FTA as an important geo-political initiative aimed at India's economic integration into the rapidly growing Asian economies and as being helpful in balancing China's growing clout in Asia. The CPI(M), on the other hand, chose to oppose the India–ASEAN FTA on the grounds that it would hurt the interests of plantation workers in Kerala and West Bengal. Keen to blunt the CPI(M)'s criticism, the Congress party in Kerala exerted pressure on the central leadership to abandon the FTA project. Sonia Gandhi's letter to the PM was written to convey these concerns. It was not normal practice for Sonia to write such formal letters to the PM. She almost always conveyed serious concerns orally and directly or through intermediaries like Ahmed Patel and Pulok Chatterjee. However, since she *had* written, Dr Singh too responded in writing, defending the FTA. He wrote:

> Our approach to regional trade agreements in general, and FTAs in particular, has been evolved after careful consideration of our geo-political as well as economic interests. Although India has a large domestic market, our experience with earlier relatively insular policies, as also the global experience in this regard, clearly bring out the growth potential of trade and economic cooperation with the global economy.

A few weeks later Sonia's confidential letter to the PM found its way into the media, with the *Business Standard* carrying a front-page story. A furious Dr Singh asked me to find out who had leaked it. I asked the editor, T.N. Ninan. Quite understandably, Ninan declined to reveal the identity of a privileged news source. However, a journalist in the know confirmed Jairam Ramesh's role. I reported this back to Dr Singh who picked up the phone and reprimanded Jairam, even as the latter denied any role in the leak.

Interestingly, the PM was amenable to the suggestion that his letter to Sonia be made public, given that her letter to him had been publicly aired. Therefore, I released his letter to the media. While such a public expression of differences between them was rare, this incident did draw attention to the role of mischief-makers in muddying the waters.

On a daily and regular basis, messages between Sonia and the PM were conveyed either by Ahmed Patel or Pulok Chatterjee. While Pulok met Sonia regularly to brief her on policy issues and seek her guidance on key decisions, Ahmed Patel was the political link between

Sonia and Dr Singh. Patel would visit South Block mainly to lobby with Pulok for the inclusion of names of Congress party members on the boards of public enterprises and nationalized banks.

Patel also met the PM from time to time and these meetings were invariably held at 7 RCR. Any increase in the frequency of his visits was almost always a signal of an impending Cabinet reshuffle. Patel was the one who carried, to and fro, the list of names of people to be included or dropped from the council of ministers. Patel was always very courteous and polite. As Sonia's trusted aide, he never behaved in a manner that would demonstrate his real power. With Dr Singh he was particularly polite and deferential in his behaviour. As Sonia's chosen courier, he acquired the power to influence decision-making in such matters till the very end. On one occasion, he arrived at 7 RCR just minutes before the PM's letter to the President listing the names of MPs to be sworn in as ministers in a reshuffle was dispatched. Since the letter had been typed and signed and was ready to be delivered, and the President was waiting to receive it, it was decided that instead of wasting time retyping the letter, the new name being canvassed by Patel would be typed over an existing name, with that name being painted over with whitener. Thus was Andhra MP Subbirami Reddy accommodated into the council of ministers in January 2006, after white paint had been applied over the name of Harish Rawat, an MP from Uttarakhand, who is now the chief minister of that state.

I had very little to do with Patel and during the few times we interacted he was always warm and friendly. I only had two substantive conversations with him during my time at the PMO. The first occurred shortly after Narasimha Rao died. I had accompanied Dr Singh to Rao's house on Delhi's Motilal Nehru Marg. As the PM entered the house, Patel pulled me aside. Narasimha Rao's children wanted the former PM to be cremated in Delhi, like other Congress prime ministers. Impressive memorials had been built for Nehru, Indira and Rajiv at the places where they had been cremated along the river Yamuna, adjacent to Mahatma Gandhi's memorial. Even former prime minister Charan Singh, who had not belonged to the Congress, and Sanjay Gandhi, who was only an MP, had been cremated and memorialized in the vicinity. However, Patel wanted me to encourage Narasimha Rao's sons, Ranga and Prabhakar, and his daughter, Vani, to take their father's body to Hyderabad for cremation. Clearly, it seemed to me, Sonia did not want a memorial for Rao anywhere in Delhi.

I reflected for a few minutes on Patel's request and felt it would not be appropriate for me to convey this message to the family. They had every right to make the demand they were making. Why should I involve myself in this matter? I kept my counsel and walked away, not saying a word about Patel's suggestion to Rao's children when I met them to express my condolences. Later that evening I was told the Congress party had got Rao's family to agree to fly his body out to Hyderabad by deploying Home Minister Shivraj Patil and Andhra Pradesh Chief Minister Y.S. Rajashekhara Reddy to persuade them to fall in line. The Congress party refused to allow Rao's body to be brought into the party's headquarters on its way to the airport, and Sonia chose not to be present at the Hyderabad cremation.

Interestingly, in 2007, the Congress party tried a replay of this stratagem with the family of former prime minister Chandra Shekhar, persuading them to take the body of the former PM to his farm at Bhondsi in Haryana. However, Chandra Shekhar's son insisted that the family would go to Delhi's Lodi Crematorium if the former PM was not given a proper state funeral in Delhi. The government fell in line and Chandra Shekhar was cremated on the banks of the Yamuna at a spot designated Ekta Sthal.

The second time Patel approached me was when the leader of the Telangana Rashtra Samithi Chandrashekhara Rao, also a Cabinet minister, demanded that I be sacked from government for issuing a denial to the media about a claim that he had made regarding the subject of his conversation with Dr Singh. Rao had claimed that he met the PM to press for an early decision on Telangana while he had, in fact, met him for some other purpose and the Telangana issue had never come up in the conversation. This is what I had said to the Telugu media when pressed by them for an account of what actually transpired at the meeting. Patel wanted me to apologize to the minister and end the controversy. I had to tell Patel that my briefing was factual and I saw no reason to apologize, but would do so if instructed by the PM. I made it clear I only took my orders from Dr Singh. The matter ended there. Rao reportedly calmed down after calling me names. A few weeks later, on a visit to 7 RCR, he hugged me warmly and offered to invite me home for a meal of Hyderabadi biryani, but the invitation never came.

The creation of the NAC in June 2004 was the first overt sign to me that Sonia's 'renunciation' of power was more of a political tactic than a response to a higher calling, or to an 'inner voice', as she put it at the time. Admittedly, she chose not to head the UPA government even after leading the Congress to electoral success in the 2004 General Elections, instead putting forward the name of Dr Singh. But, while power was delegated, authority was not. Her decisions, early on, to try and appoint a principal secretary to the PM of her choosing—the retired Tamilian official who had worked with Rajiv but declined Sonia's invitation—and to place her trusted aide Pulok Chatterjee in the PMO, were aimed at ensuring a degree of control over government. Of course, she had a decisive say in the allocation of portfolios.

The creation of the NAC and Sonia's choice of its members was explained away as a recognition of the growing importance and influence of non-governmental organizations (NGOs), that claimed to represent civil society, in policymaking. However, in actual practice it created a parallel policy structure that sought to project Sonia as the voice of civil society and Dr Singh as the representative of government. While Dr Singh realized that he had no option but to live with this situation, and never complained about it, it always seemed to me that he was not too comfortable with it, even if he was willing to see merit in the ideas that came out of the NAC.

The manner of creation of the NAC, by executive order, was no different from Nehru's creation of the Planning Commission. Many senior Congress leaders had felt unhappy about Nehru's decision to create a non-constitutional policy advisory body outside the Cabinet system, even though Nehru appointed himself as chairman of the Commission. John Mathai even resigned as finance minister from Nehru's Cabinet in protest.Yet, no one in the UPA government raised any such issues about the status and role of the NAC, a body of which the PM was not even formally the chairperson.

Notwithstanding Dr Singh's discomfort with the NAC, intellectual differences between Sonia and him were never as sharp as projected by both her supporters and critics. Such projection, when it came from her supporters, was part of her image and brand-building. Sonia was to be projected as the 'caring socialist concerned about the welfare of the poor', while Dr Singh was to be blamed for being too fiscally conservative and pro-business. Indeed, Dr Singh, essentially a Keynesian, ended up being wrongly portrayed a 'neo-liberal' economist.

Faced with this situation, the prime minister felt the need, at times, to make the point that his views were not quite as extreme as those of his friends, the economists Jagdish Bhagwati and T.N. Srinivasan, and that he did differ on some issues even with Montek. He used the opportunity provided by an episode in September 2004 to do so. Montek had come under attack from the Left for inducting what the Left dubbed 'pro-business and neo-liberal' consultants into the Planning Commission, such as Arun Maira, the chairman of the Boston Consulting Group in India, and the economist Suman Bery. Dr Singh wanted me to let it be known that he was not entirely happy with Montek's decision. On such occasions I would draw a politically savvy journalist into a conversation and say things that a good reporter always picked up and did a story on, without being explicitly told to. Montek subsequently withdrew that initiative, though Maira became a Planning Commission member in UPA-2.

When I confronted the CPI(M) ideologue and Marxist economist Prabhat Patnaik and asked him how he could dub Dr Singh a 'neo-liberal', knowing full well that his academic orientation had all along been Keynesian, Prabhat agreed that Dr Singh was intellectually a Keynesian, but claimed his policies were 'neo-liberal'. The Left found it useful to make this distinction between Sonia and Dr Singh, approvingly portraying the former as being 'socialist' in her orientation, because it provided them with a justification for continuing to extend political support to the Sonia-led UPA, while criticizing the policies of the Singh-led government.

Both the Left and Sonia, or at least her advisers, made good use of this distinction in managing the peculiar balance between two parties, the Congress and the CPI(M), that had fought each other all their lives but were now fellow travellers. The Left would be supportive of 'leftist' Sonia and critical of 'rightist' Manmohan. It suited them all to play this game till Dr Singh finally forced Sonia to choose between him and the Left in June 2008.

On the issue of the India–ASEAN FTA, the Left tried to gain political advantage by getting Kerala Chief Minister V.S. Achuthanandan to lead a delegation, including his finance minister, T.M. Thomas Isaac, and Prabhat Patnaik, who was the deputy chairman of the Kerala State Planning Board, to submit a memorandum to the PM against the India–ASEAN FTA. Dr Singh adroitly deflected this ploy. Receiving the paper, he told the delegation with his signature smile, 'But, comrades, I am told that the FTA would benefit farmers in the fraternal, socialist Republic of Vietnam.'

Everyone burst out laughing and the matter ended there.

———

With Surjeet as general secretary of the CPI(M), Dr Singh may have assumed that he would be able to manage the Left. The two Sardars had a warm relationship, testified to by Surjeet's acquiescence in Montek's appointment. Dr Singh also reached out to Jyoti Basu, who had stepped down as West Bengal chief minister, but was still a leading figure in the CPI(M), upon which Basu categorically assured him of his support 'for a full five-year term', as he put it. For the smooth functioning of the relationship, a UPA–Left coordination committee was formed. Moreover, the PMO team under Pulok that was responsible for monitoring the NCMP would pay special attention to programmes of interest to the CPM, especially in Kerala and Bengal. Dr Singh also kept in touch with the Left leadership through his own staff in the

PMO. When career diplomat Shivshankar Menon was made foreign secretary in 2006, it was hoped he, too, would be a bridge between the government and the Left because of his old friendship with CPI(M) supporters and leaders, going back to his student days and those of his sister, Saraswati Menon, a contemporary of CPI(M) politburo members Prakash Karat and Sitaram Yechury at JNU.

In the early days, the relationship did run quite smoothly. Surjeet and Basu loyalists in the CPI(M) were in general accommodating with Dr Singh. As long as this group, led by Yechury, was in control of the party's Delhi office, Dr Singh had little trouble working with the Left. Karat's takeover of the CPI(M) changed all that. His attempt to seize power from Surjeet had begun in the run-up to the CPI(M)'s 17th party congress in 2002. The 'Bengal faction' of the party, led by Jyoti Basu and including Buddhadeb Bhattacharya and Sitaram Yechury, opposed Karat's move and Surjeet stayed on. By 2004 the stakes had gone up. The CPI(M) was, after six years, once again extending support to a government in New Delhi, and it mattered who controlled the party's national leadership in Delhi.

On the eve of the 18th party congress in Delhi in April 2005, Buddhadeb met Dr Singh and assured him that there would be no change of leadership and that Surjeet would continue. Even as Dr Singh and Buddhadeb were having a private dinner at 7 RCR, the private television news channel NDTV reported as 'breaking news' that the CPI(M) party congress would see a change of guard with Karat replacing Surjeet.

I was sitting in the visitors' room at 7 RCR and watching the news while Dr Singh and Buddhadeb were having dinner. I immediately went into the dining room and informed them that NDTV had claimed Karat was likely to replace Surjeet. We all knew that NDTV had an inside line to the CPI(M) since NDTV's Prannoy Roy was married to Radhika Roy, sister of Brinda Karat, a CPI(M)leader and the wife of Prakash Karat.

The PM looked quizzically at Buddhadeb and the latter appeared surprised. He smiled and added, 'We will see.'

NDTV turned out to be right, in the end. The CPI(M) party

congress ended with Surjeet being replaced by Karat. We braced ourselves for rockier times, knowing full well that Karat and the party's hardliners disliked Surjeet's softness towards Dr Singh. Karat was among those who had been unhappy at Montek's appointment and, perhaps even more, Surjeet's acquiescence to it. Clearly, the honeymoon between the PM and the CPI(M) was now over. When Surjeet fell ill in 2008, Dr Singh was very particular that a warm tribute be paid to him in the event of his passing away. As soon as we heard that Surjeet had been hospitalized, he asked me to draft a condolence message. Surjeet survived his initial hospitalization, but finally passed away when Dr Singh was in Colombo in August that year.

With Karat at the helm, the stronger anti-Congress line of past CPI(M) leaders, the late P. Sundarayya and the late A.K. Gopalan, gained ground at the expense of the softer Basu–Surjeet–Yechury line of being more accommodating towards the Congress and Dr Singh. I warned Dr Singh that if the CPI(M) chose to move further left, partly in response to its growing unpopularity in Bengal, Dr Singh was bound to face even more difficult times.

In July 2006, when Dr Singh came under sharp attack from the CPM hardliners on the India–US nuclear deal, he called on Jyoti Basu to find out if there was any rethinking on the part of the Left on the assurance given to him that he would be allowed to serve his full term as PM. Basu reassured him that Dr Singh had his full support, as long as he adhered to the NCMP. Thus, when the Left finally withdrew support it said it was doing so because the prime minister had deviated from the NCMP, though Dr Singh had maintained all along that the nuclear deal was not a deviation from the NCMP. The NCMP had not only emphasized the importance of 'energy security' for India, a commitment this deal would address, it had also explicitly stated, 'Even as it pursues closer engagement and relations with the USA, the UPA government will maintain the independence of India's foreign policy position on all regional and global issues.'

While Dr Singh was prepared to deal with the Left's tantrums and demands, and appoint Left nominees to various positions in government and academic institutions, he was always conscious of the threat posed by the Left to his own situation. He was aware of the role the CPI(M) had played in all coalition governments that it had supported from 1977 onwards in unseating prime ministers. It had helped eject Morarji Desai and bring in Charan Singh in 1979, defending this on ideological grounds. A pro-business PM had been replaced by a peasant leader. The motive at the time was to try and make inroads into the Hindi heartland, which included the most backward and impoverished parts of India, and where the CPI(M) hardly had any presence. In 1990 the Left played a similar role, helping Chandra Shekhar displace Janata Dal leader V.P. Singh as prime minister. In 1997, it once again played a part in ousting H.D. Deve Gowda, the prime minister installed in 1996, and propping up I.K. Gujral, who replaced him.

Dr Singh had to constantly live with the assumption that the Left might try this tactic once again, securing his ouster and having him replaced by either a Bengali (Pranab Mukherjee) or a Malayalee (A.K. Antony), to win brownie points in the two states where it needed to bolster its presence. Arjun Singh tried to woo the Left with his political posturing but it never really trusted him. When the Left finally withdrew support to the government in July 2008, it tried till the very last to get Sonia to save the government by dumping Dr Singh and replacing him with a 'pro-Left' PM. Karat failed where his predecessors had succeeded, because by July 2008, Dr Singh's personal credibility and his standing as PM had reached such heights that the Congress would have been grievously wounded if Sonia had dumped Dr Singh to please the Left and retain power.

While there were formal consultative mechanisms with the Left, handling the Left was always a tricky problem for Dr Singh. He managed to keep the PMO staff on a tight leash, never allowing us to upset the Left until Karat's coup on the nuclear deal, but he did not always succeed with his Cabinet colleagues. An early incident that I got drawn into involved Finance Minister P. Chidambaram. The BJP was refusing to support some of the finance minister's budget proposals, and the Left, wanting to take advantage of the government's dependency on it to pass the budget, began arm-twisting him. One day, the CPI(M) issued a statement that it might not be able to vote in support of some of Chidambaram's budget proposals. Dr Singh called me and asked me to find out from the Left how serious it was about this threat.

Ensuring the successful passage of the finance bill in Parliament is a constitutional requirement for the survival of the government. In India's parliamentary system the government has to quit if it either loses a vote of confidence or fails to secure support for the finance bill. Not surprisingly, then, Dr Singh wanted to leave nothing to chance. At this stage, he was not seriously worried the government would fall, because both Surjeet and Jyoti Basu had personally assured Dr Singh that the CPI(M) would support him as PM for the entire five-year term. But Dr Singh wanted to be very sure that the Left would vote in favour of the budget. It seemed to me that he also wanted to make sure that the Left had the same view of the understanding with Chidambaram that the latter had claimed he had with them. Were they all on the same page or not?

I went across to the CPI(M) headquarters to meet Yechury. He replied that I should check with Karat, and went down the corridor to see if Karat was free to talk. He returned after a few minutes and said that Karat was busy but had asked him to convey a message to the PM. The message went something like this: The CPI(M) will not bring the government down. So it will not vote against the finance bill. However, the finance minister had said he would like to bring certain financial bills pertaining to the insurance and banking sectors and provident funds. The CPI(M) would vote against such bills.

Having passed on that message, Yechury came out with me as I left the building. As we walked out, he told me, 'We can only unseat the government by voting against it in Parliament. There are many things the finance minister can do without seeking Parliament's approval. Let him do those things. We will protest, but we cannot stop him.' This meant the Left would 'bark' but not 'bite', a phrase commonly used by the media to interpret its stance. It would publicly dissociate itself from the government's initiatives, but would not withdraw support.

Where a policy initiative required legislative approval and, therefore, the Left's vote in Parliament, it would support only such policies that had its prior approval.

I delivered this message to the PM. He had also seen Yechury's statement to the media that the UPA should know that the Left would remain a 'watchdog' and ensure that the government stuck to the policy parameters defined by the NCMP. Dr Singh was satisfied with this clarification and wanted to seal the deal and ensure there was no misunderstanding between the CPI(M) and the finance minister. He summoned Chidambaram and the Left leaders for a pow-wow at which the Left assured the PM that they would not vote against the finance bill. Dr Singh understood and, perhaps, was even willing to empathize with the Left's posture. This was their political compulsion, keeping their ideological hardliners happy while allowing the government to do most of what it wanted to. But he was clearly not sure if Chidambaram would adopt such an accommodating view and feared that he might be tempted to embarrass the Left from time to time to score political points.

That Dr Singh was more adept at handling the Left and Chidambaram was less so became obvious even as Chidambaram, Yechury and I walked back to the car park from the meeting. I quipped to Chidambaram that he should feel reassured by the fact that when Yechury said the CPI(M) would be the UPA's 'watchdog', he only meant that they would bark but not bite. A diplomatic finance minister would have either kept quiet or said something nice as a gesture of gratitude.

But Chidambaram, being Chidambaram, could not resist a jibe. He retorted, in Yechury's hearing, 'Either way he agrees that he is a dog!'

For Dr Singh, managing the coalition allies was less challenging than managing his own party. He was acutely aware that this was the Congress party's first attempt at stitching together and running a multiparty coalition government. Political analysts have long made the point that the Congress is itself a coalition, of various factions. It had become even more so during Narasimha Rao's tenure because the party had reverted to some of its traditional ways of functioning after Rajiv Gandhi's death, which had ended a long period of Nehru–Gandhi family suzerainty over the party. The splits that had occurred within the party during Rao's term as party president and prime minister had been reversed after Sonia Gandhi became party president in 1998. On the other hand, new splits surfaced, notably when senior Congress leaders Sharad Pawar and Purno Sangma quit the Congress and formed the NCP.

Dr Singh had played a role in stitching the new UPA coalition together. It was he who had negotiated the DMK's entry into the UPA with M. Karunanidhi in January 2004 and had gone to great lengths to be deferential to him. Announcing the new alliance with the DMK in Chennai, twenty-four years after the two parties had parted ways, Dr Singh had said, 'I have come here to establish a new relationship of trust and confidence with DMK leader M. Karunanidhi and his party.' Dr Singh went a step further and hailed Karunanidhi as not just the leader of Tamil Nadu but 'a great leader and one of the builders of the nation. His life and work has inspired many in the country.'

As prime minister, Dr Singh always received Karunanidhi at the portico of 7 RCR, and not just at the door of his room, as was the norm with most other visitors. Whenever Karunanidhi sent an emissary with a message, Dr Singh would set aside all other work and meet the DMK emissary. This made the DMK feel they had a special equation with Dr Singh. After all, the DMK's friendship with Sonia was a relatively new one. In 1996, she had rejected Narasimha Rao's proposal that the Congress ally with the DMK rather than the All India Anna Dravida Munnetra Kazhagam (AIADMK); the former were known to be sympathizers of the LTTE, her husband's killers.

The seminar room at the Rajiv Gandhi Foundation in New Delhi had framed pages on its walls of the report of the Jain Enquiry Commission on Rajiv Gandhi's assassination, in which the DMK was named a conspirator. In fact, Sonia pushed Narasimha Rao into joining hands with AIADMK leader Jayalalithaa, a deadly rival of the DMK, in the 1996 elections. This prompted P. Chidambaram, Jayalalithaa's *bête noire*, to quit the Congress and join the Tamil Maanila Congress.

Against this background, the 2004 alliance with the Congress could not have been negotiated by Sonia. It was left to Dr Singh to do that, and I was always surprised that political analysts paid little attention to these capabilities of the PM.

Initially, Karunanidhi's nephew, and the UPA government's telecom minister, Dayanidhi Maran, was the key interlocutor between Dr Singh and the DMK leader in Chennai. Maran's stars plummeted when he got involved in the DMK's fratricidal wars, joining forces with Karunanidhi's son M.K. Stalin against his other son, M.K. Azhagiri. His reputation also became unsavoury as he began using his telecom portfolio to favour his brother Kalanidhi's media business. I was not sure if Dr Singh had been alerted to this by his officials, but he certainly was by Ratan Tata in early 2007. Dayanidhi had summoned Tata to a meeting in Delhi in the latter's own Taj Mahal Hotel on Mansingh Road, and tried to browbeat him into doing a deal that would favour his brother Kalanidhi's Sun TV. Ratan Tata conveyed his disapproval of Dayanidhi's behaviour to the PM.

On 11 May 2007, Dr Singh and Sonia went to Chennai to participate in a public meeting to celebrate the golden jubilee of Karunanidhi's first election to the state legislature. At the venue itself, Karunanidhi informed them that henceforth A. Raja would be his key representative in Delhi. That same night, Dr Singh returned from Chennai and implemented Karunanidhi's request that the telecommunications portfolio be shifted from Dayanidhi to Raja. On 13 May, Raja took charge of telecom and, within months, became embroiled in the allegedly corrupt sale of telecommunications bandwidth to certain companies, popularly known as the 2G scandal.

While by February 2008 the issue of 2G telecom licences had already begun to attract political attention, with Sitaram Yechury writing to the PM on the matter, it had not become a public controversy at the time I left the PMO. In fact, no issue involving the misuse of public office became a media issue in UPA-1. There were, no doubt, rumours about the corrupt practices of some ministers. I was aware that the PM was occasionally briefed by the IB about ministers accumulating property and pursuing business interests.

However, none of this ever blew up into a public controversy, barring the Volcker Committee report charges pertaining to Natwar Singh, but that related to activities that took place in 2001. Since I was not privy to government files and the issue never became public in my time, I was blissfully ignorant of the goings-on with regard to telecom licences that have since come to light.

Dr Singh's general attitude towards corruption in public life, which he adopted through his career in government, seemed to me to be that he would himself maintain the highest standards of probity in public life, but would not impose this on others. In other words, he was himself incorruptible, and also ensured that no one in his immediate family ever did anything wrong, but he did not feel answerable for the misdemeanours of his colleagues and subordinates. In this instance, he felt even less because he was not the political authority that had appointed them to these ministerial positions. In practice, this meant that he turned a blind eye to the misdeeds of his ministers. He expected the Congress party leadership to deal with the black sheep in his government, just as he expected the allies to deal with their black sheep. While his conscience was always clear with respect to his own conduct, he believed everyone had to deal with their own conscience.

When a colleague got caught, as the DMK minister Raja finally was, he let the law take its course. Raja was arrested, placed in judicial custody at Delhi's Tihar Jail for fifteen months and is currently being prosecuted for his role in the 2G scam. Dr Singh's approach was a combination of active morality for himself and passive morality with respect to others. In UPA-1 public opinion did not turn against the PM for this moral ambivalence on his part, because the issue had not been prised out into the open. The media focus in the first term was very much on his policy initiatives.

But in UPA-2 when corruption scandals tumbled out, his public image and standing took a huge hit from which he was unable to recover because there was no parallel policy narrative in play that could have salvaged his reputation. In other words, there were no positive acts of commission that captured the public mind enough to compensate for the negative acts of omission for which he was being chastised. As his reputation fell, so did that of his government.

———

With Sharad Pawar, the boss of the NCP and Lalu Prasad Yadav, the feisty politician who headed the Rashtriya Janata Dal (RJD), both of which were constituents of the UPA, Manmohan Singh had a good equation even if he did not always approve of their conduct. With Pawar, there was a special relationship. Dr Singh often recalled how Pawar always lent support to him whenever his policies came under attack from within the Congress party. He regarded Pawar as an 'ally' against his critics in the Cabinet, like Arjun Singh, A.K. Antony and Vayalar Ravi. While Ravi maintained a low profile in the UPA government, both Arjun Singh and Antony remained difficult colleagues to handle. Arjun Singh would openly defy the PM or be critical of his policies, and Antony was guarded in public but difficult in private, often disagreeing with him on his foreign, defence and economic policy initiatives.

One day Pawar landed up at 7 RCR with a complaint. A series of anti-Pawar news reports had appeared in the media, both the national and Marathi media, and Pawar had them traced to a 'PMO source'. He wanted the PM to have this inquired into. Dr Singh asked me to find out who was behind these reports. I asked a few of my contacts in the Hindi and Marathi media to find out. They all returned with the same news: Prithviraj Chavan had planted these stories. It was a delicate issue for Dr Singh. It was hard for him to take any action in the matter because Prithvi might well have been acting under instructions from the party leadership. After all, Sonia and Pawar were not the best of friends, given his grouse that she backed Narasimha Rao against him in 1991 and her grouse that he raised her 'foreign origin' issue to split the Congress party.

As a Maharashtra politician who saw himself as a political rival of Pawar, Prithvi would have happily offered himself as a Congress party instrument in weakening Pawar's hold over the state. On the other hand, Pawar was a PMO favourite since he clearly preferred Dr Singh as PM rather than Pranab Mukherjee or any other Congress leader.

At the height of the anti-Manmohan Singh campaign by the Left, on the issue of the civil nuclear energy agreement with the United States, some critics of the PM floated the idea that he could be replaced to save the government. Political reporters would come and tell me that the names of Pranab Mukherjee and Sushil Kumar Shinde were being mentioned as possible replacements by Congress functionaries known to be close to Sonia.

One day Praful Patel walked into my room and informed me that Shinde's name was being considered more seriously than Mukherjee's by some of the 'backroom boys' of the Congress. 'But, don't worry,' he assured, 'no one can replace Doctor Saheb. We will never support anyone else.'

Thus, even as some in the Congress party targeted an ally like Pawar, Dr Singh sought to maintain good relations with him. Such relationships were Dr Singh's real source of strength. Political analysts and reporters who skimmed the surface only saw Dr Singh as 'Sonia's puppet'. Those who had a deeper knowledge of the power play within the wider coalition knew that Dr Singh had the backing of the coalition partners, some of whom were more loyal to him than to his own party leaders. Sonia chose him, no doubt, but once appointed, he became the UPA's prime minister. Dr Singh was acutely conscious of the fact that he headed a coalition and not just a monolithic party, and made sure that he maintained the best of relations with all coalition partners.

On one occasion, in 2007, when the Left and some Congressmen were raising the pitch of their anti-Manmohan Singh campaign, the usual speculation of a possible change of PM once again surfaced. Dr Singh was very upset with such speculation. One evening I found him seated alone in the living room of 7 RCR, looking grim. I could see he was upset about something.

'I cannot go on like this,' he remarked, as his eyes became moist. I felt he was holding back tears. When I asked what had happened, he kept quiet. I just sat with him and tried to lighten the atmosphere by cracking a joke. It was common for Subbu to summon me whenever he found the PM looking depressed or unhappy and say, 'Please go and cheer him up.' I would refer to myself as the court jester, summoned to entertain a morose king. My usual formula was to pass on some gossip from the media about the shenanigans of his ministerial colleagues or about Advani's latest attempt to unseat him and become PM. That kind of gossip always made him chuckle.

This time his unhappiness seemed to have been triggered by the renewed speculation about the Congress party seeking a change of PM, rather than parting ways with the Left. A political journalist gave me the name of one senior Congressman who was indulging in such talk. That week there was to be a meeting of the UPA coordination committee. To quell such idle talk I encouraged Lalu Prasad Yadav to reiterate the UPA's confidence in Dr Singh's leadership at this meeting. Lalu, rubbishing the idea of any change of leadership, went on to make a statement to that effect at the coordination committee meeting and, in a grand gesture, said he would like to place on record his appreciation of the PM's stewardship of the government. Others joined in and reiterated their confidence in Dr Singh's leadership.

The UPA coalition, many believed, was handicapped by not having an active coordination committee and not naming a senior leader as its spokesperson. The NDA benefitted from the institution of a coalition spokesman and George Fernandes did a good job in this role. The United and National Fronts had Jaipal Reddy as their spokesperson. In the NDA, it was the personal equation and chemistry between Vajpayee and Fernandes that had enabled the latter to function effectively. The absence of an effective coalition management mechanism and a coalition spokesperson made the UPA less cohesive than the NDA, and this became more manifest in UPA-2.

To compensate for this organizational weakness, Dr Singh took care to regularly brief the UPA leaders about every important decision his government would take, and they liked him for that. He would do nothing politically significant without informing, not just Sonia but also Karunanidhi, Pawar and Lalu. On many occasions, after a major decision was taken at the weekly meeting of the Congress party 'core group', Dr Singh would personally inform the three coalition leaders before letting me inform the media.

In that sense, Dr Singh was a truly 'consensual' PM. His success in UPA-1 derived largely from the fact that he invested enormous time and energy into building the required consensus around every important political decision. The criticism sometimes levelled against him that he had taken a particular decision without consulting anyone was never really true. His fault, if anything, was that he spent far too much time building consensus, rather than doing what he thought was right and then demanding that the coalition support him.

In the end, Dr Singh was always conscious of the fact that while he may have been 'chosen' by Sonia to become PM, he had, in fact, become PM as a consequence of an implicit consensus within the UPA coalition as a whole that he was the best man for the job. In other words, he entered office as Sonia's nominee, but he settled down and retained his office as the consensual and implicit choice of all the UPA allies, especially Karunanidhi, Pawar and Lalu, and indeed even the 'Bengal faction' of the CPI(M).

His name had presented itself as an obvious 'compromise' between Sonia on one side and Pawar, Karunanidhi and Surjeet on the other. Sharad Pawar's opposition to Sonia being PM had been openly stated and was the reason for his quitting the Congress in the first place. The CPI(M) claimed it was open to supporting Sonia as PM, though this has been disputed by I.K. Gujral in his autobiography. Gujral claims that it was Surjeet who was instrumental in getting Mulayam to step back and not support Sonia when she tried to form a government in 1999. But there is no argument that in 2004 Surjeet, as CPI(M) general secretary, enthusiastically endorsed Dr Singh's nomination to the job. So, there was considerable truth to Dr Singh's self-perception in UPA-1 that he was not just the 'nominee' of Sonia, but was someone acceptable to other stakeholders in the coalition.

The phenomenon of prime ministers being named by a clique of leaders and compromise candidates coming up from nowhere was not new to Indian politics. That is how Lal Bahadur Shastri, Charan Singh, Narasimha Rao, Deve Gowda and I.K. Gujral were named. Indeed, even Indira Gandhi was 'nominated' by the so-called 'syndicate' that ran the affairs of the Congress party after Nehru's death. However, both Indira and Rao staged coups and took charge of the party organization, by getting themselves elected as party president. Every now and then, the party experimented with separating the two posts but no one was left in doubt that the real power lay with the PM. Congress party president Dev Kant Barooah's infamous statement, during the time of Indira Gandhi's prime ministership, that 'Indira is India and India is Indira' showed who the real boss was even when the two posts were separated.

Given this background, it was not surprising that many initially believed the BJP charge that Dr Singh was a *mukhota*, a mask, for the Congress president. In August 2004 Yashwant Sinha dubbed him Shikhandi, the man–woman character in the Mahabharata whom Bheeshma refused to fight because it was against his principles to fight a woman. There was a double entendre in that metaphor, implying that the prime minister was controlled by Sonia Gandhi, and it was a damaging allusion. Clearly, my biggest challenge as media adviser was to firmly establish in the minds of ordinary people the credentials and credibility of Dr Singh as PM.

5

Responsibility without Power

'I am an accidental prime minister.'

Manmohan Singh

No one in Dr Singh's council of ministers seemed to feel that he owed his position, rank or portfolio to the PM. While his role in the formation of his original team was understandably marginal, he was increasingly consulted in subsequent reshuffles, but the final word was always that of the leaders of the parties constituting the coalition. That is how all coalitions came to be constituted since Deve Gowda's time. Quite understandably, in a parliamentary democracy a prime minister never has the kind of free hand that a President enjoys in a presidential system. In India, even Jawaharlal Nehru did not have too much freedom of manoeuvre and his daughter gained space only after 1971, when she was re-elected with a landslide vote on the back of the victory in the Bangladesh war. Rajiv Gandhi, who became prime minister after winning nearly four-fifths of the seats in Parliament, after Indira's assassination, may have had much greater freedom in constituting his council of ministers, but even he had to accommodate ministers he did not like, Delhi's H.K.L. Bhagat being a case in point. Narasimha Rao and Vajpayee, not to mention Deve Gowda and Gujral, had to also yield to such political pressures, with Vajpayee forced to drop a colleague, Suresh Prabhu, whom he clearly wished to retain in his team.

While Narasimha Rao established control over his team by getting himself elected Congress president in 1992, Vajpayee did so by his decision to conduct nuclear tests within weeks of becoming PM. His decision to test and declare India a nuclear weapons power was both strategic, that is, a response to what was happening globally on the nuclear non-proliferation front and in India's neighbourhood, and political, namely an attempt to raise his profile as the head of government and a national leader. Vajpayee's term began with his inability to get the finance minister he wanted, when his party rejected his initial nominee, Jaswant Singh, and he was forced to appoint Yashwant Sinha. So he chose to establish his leadership of the coalition, outpacing Advani and other challengers to his authority by becoming a national hero.

Well into Vajpayee's tenure, he was taunted, as Dr Singh would later be, by being called a *mukhota*, a moniker bestowed on him by senior BJP functionary Govindacharya in the 1990s. The suggestion was that the real power lay elsewhere, with the party's hardline president L.K. Advani, and with the RSS. However, Vajpayee was quick to give the impression that he was *primus inter pares*, or first among equals, which is how a prime minister is viewed in a parliamentary system, by declaring India a nuclear weapons power. He also took, before this, another important decision in appointing Brajesh Mishra, a trusted friend and fellow Brahmin from Madhya Pradesh, as his principal secretary. Mishra had not only built relationships within the BJP through his chairmanship of the BJP's foreign affairs cell, but had also developed a wide range of power relationships over the years, including with senior editors.

In the UPA, however, Congress party spokespersons let it be known to all concerned that Sonia Gandhi would remain the boss even though she was not the PM, despite her 'renunciation' of power. Even a Left Front leader like Sitaram Yechury, though not as inimical to Dr Singh as some of the hardliners in his party, would remind political reporters that this was not the first time that the head of the party was seen as more important than the head of government, recalling Jyoti Basu's early days as CM. In the case of UPA-1, what the arrangement also implied was that the credit for all the good work done by the government would go to Sonia, and all the blame for any mistakes or failures would go to Dr Singh.

Dr Singh never shied away from this political reality. When confronted with a difficult political demand from an ally, or from leaders of other political parties, he would confess to them that he did not have the last word on the matter, that he was an 'accidental prime minister' and that the buck stopped with Sonia. Fully conscious of this political Achilles' heel, he nevertheless tried bringing into line difficult colleagues.

With his hands tied in other areas of governance, he decided that foreign policy was one area where he would be the boss, and used an early opportunity to let his foreign minister Natwar Singh know that. Natwar told the media on 11 June 2004 in Washington DC that India would take a 'new look' at the question of sending troops to Iraq to support American-led forces in the war that began in 2003. The Vajpayee government had been divided on the issue, with L.K. Advani and Jaswant Singh in favour of sending troops and Vajpayee and Brajesh Mishra opposed to the idea. Vajpayee finally chose not to send troops. While the earlier request for troops had come directly from the US, making the decision politically sensitive, the UPA government was offered the fig leaf of a UN Security Council resolution that could have helped justify sending troops if India so wanted.

Those who advocated that India should send troops pointed to the historical precedent of Indian soldiers fighting in Iraq in the early part of the twentieth century. Iraq had an intimate relationship with India for centuries, and in the period between the two World Wars, the Indian Rupiah was even legal tender in Iraq. Some felt sending troops would demonstrate a widening of India's strategic footprint. Those opposed to the move believed India would get drawn into intra-Muslim sectarian conflict which would invariably have echoes back home. The naysayers prevailed then, as they did again in 2004.

Dr Singh was not in favour of sending Indian troops to Iraq, nor was the Congress party. There was surprise in Delhi at Natwar's remarks and uproar in Parliament. The government denied that it was reconsidering the earlier decision and Dr Singh forced Natwar to recant in Parliament.

Bringing Natwar into line was not a problem, but bringing the politically ambitious Arjun Singh, the left-of-centre Antony and the presumed 'PM-in-waiting' Pranab into line was always a challenge. Each had a mind of his own and each was conscious of his political status and rank. Pranab had no ideological problem with Dr Singh's policies but reportedly nursed the grievance that he was now serving under a person who had served under him many moons ago—Pranab was finance minister when Dr Singh was governor of the Reserve Bank of India in 1982–84. Antony was not a member of the original UPA ministerial team in 2004 and became defence minister only in 2006, when Pranab moved to external affairs. These decisions were essentially Sonia's, though sometimes taken in consultation with Dr Singh, who generally went along with her suggestions in these matters.

Not having allocated portfolios, Dr Singh did not always find it easy to impose his will in the Cabinet. While he ensured that the Cabinet met regularly, once a week every Thursday, and deliberated at length on issues, Dr Singh would rarely intervene in Cabinet meetings to shape a discussion. Ministers were even known to absent themselves if the agenda did not interest them. However, if he had a firm view on a subject, he would ensure support for it before the Cabinet met, or allow a senior minister like Pawar or Chidambaram to articulate his point of view. This made his pre-meeting consultations with Cabinet ministers more important than the meeting itself.

While the Congress 'core group', that met every Friday evening at 7 RCR, became the effective management board of the party and the government, it did not include alliance leaders. Traditionally, the Cabinet Committee on Political Affairs (CCPA), consisting of senior Cabinet ministers, used to take high-level policy decisions with a political edge. The CCPA was the equivalent of the communist politburo. However, as a consequence of the PM's non-existent political standing within the Cabinet, and the fact that Sonia, not being a Cabinet minister, was not a member of the CCPA, this once-powerful arm of the Cabinet hardly ever met during Dr Singh's tenure. The core group became the de facto CCPA.

Dr Singh deployed an institutional innovation, first created by Vajpayee to involve senior coalition leaders in policymaking, called the groups of ministers (GoM). GoMs were meant to facilitate consensual decision-making within smaller groups. Those on policy issues would include at least one minister from each major party in the coalition. They enabled coalition partners to participate in discussions on policy pertaining to other ministries before policy decisions were brought to the Cabinet for its approval. Scores of GoMs were set up, with Pranab, Pawar, Antony and Chidambaram being the key chairs. The only important GoM that Arjun Singh chaired was on the 2010 Commonwealth Games. The poor frequency with which it met provided an early signal that the preparations for the Games would not be on track.

In itself, the GoM was a good idea. However, Dr Singh went a step further and created the EGoM—empowered GoMs—which effectively undermined prime ministerial authority. The EGoMs, constituted around key policies, projects and issues, became substitutes for the full Cabinet because they were empowered to take decisions that the Cabinet then only ratified. They effectively weakened the authority of the prime minister since they were chaired by senior Cabinet ministers and could approve policy without further reference to the PM. This was especially the case with EGoMs chaired by Pranab Mukherjee, the seniormost minister in the Cabinet. Every now and then a journalist would ask me how many GoMs/EGoMs had been constituted and each time I sought this information from the Cabinet secretariat I would myself be taken aback by the number. At one point in 2007 there was a total of over fifty GoMs, a number that only increased with time.

While the EGoMs may have been created to either share power with senior colleagues like Pranab or pass the buck on tricky issues where he did not want to be seen taking the decision, the fact is that they were a self-inflicted wound on prime ministerial authority. I was puzzled by Dr Singh's move because, as a long-time player in government, he understood only too well the importance of protecting turf. Once, when I told him I might not be able to accompany him on a foreign tour because of my daughter's school examinations his uncharacteristic reply, delivered with a smile, was, 'If you don't come, someone else will end up doing your work. Never yield space!'

The subject-specific committees of ministers, officials and experts did enable greater intellectual input into policymaking and facilitated the resolution of inter-ministerial differences on policy issues. Thus, to resolve the problem created by the multiplicity of ministries dealing with energy (petroleum and gas, power, coal, nuclear, non-conventional energy and so on), the Energy Coordination Committee (ECC) was created. The ECC, which included the finance minister, also enabled the PM to push through his initiatives on civil nuclear energy development by ensuring a wider consensus within government, going beyond the more conservative DAE. The Agriculture Coordination Committee and Trade and Economic Relations Committee were two other forums that brought several senior ministers and members of the Planning Commission around one table and enabled important initiatives like the India–ASEAN FTA negotiations to be taken up.

The composition of these various committees revealed who Dr Singh felt most comfortable working with. His A-team in UPA-1, if one can call it that, included Pawar and Chidambaram. They had been his colleagues in the Narasimha Rao government and while they had a rocky relationship with Rao, they had a good one with Dr Singh. He also had a satisfactory working equation with senior colleagues like Shivraj Patil and Lalu Yadav, but remained wary of old critics like Arjun Singh and Antony. Among the younger lot, such as Kamal Nath, Dayanidhi Maran and Praful Patel, his affections waxed and waned, and he would balance his disapproval of their ways, expressed only gently, with effusive appreciation of their work when they did something he approved of. From among the allies, a minister he held in high regard was Rural Development Minister Raghuvansh Prasad Singh, who was from the RJD. This was the minister who implemented the rural employment guarantee programme, an important initiative for UPA-1. Dr Singh was not overly impressed by the administrative capacity of most other senior Congress ministers.

While Home Minister Shivraj Patil was perceived as inefficient and ineffective in the public mind, Dr Singh found him an easy person to work with. At one point in 2006, when Patil was facing a terrible media onslaught, with widespread criticism of his handling of terror attacks and the Naxalite problem, he asked me to meet Patil and offer him advice on how to handle the media. Patil was very courteous and thanked me profusely for my offer to help but was not willing to be proactive. Once, finding both Patil and a bitter critic of his, Shekhar Gupta of the *Indian Express*, present at a function at 7 RCR, I suggested to Patil that he disarm the editor by walking across to Shekhar and chatting him up.

His reply was classic Patil: 'It is better you bring him here.'

I had to hold him by his hand and virtually drag him to Shekhar and make them shake hands.

What this incident showed was that the home minister was more concerned about protocol than about winning over a critic. For him, it seemed, form mattered over substance. This also explained his penchant for looking dapper at all times of the day, even if it meant changing his clothes frequently. In the PMO, we would quip that while he might not, despite being home minister, be a 'man for all occasions', he was certainly dressed as if he was ready for any occasion.

Both Subbu and I would encourage Dr Singh to interact more with junior ministers like Sachin Pilot, Purandeswari, Jyotiraditya Scindia and Pallam Raju. But he rarely did so, perhaps not wanting to upset his senior colleagues by appearing to be too friendly with their juniors. Faced with complaints from junior ministers that they were not being given enough work, he tried to boost their morale by interacting with them when he convened a meeting of the entire council of ministers and urged their senior ministers to share more work with them. This never did happen in practice, not even in the

PMO. The prime minister evidently found it hard to delegate much work to his MoS, Prithviraj Chavan.

Cabinet reshuffles were an elaborate exercise. Every now and then, Dr Singh would seek feedback on the performance of his ministers. These were more in the nature of informal assessments rather than a 'report card', as the media imagined them to be. In May 2005, as the UPA approached its first anniversary, reports began to appear that the PM was reviewing the performance of his ministers. On 9 May, when he was in Moscow, NDTV ran a story that External Affairs Minister Natwar Singh had secured a low 'score' on the PM's 'report card' and was likely to be dropped from the Cabinet. Natwar was most unhappy and took the day off on 'health grounds'. This news reached the PM in Moscow when he was in the midst of a briefing at his hotel. He asked me to find out what exactly NDTV had reported.

When I briefed him he burst out angrily, 'Tell Prannoy to stop reporting these lies.'

I called Prannoy Roy, the head of NDTV, and had just begun speaking to him when the PM asked for my mobile phone and spoke to Prannoy himself, scolding him like he was chiding a student who had erred, saying, 'This is not correct. You cannot report like this.' Indeed, the relationship between him and Prannoy was not that of a prime minister and a senior media editor but more like that of a former boss and a one-time junior. This was because Prannoy had worked as an economic adviser in the ministry of finance under Dr Singh. After a few minutes, Prannoy called me back.

'Are you still with him?' he asked.

I stepped out of the room and told him that I was now alone.

'Boy, I have not been scolded like that since school! He sounded like a headmaster, not a prime minister,' complained Prannoy.

After the meeting with his aides was over, Dr Singh called Natwar and inquired about his health and let him know that he looked forward to meeting him on his return.

I could see why Dr Singh was livid with Prannoy and gentle with Natwar. By then, he had Natwar on his side and his support was needed for the major initiative he was about to launch in the summer of 2005 with the US, and he could not afford a sulking foreign minister. When Natwar did get involved in the controversy generated by a United Nations commission report on entities that had profited from Iraq's oil-for-food programme during Saddam Hussein's time, Dr Singh did seek Natwar's immediate resignation but responded, many thought, leniently to Natwar's request that he be allowed to remain in office till the charges had been verified. Finally, when Natwar did leave, Dr Singh retained the external affairs portfolio, signalling the importance he attached to keeping the foreign affairs portfolio under his control.

Natwar came in handy in dealing with the tricky issue of India's vote at the International Atomic Energy Association (IAEA) against Iran's nuclear programme. The IAEA vote on Iran's nuclear programme became a political hot potato. The US wanted India to prove its non-proliferation credentials by supporting its stance. It was also the view of all the signatories to the Non-Proliferation Treaty (NPT), of which India was not a signatory, that Iran stand by its NPT commitments. In itself this was a simple demand. However, in India anti-US elements projected it as a surrender of sovereignty to the US, and an act which would displease a friend, Iran, and Shia Muslims in India. Given the political sensitivity around what ought to have been a routine vote, Dr Singh wanted all his senior colleagues, including Sonia, on board.

Natwar called the PM from New York one night saying the Indian ambassador at the IAEA was awaiting instructions on how to vote. Dr Singh was in Chandigarh and chose to keep his opinion to himself. He instructed Natwar to find out what other members of the CSS felt. Natwar then called Pranab, Chidambaram and Shivraj Patil and all three suggested that India should vote along with other permanent members of the United Nations Security Council (UNSC). Finally, Natwar called Sonia and ensured she was also on board. Natwar then called the PM back and reported this. Dr Singh asked him what he himself felt. Natwar said he agreed with the others. 'Then do so accordingly,' was the PM's instruction.

Even while working with the PM on this issue, Natwar wanted to keep his non-aligned, left-of-centre credentials intact, and therefore tried to give the impression to the media that he was not really on board. A story appeared in the *Asian Age*, under Seema Mustafa's byline, that it was the PM who had instructed Natwar, against the latter's wishes, to vote against Iran. I had to write a letter to the editor protesting against this distortion of facts. When the letter did not appear in print the next day, I issued a press release to all media. Taking a public stand on such matters helped. It put ministers on notice that if they briefed the press wrongly, the PMO would not hesitate to state facts as they were, even if this embarrassed the minister concerned.

In defending Dr Singh's policies I found myself getting into many such arguments with Congressmen. Once on a flight with the PM on an Air Force aircraft, Mani Shankar Aiyar was holding forth on the problems of the nuclear deal. Aiyar was not a supporter and had even said to some journalists that if the PM threatened to resign on the issue he should be allowed to go. On this flight he was openly critical of the US and said he was a proud communist who would rather have the old Soviet Union back than befriend the US.

I had to tell the outspoken Congressman that if he were a minister in Stalin's Cabinet then the official who would have been my equivalent, Stalin's media adviser, would simply have opened the door of the aircraft and pushed him out. I reminded him that he felt secure criticizing the PM on the PM's official aircraft because Dr Singh was a gentleman, not a dictator, nor a party boss!

This, indeed, was at once Dr Singh's strength and weakness. His soft touch and his unwillingness to confront and discipline his detractors in the party encouraged many of them to run with the hare and hunt with the hounds. On the other hand, his willingness to give them political space despite their mischief and worse disarmed them and often made them look foolish.

Dr Singh rarely chided his ministers. His strategy was to simply do other people's work when they were not doing it themselves. If he was not happy with Shivraj Patil's handling of internal security, he would rather step in and do the home minister's job himself than reprimand him. On one occasion, after a terrorist attack the PM summoned a meeting to get himself briefed. The home secretary and IB chief reached 7 RCR in good time but Patil was delayed. We quipped that he must be changing his clothes. Instead of waiting for Patil to arrive, the PM insisted that the meeting begin. If he was unhappy about the way Kamal Nath was handling trade talks at the World Trade Organization, he would summon the commerce secretary and instruct him on how to handle a particular issue, rather than seek ways to win Nath over. Stepping in to do a minister's job for them was his characteristic way of expressing displeasure at the minister's work, but it wasn't necessarily an effective one.

I would only find out what Dr Singh really thought of a minister when I sat down with him to discuss ideas for a Cabinet reshuffle. When I would suggest a minister's name for a better portfolio or an elevation in rank he would, every now and then, say what he felt about the person. Sometimes, he would just make a face that conveyed disapproval. Over time, I realized that there were few members of his council of ministers that he truly valued as administrative assets. His constant refrain was that there was a paucity of administrative talent in the Congress and among the allies.

Whenever a reshuffle was being considered, Dr Singh would ask for lists of MPs, their résumés and any other relevant information. He would also like to be kept informed on changes in power equations in the states to understand the political weight of ministers belonging to different states and caste groups. Several people in the PMO, including Narayanan, Nair, Subbu and myself, would be asked for such information. His grasp of caste and social dynamics was good but not as sound as that of a regular politician. On occasion I would take a senior editor from an Indian-language publication from one or another state to him, and request him to brief the PM on local politics.

———

Much could have been done to improve governance and to make the PMO the instrument of governance reform, had Dr Singh had political authority or was willing to invest more effort. In June 2004, in his very first address to the nation, he had said, 'No objective in this development agenda can be met if we do not reform the instrument in our hand with which we have to work, namely the government and public institutions. Clearly, this will be my main concern and challenge in the days to come.' Failure to act on this assurance remained a major weakness of UPA-1.

Some initiatives were taken, like declaring 21 April as Civil Services Day, with the PM giving away awards to the best civil servants, who were identified through a nationwide effort. But there was no attempt to undertake major administrative reform. An administrative reforms committee, headed by Veerappa Moily, produced many voluminous reports but there was very little follow-up.

In the context of growing concern about the inadequacies of Indian diplomacy, I had suggested the PM constitute a high-level committee on the reform and modernization of the foreign service. He liked the idea but was not sure if he could secure the desired result without the active cooperation of the foreign minister. And he was never sure that Natwar, or Pranab after him, would go along with the kind of reforms he may have had in mind.

Ostensibly, the most important governance reform was supposed to be the Right to Information (RTI) Act that aimed to impose greater accountability on the government. It was an NAC initiative. Several senior and retired civil servants cautioned Dr Singh against the RTI, worrying that rather than expose corruption and sloth in government, it would sap initiative and encourage officers to pass the buck.

The jury is still out on whether or not RTI was a wise move and what its impact on governance has been. Has it made the government more transparent and accountable or has it made civil servants risk averse and unwilling to take difficult decisions? In UPA-1, when there was considerable euphoria over the RTI Act, few would have imagined that analysts would hold the RTI Act responsible for at least some of the so-called 'policy paralysis' that UPA-2 came to be charged with.

In the PMO, some officials shared my unfashionable scepticism about the efficacy of the RTI Act but Sonia was so committed to this initiative that no one seriously resisted it. I was not convinced that transparency, in terms of public access to internal government communication, was a necessary condition to making the government more responsive to people's needs, and to good governance. By this token, few organizations, including most NGOs and the media as an institution, were 'transparent' even though they were more 'responsive'. The glare of public scrutiny would not scare corrupt and inefficient officers, who would always find new means of playing old tricks, but it would certainly discourage honest officers from stating in writing views that might later be used to question their motives. I felt Dr Singh was sympathetic to my view though he never explicitly said so.

———

At the heart of the governance reform failure lay the weakening of the PMO. Dr Singh's deliberately low-profile style was compounded by the relative inexperience of Principal Secretary Nair, who lacked the confidence of some of his distinguished predecessors, and had not been able to build up the kind of networks they had developed. Despite these weaknesses, and its limited political power and influence within government, internally, the PMO functioned efficiently. Pulok and his assistant Amit Agarwal listed every promise made in the NCMP and created a spreadsheet on which responsibilities were assigned to individual ministries. The PMO would seek a status report from each ministry from time to time and report back to the PM. This was the first time such a review system was devised and systematically implemented.

The sense of purpose this regular monitoring imparted to the PMO team was palpable, but it also meant that Dr Singh would himself chair long meetings to review the NCMP, getting into too much micro-management. Moreover, monitoring what others were doing was one thing, getting others to do what the PM wanted, quite another.

At the time I did not realize how the limits to the PM's political authority and the PMO's institutional weakness in fact meant that there was very little control of the PM and his office over the misdemeanours of ministers. Whenever I heard a tale about ministerial corruption that was credible enough to bear repeating, I would relate this to Dr Singh. He would always listen with attention. Most of the tales related to ministers belonging to parties that were allies in the coalition, but a good many also related to Congress ministers. It was clear that Dr Singh wanted to know what was happening. I assumed this information would help the PM to remain alert, especially when signing files, and that he would perhaps pull up the minister concerned.

All coalition PMs found their power limited by political compulsions, but none of them exercised as little power while taking on as much responsibility as Dr Singh. With the benefit of hindsight I would say that Dr Singh has to take some of the blame for this. If he had stuck to the dictum he quoted to me, 'Never yield space' and ensured that the PM and the PMO played their due role in decision-making, Cabinet formation and political communication, he may not have felt as disempowered as he came to be.

The politically fatal combination of responsibility without power and governance without authority meant that Dr Singh was unable, even when he was aware, of checking corruption in his ministry without disturbing the political arrangement over which he nominally presided. Political power resided with the heads of parties of the coalition and, as PM, he could not dismiss ministers at will. He could, perhaps, have done more to discipline his ministers. One way in which this could have been done would have been to appoint upright and effective officers as secretaries under corrupt ministers. Here too the PM often failed to assert his authority, appointing as secretary a person that the minister concerned preferred.

The consequence of all of this was to bring the PM into disrepute despite his own impressive record and reputation for personal probity and integrity. Still, I never imagined that charges of corruption of the kind that came to haunt him, in the manner they did, in years to come would so sully his reputation. For a long time the media was willing to give him the benefit of doubt on his role in questionable decisions by accepting the view that his lack of political authority prevented him from disciplining his wayward ministers. But when the issue of corruption took centre stage in public discourse, the question that was relentlessly asked was why had the PM not prevented what was going on. That he had 'yielded so much space' to other centres of power, so that he had little of his own to act, was not viewed as an adequate defence.

6

Brand Manmohan

'There is no foundation to the insinuation that
there are two power centres. I am the prime minister.'

Manmohan Singh, first national press conference
4 September 2004

Manmohan Singh began his tenure with a problem. Even though many coalition prime ministers before him had come to that office as the result of a political compromise between various power brokers of different parties and factions, Dr Singh was the first one to be seen as being 'nominated' by one person. Moreover, while he was not the first PM to be a member of the Rajya Sabha at the time of taking office, he was certainly the first to not seek a Lok Sabha seat after being elected PM. While there was no legal impediment to remaining a prime minister indirectly elected to Parliament through its Upper House, the Rajya Sabha, most prime ministers were directly elected by 'the people' to the Lok Sabha, the House of the People, which is the normal practice in all parliamentary systems.

I assumed at first that Dr Singh saw an election to the Lok Sabha as a risky venture, given his experience of 1999. This time around the stakes were infinitely higher: he was not just a Congress leader, but a prime minister. So perhaps, I thought, it was a case of better safe than sorry. However, Dr Singh's decision—or was it Sonia's, I was never too sure—that the prime minister not contest in the General Elections of 2009 suggested, with hindsight, that it was not just risk-aversion that led Dr Singh to not seek re-election to Parliament through the Lok Sabha in 2004. This, I concluded, was to be the nature of the arrangement. In 2004 he was, without doubt, an 'accidental prime minister' and, it would appear, neither he nor Sonia wanted to alter the arrangement in UPA-2. In an early conversation with him, I asked if he was considering seeking a seat in the Lok Sabha and his answer was that it was for the party to decide. I never raised the question again in UPA-1, though I insistently advised him in early 2009 that he seek a Lok Sabha seat in the approaching General Elections. Regrettably, he did not take that advice.

Despite the obvious existence of two centres of power, I took the view that the office of the prime minister is sacrosanct in the Indian system of governance and there should be no doubt in people's minds who the 'leader' of the 'country' was. Sonia was the leader of the Congress and had been designated chairperson of the UPA. However, I believed that as head of government Manmohan Singh was the coalition's leader, and that is how I would project him to the public.

I had observed, as a journalist, how both Narasimha Rao and Vajpayee had asserted their authority as PM. One began as the head of a minority government and the other as the head of a coalition. Both had factions and coalition partners to contend with. Both knew the limits of their power. Yet, both managed to project themselves as prime ministers in their own right. They zealously guarded their turf. How was I to project this image of the PM without bringing him into the party's line of fire? This was my challenge as Dr Singh's 'brand manager'.

UPA's first Parliament session began on a rocky note. From the prime minister's point of view, it was a sad note. For the first time in parliamentary history, a newly elected prime minister was neither allowed to introduce his council of ministers to Parliament nor given the privilege of replying to the debate on the motion of thanks to the President for his address to Parliament.

The very first session of a new Parliament was rudely disrupted in this manner because the main Opposition party, the BJP, was still not reconciled to its surprise defeat in the General Elections. It made an issue of the induction into the Union Cabinet of Shibu Soren, leader of the Jharkhand Mukti Morcha (JMM), and a few others who were facing criminal charges. When, on 10 June, the last day of the opening session of the new Parliament, Speaker Somnath Chatterjee invited the PM to speak, and the Opposition did not allow it, Dr Singh was disturbed. He was both angry and deeply unhappy that the BJP remained in denial about its defeat and was refusing to extend to the new PM the basic courtesy of letting him speak in Parliament. Finally, a most unsatisfactory compromise was arrived at by which the BJP agreed to allow the PM to seek the House's approval of the motion of thanks. A visibly disturbed Dr Singh finally stood up and made his statement in a voice touched by sadness:

Mr Speaker Sir, I learn that there is an understanding among the political parties on both sides that the Motion of Thanks on the President's Address be put to vote straightaway and passed unanimously. Therefore, Sir, I request you to put the Motion to vote. I take this opportunity to thank all the honourable Members of the Lok Sabha.

Dr Singh returned home upset at the turn of events. It was then decided that the statement he had intended to make in Parliament be read out as an address to the nation on television. Mani Dixit and I were asked to redraft it as an 'Address to the Nation'. The template for the address was the NCMP. After listing the new government's agenda, I added a paragraph that said, 'No objective in this development agenda can be met if we do not reform the instrument in our hand with which we have to work, namely the government and public institutions. Clearly, this will be my main concern and challenge in the days to come.' It is a paragraph that many have pointed to over the years as the one that gave them great hope and the one agenda item on which the PM failed to deliver.

On foreign policy and national security, the address reaffirmed UPA's commitment to the 'no first use' nuclear doctrine enunciated by the Vajpayee government, with the proviso that India would continue to work for universal nuclear disarmament. The speech also included an early hint that the UPA would continue the dialogue with the United States on removing barriers on high-technology trade. It was with this objective in mind, and in the context of India declaring itself a nuclear weapons power, that the Vajpayee government had started a dialogue with the US on Next Steps in Strategic Partnership. Dixit and the PM were clear in their minds that they would take this dialogue forward.

Once the draft was approved, I advised the PM to practise delivering the speech on television, using a teleprompter. This would not be like reading out a budget speech, I pointed out. There is an intimacy to a TV broadcast. He would be talking to families across the country sitting in their living rooms and bedrooms. Even the best public speaker could fail to connect with a TV audience if he did not understand the medium.

Dr Singh readily agreed to practice sessions. We installed a TV camera in 7 RCR and every afternoon, after his lunch and siesta, he would devote an hour to reading the speech out in front of the camera. At the end of the working day, before he went home to 3 RCR for dinner, I would play the recording back to show him the defects so that he could improve his style. His voice was far too soft and he did not have the debater's knack for emphasizing important words. He would not pause after making an important point but move on to the next sentence.

Later, while preparing him for his address to the US Congress I had to indicate in the written text where he should expect applause from the audience and, therefore, pause before moving to the next sentence. Important sentences would be underlined so that he knew where to be more emphatic, though he rarely managed to be so. Whenever he recorded a TV interview or just a statement for telecast I would decide camera angles and also insist on re-recording if the PM made any mistake. Once the recording was done I would ensure that only the final approved version was available for telecast.

His first televised address to the nation required three days of practice and the speech was recorded on the morning of 24 June in the conference room at Panchavati, 7 RCR, and telecast that night. Next morning, *The Hindu*'s lead story said: 'Dr. Singh's first public address was marked by an equanimous tone, thoughtful content, competent articulation and a tightly-written prose avoiding rhetorical flourishes, reflecting the Prime Minister's own personality.'

The Hindi part of the speech was written in the Urdu script. Born and educated in western Punjab, now Pakistan, Dr Singh had never learnt to read Hindi. His mother tongue was Punjabi, written in the Gurmukhi script, while Urdu was his language of instruction at school. Dr Singh was not merely proficient in Urdu, he was also very well versed in Urdu literature and poetry.

Dr Singh deployed with skill his knowledge of Urdu poetry during his interventions in Parliament. He had a good repertory of appropriate quotes from such great poets as Ghalib, Faiz and Firaq. One of his favourite couplets, by the poet Muzaffar Razmi, which he quoted on more than one occasion, in Parliament and to Pakistan's President Pervez Musharraf, was: '*Ye jabr bhi dekha hai, taareeq ki nazron ne / Lamhon ne khata ki thi, sadiyon ne saza payi*' (Much injustice / has been seen in the saga of history / When for a mistake made in a moment we are punished for centuries).

Dr Singh's Independence Day speech would always be written in Urdu, though some of his other Hindustani speeches were also written in Gurmukhi. While he would try from time to time to improve his delivery in public speaking and TV appearances, this never came naturally to him. Even a smile before TV cameras, a basic requirement for a politician, never came easily to him and I had to often get close to him, sometimes worrying the SPG guards, standing just a step away, to whisper in his ear, 'Smile'.

When the PM had to appear on TV to condemn a terror attack or express his grief I would insist he not read from a prepared text and speak to the camera. Over time he had become adept at reading from a teleprompter, but he never evolved into a good public speaker, either at large gatherings or on television.

———

Before his first interaction with the media in July in Bangkok, I had gone into the PM's room to ask him if he would like to freshen up before facing the media. His instant reply, with a smile, was, '*Kya sher kabhi apne dant saaf karta hai?*' (Does a tiger ever brush its teeth?) I spun this as evidence of a new, confident Manmohan and many in the media lapped it up. But by the time Parliament met again, the Opposition was quick to resume its attack on the 'weak PM'. Moreover, his decision to induct his own man, Montek, as deputy chairman of the Planning Commission, was countered by Sonia's decision to create an NAC filled with critics not just of Montek but also the PM. This did nothing for his image.

What could Dr Singh do to show that he was the boss? Indeed, was he prepared to do anything at all? His shy and introverted personality was a barrier. His unwillingness to assert himself vis-à-vis senior Cabinet colleagues imposed limits on what a subordinate could do to project his image. There was also the additional problem of the Opposition painting him as an interloper because he was a member of the Rajya Sabha and not the Lok Sabha. After disrupting his opening address to Parliament, the BJP once again prevented Dr Singh from addressing Parliament when it reconvened in July.

Dr Singh's own attitude to the situation he was placed in was puzzlingly ambiguous. On occasion he would get irritated by suggestions that he was not his own man, at other times he would opt for a low profile and shy away from asserting his authority. Sometimes he would deliberately say or do things to establish his independence. A trivial but telling example was his angry response, still in the early days of his first term, to my question on whether a particular proposal that he was approving had Sonia Gandhi's approval, and whether we should have it checked through Pulok.

Dr Singh retorted, 'I am the prime minister!'

Yet, on another occasion, in September 2004, when a front-page report in the Hindi newspaper *Punjab Kesari* announced my imminent dismissal from the PMO ('*Sanjay Baru ki Chutti Hogi*') because, as it claimed, the Congress party leadership was unhappy with my style of functioning, Dr Singh said to me, 'Why don't you call on Sonia? They will stop bothering you.' The reference was to those around

Sonia who were seen to be planting stories in the media against me and the suggestion was that once I was seen having access to her all the sniping would end.

I first responded by saying, 'If you want me to, I will.' He said he would secure an appointment for me. But I had second thoughts and suggested he drop the idea. My meeting her when I was under attack would be interpreted as my seeking her blessings to remain in office. I told him I took the PMO job because he asked me to work for him and I would leave the day he wanted me to. Why should I now seek her protection and be beholden to her? He remained silent. The subject was never raised again and I never called on Sonia during my entire tenure at the PMO.

There was a trivial episode in the first few weeks after he assumed office that had me deeply worried because it not only drew attention to the PM's excessively careful approach towards junior ministers known to be close to Sonia but also pointed to a willingness to look the other way when such ministers were accused of wrongdoing. The media reported that a junior minister of the Congress, Renuka Chowdhury, had written a letter to BJP leader Jaswant Singh seeking an appointment for an arms dealer when Jaswant was defence minister. There had been some criticism of this in the media. A reporter from a Telugu newspaper asked me whether the PM was aware of this and whether he had approved of her conduct. I saw no point in going to the PM for a reply. Moreover, I did not see how I could say the PM would approve of such conduct. So I offered a wishy-washy reply saying that while the PM was too busy and had not yet seen the news reports, he would of course never approve of any MP seeking an appointment for an arms dealer. Maybe I should have just kept my mouth shut, but these were early days in the job.

The next day, the Telugu media reported that the PM had disapproved of Renuka's interest in arms deals. That evening she called me and asked me if I had made that statement with the approval of the PM. I said I had not spoken to the PM and had made a general statement that the PM would not approve of such things. She then claimed that she had not written any such letter and that this was all fictitious stuff aimed at maligning her. She wanted me to issue a clarification stating that the PM had not said anything against her.

I told her that I could not issue any such statement without the PM's explicit instruction. She said she would meet the PM and ask him to instruct me. I waited anxiously for a summons from Dr Singh after her meeting with him. That did not happen. A few days later, Dr Singh asked me for my version of what had happened. After I offered it, he said with a smile, 'Maybe you should go and make up. She is very angry.'

I was flabbergasted. Renuka was not a senior enough party leader for a PM to worry if one of his officials had offended her. I told him that if I apologized to her, Renuka would go to town and not just claim that the PM had not reprimanded her for lobbying for an arms dealer, but, much worse, that the PMO had said sorry to a junior minister. I felt this would damage the PM's image. I told him that the media would be happy to see him disapprove of such conduct and it was best to let matters rest there. He did not press me. The next day, Nair asked me if I was going to see Renuka to clear the air. A bit irritated, I asked him why she was considered that important.

'Because she is close to the party leadership,' he replied.

These incidents captured the limits the PM was willing to impose on his authority. It was not as if the PM condoned what Renuka had been accused of, it was just that he did not want to make a point of admonishing her publicly because she was regarded as being close to Sonia. This, I realized early, would be the source of his image problem, given that his political USP was the image of being a man of integrity.

His personal integrity was, of course, never questioned. His driving his own Maruti 800 as the leader of the Rajya Sabha was a legend among Delhi's journalists. Mrs Kaur serving tea herself to visitors to their home was another. He was probably the first prime minister in a long time who did not have a son or son-in-law in business or real estate. His daughters and sons-in-law were all salary-earning professionals. Which is probably why he felt no scandal would ever touch him even if he had not intervened to prevent it.

This was the image that worked. Through UPA-1 that image sustained. Vidya Subrahmaniam of *The Hindu* reported from a village in Uttar Pradesh during the 2009 election campaign that when she asked several poor villagers whom they would vote for, they would say, '*Congress ko. Sardarji ko,*' and that, she reported, was because the PM was seen by these simple folk as a '*neyk aadmi*' (good and honest man). The 'good man' image had to be converted into a political asset and he had to be shown to be his own boss. That, I saw as my task as media adviser.

Sharada Prasad agreed with me. 'Tell the prime minister,' he advised, 'that he should be politically active, and do what he can and must as PM, without necessarily challenging her authority as party president.' He suggested that the PM should meet chief ministers and write letters to them on matters of national importance. 'Maybe you should arrange a press conference where he takes political questions and gives his personal views. The nation should know that the PM has a mind of his own.'

The next day, I conveyed the gist of this conversation to Dr Singh. Without my having to persuade him too much, he agreed to address a press conference. I viewed the press conference as part of a larger strategy to build a credible Manmohan Singh brand. Unless people across the country had an intimate understanding of who this man was, it would never be possible to convince them that he was his own boss.

There was no doubt in my mind that the PM needed to build his own personal credibility to be able to ensure the credibility of his government and of the country. I did not view the task of building his image as a personal favour to him; I saw it as a national duty. As Pranab Mukherjee put it to me emphatically years later, the country's credibility depended on the PM's credibility. What would the world think of India if it saw its PM as a political puppet?

A short while later, during the budget session of Parliament in August 2004, an ill-considered initiative by L.K. Advani and George Fernandes offered a welcome opportunity to project the PM as a tough guy with a mind of his own. Advani and Fernandes led an NDA delegation to the PM suggesting changes to the finance bill. An irritated Dr Singh did not even invite his visitors to sit down, leave alone offering them a cup of tea. Dr Singh was not inclined to be kind to an Opposition that had ruined his first day in Parliament. He received them standing in his room and continued to stand so that they, too, had to present their letter standing. He accepted their file, but threw it down on the table without even reading it. Nonplussed, the delegation left the room.

The NDA leaders went to the TV cameras outside the Parliament building and lodged a complaint that they had been 'insulted' by the PM. I was in South Block at the time. Subbu called me from the PM's office in Parliament to explain what exactly had happened, in case the media asked me for a comment. He explained that the PM had not in fact 'thrown' the file down, as being alleged on TV, but that he had only 'dropped' it, since he was standing and the table was at a lower height. I grabbed the opportunity. I suggested to Subbu that we need not be defensive. Why explain that the PM meant no disrespect to the leaders of the Opposition, and that he had not 'thrown' the file down? Let us confirm what is being alleged and claim the PM was angry, irritated and tired of the Opposition's disruptive ways.

The media loved the story and interpreted it as evidence of a new 'enough-is-enough, no-nonsense' Manmohan Singh. *Outlook* magazine commented: 'For Manmohan's media managers, long despairing of changing their shy, workaholic and stiff boss into a more popular prime ministerial mould, this was the one opportunity they had been waiting for over three months. And far from glossing over the incident as his party colleagues were so desperately trying to do, they were convinced that this could be the making of a brand new image: a confident, relaxed, assertive Manmohan—under no one's shadow but his own man at last. . . . A flash of temper was just what his spin doctors had been waiting for.'

There were other positive developments in the run-up to the press conference. Dr Singh accepted Sharada Prasad's suggestion that he should write letters to chief ministers on important issues of the day. The practice of prime ministerial letters to chief ministers was an institution created by Nehru, but other PMs had not followed it regularly. Two considerations went into the decision to reintroduce the practice. First, since many of the chief ministers belonged to either regional parties or the BJP, it would enable the PM to directly communicate with leaders of other political parties. Secondly, the move would emphasize his stature as a leader of the nation and not just of the Congress party. Finally, since all Indian-language newspapers would translate and publicize the PM's letter to chief ministers, this would be one more avenue for communicating with people across the country.

On 18 July 2004, the prime minister wrote his first letter to CMs on the theme of the delivery of public services. The letter got good play in the media, with many newspapers pointing out that Dr Singh had revived a practice first started by Nehru and noting that his letter was 'non-partisan'. Building Dr Singh's image as a 'non-partisan' PM had been one of my objectives. After all, Sonia, party president and UPA chairperson, was asserting her political leadership of the party and Dr Singh could not compete with her for that role. Rather, he had to assert his leadership as PM by dealing directly with chief ministers. It was a popular saying that in India's power structure only three institutions mattered—the PM, the CM and the DM (district magistrate or collector). Many CMs consolidated their power in state capitals by dealing with DMs directly, and not through the administrative chain of command. I saw the PM's direct communication with CMs as a similar exercise.

Unfortunately, while Dr Singh was happy to write letters, he was not enthusiastic about the second leg of this strategy, namely having quiet one-on-one meetings, preferably informal ones over breakfast or a meal, with chief ministers. He did have private dinner meetings with West Bengal Chief Minister Buddhadeb Bhattacharya, with whom he felt comfortable, on a couple of occasions, but was not keen to repeat this with any other chief minister.

While generally non-partisan, once in a while Dr Singh would adopt a more partisan stance, getting tough with state governments run by political opponents. On one such occasion, when Orissa chief minister Naveen Patnaik, then an ally of the BJP, called on him and sought a financial package for Orissa on the same lines as what was given to Bihar, a state ruled at the time by a UPA ally, Dr Singh delivered an uncharacteristic snub, saying, 'Does money grow on trees?' I was happy to share this with the media to show that if he so wanted, the mild-mannered PM could get rough.

Outlook magazine's cover story, appearing on the morning of the first national press conference, Saturday, 4 September, focused on Dr Singh's new 'assertive personality', using the encounter with Advani and Fernandes as an example of Dr Singh meaning business. *Outlook* dubbed the PM as being 'Stronger, Firmer, Tougher'. The story's strapline was: 'He doesn't take things lying down anymore. Both the Opposition, and his partymen, better beware.' *Outlook*'s Sheela Reddy wrote: 'The days of the faceless, shy and unassuming Manmohan are over. The PM will interact with the media and the public more. Will take a tough stand with the Opposition when it is required. Won't tolerate ministers getting out of line.'

But the report went on to add, 'Given a free hand by Sonia Gandhi to iron out policy matters with allies and the Left. Will chair coordination committee meetings in Sonia's absence. Activities will be broadened from governance to include issues like Kashmir. Sonia wants him to be a political PM, not function like a mere given administrator.' I saw in this small concession to Sonia, and the message that the PM was being assertive with her approval, the hand of *Outlook* editor-in-chief Vinod Mehta. He would, I knew, not want to be on the wrong side of the Congress 'High Command'.

The report quoted CPI leader D. Raja as saying that he was now convinced that Manmohan was gradually emerging as a 'real prime minister' and that 'History has given him a new role and he is changing to fit into that role. There is no such thing as a political lightweight or a nominated prime minister. He is the head of the government now and he is behaving like one.' I called Raja and thanked him for that endorsement.

The other positive development in the run-up to the prime minister's press conference was that Sonia, while happy to make it clear that she remained the boss, as party president, did take several steps to ensure that other senior party leaders and ministers publicly accepted Dr Singh as *primus inter pares*. Her first visible step was to get the entire Cabinet to line up at 7 RCR and bid the PM farewell when he went abroad. This was seen as a public gesture of deference to the PM. She then encouraged her senior colleagues, or so I gathered, to be more deferential to the PM in their dealings.

For example, in the early days of government, External Affairs Minister Natwar Singh would refer to Dr Singh as Manmohan. He was gently told that equations had changed. Human Resources Development Minister Arjun Singh would not stand up in Cabinet meetings or at public functions when the PM arrived. After Sonia's intervention, he began doing so, even if half-heartedly. Sonia let it be known that, in her absence, party and UPA coordination meetings would be chaired by Dr Singh. At the AICC session in August 2004, Dr Singh was projected by Sonia as the second in command. I chose to draft an overtly political speech for the PM for the AICC session. Coming just a week after his first Independence Day address from the ramparts of the Red Fort, the AICC address would reinforce his prime ministerial image. In his Independence Day speech he re-crafted the NCMP into 'Saat Sutra', seven priorities, and spoke of a 'New Deal for Rural India'. His declaration that he had 'no promises to make, but only promises to keep' was widely appreciated.

Considerable work went into preparing Dr Singh for his media interaction in September 2004. Several ministers and senior officials and editors were consulted for advice both on likely questions and possible answers. I personally spoke to several ministers and editors. Mani, Nair and Narayanan worked with PMO officials to put together their own set of likely questions and suggested answers. A final list of seventy-five likely questions and answers was prepared and these were discussed with Dr Singh over several sessions in the preceding week. These sessions proved most instructive because Dr Singh revealed his mind on many issues, rehearsing his replies to potential questions. The internal debate among his key aides on what each thought he should say was the first structured conversation on policy in the PMO.

While my approach was to read out a set of likely questions to him and let him identify the questions for which he needed written draft replies from the PMO, my colleague Sujata Mehta, the joint secretary from the foreign service, prepared elaborate answers for every likely question on foreign policy. The foreign service had got used to tutoring the PM on what he should or should not say to the media. Dr Singh was not someone who needed tutoring, especially on foreign policy. He knew well what to say on key issues and had a mind of his own. But he would never snub an official engaged in tutoring him. He would hear her patiently and say precisely what he wanted to. Every once in a while, though, he would respond to advice from officials on what they thought he 'should say', to the media or to a visiting dignitary, by snapping, 'Tell me what I should know, not what I should say!'

It was decided that the press conference would be in the large hall of Vigyan Bhavan, the premier sarkari conference hall, and would be open to all accredited journalists, Indian and foreign. In order to make the event more inclusive, those not accredited could secure an invitation card. Over 500 journalists trooped into the hall, filling it up. Dr Singh suggested the press conference should be in the morning. Both Mani and Vikram agreed, saying he would look fresh and rested in the morning. I disagreed and told them that in the age of live television Saturday morning was not 'prime' time and a pre-lunch event would enable the Opposition to dominate the airwaves at prime time in the evening. The headlines in the evening news bulletins would not be about what the PM said, but about what his critics were saying. The PM agreed to schedule the event at 5 p.m. This would give TV journalists headline material and print journalists enough time to file their reports for the next day's papers.

On the morning of the press conference, I found only half an hour had been allotted for the interaction. I was dismayed. I was told that Mani and Nair had decided between them that it was best to restrict the press conference to thirty minutes so that nothing went wrong. I went to the PM and told him this would be counterproductive. At least fifty of the 500 journalists expected should be allowed to ask questions, I pointed out. I reasoned that even if each question took a minute to answer, the press conference would have to go on for an hour. To my relief, Dr Singh readily agreed. He asked Vikram Doraiswamy not to schedule any meeting for that evening. I saw this as a welcome signal of his willingness to spend even more than an hour with the media. As it turned out, the press conference lasted for ninety minutes and fifty-two questions were asked.

Later that morning, I went across to Vigyan Bhavan along with my colleague Muthu Kumar, a very competent information service officer with an impressive record at Doordarshan, to arrange the dais and the positioning of the Doordarshan camera. The public broadcaster's cameras were the only ones to be placed in the hall and private channels would get free live feed from them. This arrangement enabled me to fix the frame to the PM's advantage, rather than leave the angles to be determined by the private channels. The viewer would see only the PM's face on television in a close shot and the size of the audience in a long shot. The PM would speak against the backdrop of the Tricolour and the three lions on the Ashoka Pillar—both symbols of the Indian state.

All officials would be seated in the audience. On hearing about this, Minister for Information and Broadcasting Priya Ranjan Dasmunshi called to object. How could the PM address a press conference without the information and broadcasting minister sitting next to him, he protested, when his ministry was the official event organizer. I told him that I had taken this decision on the advice of Sharada Prasad, who had informed me that Indiraji and Rajivji had addressed the media in this manner. He mumbled something and hung up.

Muthu ensured that the journalists were seated in groups, with English-language print in one section and TV in another, the Hindi media in one section and other Indian languages grouped together, and Urdu media given a separate row. Foreign media was seated at the back. This way, I could call out names, or numbers (since every journalist had been given a placard with a number on it), from different sections of the audience, to ensure that every segment of the media got a chance to ask a question.

Logistics were important, no doubt, but the key strategic consideration was that Dr Singh should be seen answering every and any kind of question without reference to officials. By doing so, he was meant to establish that he had command over the entire gamut of policy. He needed to show that he knew as much about nuclear policy as he did about river water disputes; was as familiar with farmers' issues as with fiscal issues; knew as much about Kashmir as he did about Telangana. In order to save time, the standard opening statement was abandoned. A 1000-word statement detailing what the UPA government had done in its first 100 days in office was circulated and taken as read. The conference went straight into question time.

At the end, I was pleased at our hit rate: we had anticipated fifty-one of the fifty-two questions. The one unanticipated question was from Jay Raina of *Hindustan Times*, who wanted to know what the PM thought of his 'spin doctor's work'. The PM smiled, even as the audience laughed, but gave a quizzical look. It appeared he was not aware of the term 'spin doctor'.

By the end of the press conference, the media was astounded. Dr Singh had proved the *Outlook* story right. He had not come across as weak or unsure, and did not appear to need help in answering a question. No one disrupted the press conference. As he left the dais, the entire media stood up as a sign of respect. The first step in branding Manmohan Singh as a man of prime ministerial timber was taken.

That evening Mani Dixit hosted a dinner at his home. When I reached, he held out his hand and hugged me and said he was wrong to have been worried. He conceded that I was right to have adopted a 'high-risk' strategy, as he put it. Mani and some others in the PMO had thought that exposing the PM to media scrutiny in the manner I did was fraught with the risk of Dr Singh coming across as inadequately aware of the range of political and diplomatic issues that would be brought up.

'If it had failed, everyone would have asked for your head,' said Mani. 'You deserve a drink. Come in.'

My phone kept ringing through the evening with friends from the media complimenting the PM and congratulating me for getting him to address the media. I took every call. As I walked into Mani's living room an RCR number flashed on my mobile. It was Dr Singh himself.

'I was watching TV,' he said, adding in his economical way, 'I think they are all happy. There is nothing negative so far.'

I told him he was superb and that I had spent much of the evening responding to callers complimenting the PM. Mani placed a much-needed glass of single malt in my hand.

———

The national press conference was not an exercise in transparency and accountability. It was meant to demonstrate to the country and even to the media that Dr Singh had a mind of his own. That he was not a 'rubber stamp' PM but was in fact 'in charge' and *au fait* with his brief. That he had a prime minister's grasp on a wide range of national and international issues and was not some academic economist or a file-pushing government official.

While Dr Singh was pleased that night with the generally favourable TV coverage, the next morning's headlines pleased him even more. Most papers highlighted Dr Singh's answer to the very last question of the press conference, from a woman journalist. 'Mr Prime Minister,' she asked, 'it is being said in certain quarters that the threat to Dr Manmohan Singh comes not from the Left or from the Opposition, but from Dr Manmohan Singh himself and that if you are pushed against the wall and compelled to do things that go against your grain in the course of keeping the coalition together, you might just decide to put in your papers. Could such a thing happen?'

The PM's reply was candid and assertive. 'Well, Madam, I believe our government is going to last for full five years, and let there be no doubt or ambiguity about this. Therefore, this misconception that I can be pressured into giving up is simply not going to materialize.' Newspapers also highlighted his assertion that 'The insinuation that there are two separate centres of power is not true.' Chandigarh's

Tribune, a newspaper that Dr Singh grew up with and which was his first morning read with a cup of tea, opened its report with 'Prime Minister Manmohan Singh . . . dismissed as "without foundation" the Opposition charge that Congress president and UPA chairperson Sonia Gandhi is the "super Prime Minister".' *The Hindu*'s headline summed it up pithily: 'I am in charge, and will last'.

A fortnight later, when he arrived in New York, *Time* ran a cover story on Dr Singh's prime ministership with the headline: 'His Own Man'. The message had gone out to the world. Most reports and editorial comments drew attention to three aspects of the press interaction. First, that it was wide-ranging and the PM answered every single question. Second, the PM's 'political personality' came through. Finally, that he had a clear view of his agenda and his priorities.

The key to 'Brand Manmohan' was his projection as his own man. His Achilles' heel was the equation with Sonia. He would always be tormented by the question of whether he was his own man, or just her puppet. Throughout his two terms, this was always the most difficult and delicate issue for him to handle.

Whenever he asserted prime ministerial authority his image shone. Whenever he shied away from doing so, it took a beating. Creating, building and protecting this image, without necessarily allowing a situation where he would have to publicly differ or confront Sonia or his senior colleagues was the key to his success, his image and his power. With mischief-makers aplenty, protecting the PM's image required constant vigilance.

Apart from projecting Dr Singh as a 'national' leader, and not just a partisan politician, I also aimed to project him as a 'consensual' leader. The purpose of this, too, was to show that like Vajpayee and Narasimha Rao, Dr Singh was a prime minister who tried to build support for his policies cutting across factions within the Congress and across political parties. Whenever he acted as an arbitrator between warring ministers, like Chidambaram and Kamal Nath, or between senior and junior ministers, like Pranab Mukherjee and Anand Sharma, or between the leader of an alliance partner like Sharad Pawar and his own party member Prithviraj Chavan, I would let political reporters and analysts know how the PM was mediating between them and building consensus. Even with the Left, his inveterate critics, he took a conciliatory stance through the first half of his tenure. He would ensure that the PMO acted on every request that came from Left leaders, be it the nomination of a Left-leaning academic to some institution or the clearance of a project in a Left bastion in West Bengal or sending Left MPs off on foreign junkets.

By the time Dr Singh travelled to New York to attend the United Nations General Assembly in September 2004, he had acquired the image of being a businesslike, consensual and capable PM. The September press conference was not planned with a view to projecting the PM's image to the world. My focus was entirely on building his image at home. However, it was Mani Dixit who made the point to me that by firmly establishing his image as PM at home, we had also sent a message to the world that this was a PM the world could do business with. Given our parliamentary system, it's important that heads of government of other countries felt confident that an assurance from the Indian head of government was backed by his entire government.

After the first national press conference, few saw Manmohan Singh as a 'puppet' PM, or as a novice, a 'weak' leader, or just an 'academic' or 'bureaucrat'. Both US President George Bush and Pakistan President Pervez Musharraf met him in New York and had substantial conversations. The success of those meetings, which we shall discuss later, bolstered his public image at home.

Flying back home on his seventy-second birthday, Dr Singh looked relaxed as he cut a cake and shared it with the media on Air India One. The phase of teething troubles was over. He was now firmly ensconced as prime minister.

Given that I had mainly been a financial journalist in the print media,

I had to get to know a lot of new media personnel in TV, on the
political beat and in Indian-language media. It became apparent to
me fairly early in my tenure that a large majority of journalists were
just professionals doing their job and as long as one dealt with them
with courtesy and regard for their need to get a good story they would
always be objective in their reporting, often even supportive without
my trying very hard. A second category of journalists were those who
liked being pampered and given additional attention. A junket here
or an exclusive story there and one had no problem with them. The
third category were partisan journalists—pro-BJP, pro-Left, pro-Sonia,
pro-Arjun, pro-Pranab and so on—and my approach was to keep them
at a distance. This did upset some, especially those close to Sonia who
assumed the government was theirs and the PMO should treat them
with deference. Finally, there were the prima donnas. Media baron-
editors, editor-CEOs, columnists with a brand name.

In Vajpayee's PMO, the SPG had a list of senior editors who were
given various privileges, including being allowed to carry their cell
phones into South Block, an entitlement denied to other visitors for
security reasons. I discovered that there were even nicer ones, when at
a foreign airport I saw a Mercedes car draw up for one editor while
the rest of the press contingent accompanying the prime minister filed
into a bus. On making inquiries I discovered that the car had been sent
by the local embassy and that it was standard practice in the Vajpayee
PMO for some journalists to get such limousines when travelling abroad
with the PM. I was told that Vajpayee's son-in-law, Ranjan Bhattacharya,
who had befriended many senior editors, had taken personal interest in
ensuring that the PMO's favoured journalists were well looked after. I
brought to an end all such privileges and incurred the wrath of some
professional peers. The only privilege I retained was the serving of
good-quality alcohol on the PM's plane.

On the first trip out to Bangkok in July 2004 I noticed that drinks
were not being served. I was told the PMO had issued instructions
that no alcohol be offered on the PM's plane. This was ridiculous.
We were clearly swinging from one extreme, of the Vajpayee days, to
the other. The air hostess told me that they had drinks in stock and

could serve them if instructed. Mani Dixit thought it would not be appropriate. Not wanting to waste time convincing the bureaucrats on board, I walked into the PM's cabin and asked him if he had any objection if drinks were served to the media. Dr Singh was engrossed in some official papers. He looked up, thought for a moment and said, 'You decide.' When the drinks finally came out, several officials on board also raised a toast.

Dr Singh always made it a point to meet journalists accompanying him on foreign visits and would always ask me if they were being well looked after. On board he would spare time for a private chat with just one or two senior editors. It was a privilege that journalists, especially from regional Indian-language media, valued enormously. Apart from interacting with journalists accompanying him on foreign trips, Dr Singh always made time to meet representatives of the media in every state capital. Finding him more relaxed on these visits outside Delhi, I told a correspondent of the *Economic Times* who had been seeking an interview for a long time to find his way to Gandhiji's ashram at Wardha. The PM was scheduled to visit the ashram, have lunch with its residents and rest for a while before moving on to Nagpur. Sitting in a modest hut, under a fan, on a warm July afternoon in 2006, Dr Singh gave an extensive interview to *ET*. It was perhaps his only lengthy interview to an Indian newspaper and the only one given by an Indian PM at Gandhiji's ashram.

As a former editor I was able to relate to most editors and I managed to befriend several media owners as well, giving them time with the PM or helping them out whenever they had problems with one ministry or another. However, the bulk of my time was spent just chatting up reporters and establishing a personal bond with them. When Parliament was in session, I would visit the media gallery regularly and spend time gossiping with reporters, planting stories and picking up information. On the PM's aircraft, travelling abroad, I would spend a few minutes with every one of the forty journalists on board, including Doordarshan cameramen and wire-service reporters, regarded as the lowest rung of the media's social pyramid. All of this came in handy in times of crisis and need. There were always those who took favours but never returned them. But more often than not, one could encash an IOU, earned by nothing more than a show of courtesy and friendship.

Consequently, it was a relatively smooth ride with the media for Dr Singh in UPA-1. His problem always was that he did not want to become more popular with the media and the general public than Sonia. Whenever a TV channel or newsmagazine conducted an opinion poll and showed that his popularity, while rising, was a few notches below that of Sonia, he would feel relieved. 'Good,' he would say, with a mischievous smile. That defined the limit to his projection and brand-building.

Dr Singh's 'silences' and his unwillingness to project himself became more manifest in UPA-2 and were more widely commented upon. His penchant for a 'low profile' was seen in UPA-1 as a defence mechanism, part shyness and part self-preservation, but in UPA-2 it came to be seen as escapism, as shirking responsibility and an unwillingness to take charge. The same trait of self-effacement was seen as a virtue in UPA-1 and a weakness in UPA-2.

7

Manmohan's Camelot

*'Public office offers the opportunity
to be educated at public expense.'*

Manmohan Singh

At a meeting of business leaders from India and Southeast Asia in Kuala Lumpur in 2005, the secretary general of the ASEAN, Ong Keng Yong, introduced Dr Singh as 'the world's most highly qualified head of government'. A standing ovation followed.

Dr Singh's academic and professional credentials had by now become legendary. Intellectuals around the world wanted to meet him. At the Indian Science Congress in Ahmedabad in December 2004, and at subsequent congresses every year, Nobel Prize-winners wanted to be photographed with him. Visiting scholars from around the world sought appointments with him. It is the practice in the PMO that the joint secretary concerned is required to be present when the PM has official visitors. But when the visitor was neither 'official' nor 'personal' I would often get summoned instead. Thus, I was fortunate enough to be present when an Eric Hobsbawm, or a Norman Borlaug or a Roderick MacFarquhar or even a George Soros came calling.

It was not just his academic credentials or his continuing interest in engaging academics that attracted so many thinking people to Dr Singh. It was also the fact that many around the world had come to see him, as indeed many at home did, as a thinking man's political leader. The world had many such leaders in the early post-colonial era. Jawaharlal Nehru himself was one such. Even small countries in obscure parts of the world had produced leaders who were seen by their people as 'teachers' and 'thinkers'. That era seemed to have ended as more practical, tactical and manipulative politicians came to the fore.

The Indian and Western elite did not regard any of Nehru's successors as 'thinking' leaders. Indira Gandhi tried hard to win over India's intellectual elite, but the Emergency broke a nascent link. When men like P.N. Haksar and P.N. Dhar were hounded out of her inner circle, India's intellectuals deserted her. Rajiv Gandhi was never taken seriously by this elite. Narasimha Rao may have been a scholar in his own right, but he was an 'outsider' to India's metropolitan elite. In Andhra Pradesh, among the Telugu-speaking elite he was known as an *ashtavadhani*, a literary master. But Delhi's elite tended to conflate his intellectual achievements with the fact that he was fluent in many languages. Vajpayee too was a highly regarded poet. Indeed, Rao and Vajpayee enjoyed the company of intellectuals and could count many professors among their friends. But in the snobbish world of the metropolitan elite, an Oxbridge type like Dr Singh was regarded as a class apart from these home-grown politician–intellectuals.

Whatever the ups and downs of the daily drill of being PM, Dr Singh enjoyed these intellectual engagements. Every now and then, he would summon me and ask, 'Who are the wise men I can consult?' on some issue or the other that he was grappling with. Apart from the distinguished visitors who sought appointments with the PM and the 'specialists' who were invited to meet him, he also had his own set of friends from the world of academia and policymaking who would meet him every now and then. This was a long list, including Amartya Sen, Jagdish Bhagwati, Padma Desai, I.G. Patel, Meghnad Desai, H.M. Sethna, M.S. Swaminathan, K. Subrahmanyam and V.S. Arunachalam. Hoping to secure US support for a 'Second Green Revolution' in India, a favourite theme of his, Dr Singh met Norman Borlaug, the 'father of the green revolution', and talked about agricultural research and ways in which India could boost farm productivity once again. Given his academic bent, he took a keen interest in academic achievements across disciplines. When mathematician S.R. Srinivasa Vardhan was awarded the Abel Prize, the Nobel equivalent in mathematics, Dr Singh shot off a letter of congratulations. Dr Vardhan was reportedly surprised, for he had never before had a letter from a head of government.

Dr Singh also inducted several experts into various government bodies like the Prime Minister's Economic Advisory Council, the Science Advisory Council to the PM and advisory groups on a range of issues dealing with domestic and foreign policy. Some of the prominent names were C. Rangarajan, V.S. Vyas, Suresh Tendulkar, A.Vaidyanathan, Palle Rama Rao, C.N.R. Rao, R.K. Pachauri, Roddam Narasimha, V.S. Ananth, Andre Beteille, P.M. Bhargava and Deepak Nayyar. He would patiently sit through long meetings with them and listen to contending viewpoints. When the tiger population in India was threatened, he set up an expert group that included wildlife expert Valmik Thapar and Sunita Narain of the Centre for Science and Environment and heard both sides of what was a particularly sharp argument. In the National Knowledge Commission, he would listen to the 'left-wing' scientist P.M. Bhargava with as much interest as to the liberal sociologist Andre Beteille.

When Soros sought an appointment, Dr Singh wanted to know what he wished to talk about. Was Soros going to invest in India? Would he want to know about Indian policies? Soros did not have money on his mind. He wanted to meet Dr Singh, not the PM, and discuss his books! I had to quickly read and brief the PM on the key arguments of Soros' books on globalization, capitalism and terrorism. Soros meant what he said—he did actually talk about his books—but Rupert Murdoch tried a trick to secure an appointment. Having failed on one occasion to meet Dr Singh, he made a second attempt by letting it be known that he was not interested in talking about his media business. Rather, he wanted to talk about China. The PM was amused and granted him an appointment. Murdoch did discuss China and explained where he saw China going. But, as he got up to leave, he expressed the hope that the Indian government would be more receptive to his media plans than China had been.

On China, Dr Singh was an eager learner. For him, China remained an enigma and he eagerly sought out people who were knowledgeable about it. He spent two long afternoons with Singapore's leader Lee Kuan Yew getting tutored about China and its new generation of leaders. Lee knew the country better than most world leaders. He also invited Harvard professor Roderick MacFarquhar and Opposition politician and India's China-watcher Subramaniam Swamy for long conversations on the subject.

He followed these up by doing his own homework, devoting several days to a thorough reading of all the Nehru papers. 'I do not want to make the mistakes Nehru made, so it is important that I understand his own thinking at the time,' he once said to me, explaining how he painstakingly read through the official record of what happened between China and India in the years 1957 to 1962. In his second term, as he familiarized himself with China's new leadership, he read with interest Ezra Vogel's authoritative biography of Deng Xiaoping. He knew the West and much of East and Southeast Asia well. His stint in the South Commission had given him a good grasp of the developing world, especially Africa.

Before a visit to Russia, he sought out the economist Padma Desai, an acknowledged authority on Russia. He would, of course, also read widely and extensively the biographies of important leaders he had to meet, picking up information about his interlocutors that no Indian diplomat was able to put into his brief before a meeting. Dr Singh was a voracious reader and his living room table always had on it a new book that he was reading. Weekends were mostly spent reading.

Over time, I consulted a wide range of scholars and policy experts when writing the PM's speeches, sometimes seeking draft texts, and would keep him informed of the names. These included scientists like C.N.R. Rao, R.M. Mashelkar and M.S. Swaminathan, strategic affairs guru K. Subrahmanyam, Kashmir expert Amitabh Mattoo, bureaucrat and diplomat Gopalkrishna Gandhi, historian–journalist Rudrangshu Mukherjee, and my father, who had been a speech-writer for Narasimha Rao. It was, on occasion, amusing to see some of our most distinguished scientists and academics sending draft speeches full of self-praise that read more like their résumés, hoping the PM would read them out.

For his first major speech abroad, at New York's CFR, he wanted me to consult people with specialist knowledge of India–US relations outside government and also find out from those familiar with the event who would be in the audience, and what they might expect to hear from the Indian PM. Accordingly, I consulted Sunil Khilnani and Fareed Zakaria. Not surprisingly, Mani Dixit disapproved of the idea. Reflecting the traditional Indian establishment view, he asked, 'Can we not write a speech for the PM? Why do we need external advice?'

There was a bit of Camelot in UPA-1. Like John Kennedy's circle of the 'best and the brightest', which included East Coast academics like John Kenneth Galbraith, Walt Rostow and Arthur Schlesinger, Dr Singh too had created a circle of intellect around himself. In the latter half of his first term, as Indian ambassadors began to understand this side of the PM's personality, they would make sure to offer the PM some time with local scholars and public intellectuals, albeit mostly economists. In Paris he would meet with Alice Thorner, the widow of Daniel Thorner. Both were economists who had researched deeply on India. In New York he would meet Paul Volcker, former chairman of the Federal Reserve; in London he would meet economist Nick Stern and scholars from Cambridge and Oxford.

With his many friends, admirers and students dropping in every now and then, the visitor's room at RCR became a school at which one learnt a lot, validating one of Dr Singh's favourite lines, 'Public office offers the opportunity for private education at public expense.'

———

His flaw was, of course, the weak follow-up. The original intention of setting up the National Knowledge Commission was to seek ideas on improving the quality of higher education in India and strengthening the public library system around the country. But the commission got itself embroiled in avoidable controversies, with two members quitting and another becoming a permanent dissenter. Appointing an NRI technocrat like Sam Pitroda, who did not command much respect among liberal academics, was probably a bad idea to begin with.

While Dr Singh valued inputs into policy he would become impatient with purely academic solutions that were not adequately grounded in political reality. However, he did come to appreciate the fact that while the gap between the academic and the policy worlds was not very wide in the field of economics, his own example being a case in point, in other fields, like foreign affairs, the gap was very wide because policymakers rarely shared information with scholars. Releasing a book by diplomat Jagat Mehta in April 2006, Dr Singh regretted the fact that scholars had to depend on the memory of retired civil servants to get a glimpse into the thinking that had gone into policymaking. While agreeing that memoirs like Mehta's were very useful for scholars, he said, 'I do hope that we do not have to depend only on memory and personal notes for a record of policymaking. I think the time has come for us to have at least a fifty-year rule, if not a thirty-year rule, that allows scholars and researchers free access to declassified official papers. I would like to have this issue examined so that we can take an early and informed decision. In the long run, this will make it possible for us to draw appropriate lessons from the past and make effective decisions for the future.'

The next day, I took a printout of the PM's speech and put up a note for his approval saying he might wish to instruct the principal secretary to follow up on this statement and take the necessary steps to have this new policy announced. I heard nothing about this afterwards. Years later, after I left the PMO, I asked Dr Singh why he never followed up on that announcement. His matter-of-fact reply was, 'This should have been done by the BJP when they were in office. The Congress party is not yet ready to take this step.' The implication of his remark was that any declassification of official papers based on a thirty-year rule would begin to throw more light on Nehru's and Indira's time in office.

The two key initiatives of the PM for which he sought expert opinion in a systematic fashion were his dialogue with Pakistan's President

Pervez Musharraf on Jammu and Kashmir and the initiative he took with the US on civil nuclear energy.

In November 2004, Dr Singh was to make his first official visit to Jammu and Kashmir. He had returned from New York in September 2004 after a useful meeting with President Musharraf and felt the time was ripe for a new initiative on Kashmir. Addressing the students and faculty of the Kashmir Institute of Medical Sciences, he spoke of his vision of a 'new Kashmir' (naya Kashmir) and said that the 'time has come to put forward a new blueprint, a fresh vision for Kashmir and for the Kashmiri people, free from the fear of war, want and exploitation'.

Those following the Kashmir issue understood the significance of both the phrase 'naya Kashmir' and, even more importantly, the term 'new blueprint'—a reference to the Manmohan–Musharraf formula that I will discuss in the next chapter. The speech was drafted by Mani Dixit and Amitabh Mattoo, then vice chancellor of Jammu University, and a Kashmiri Pandit. A few weeks later Mani died and in the transition from Mani to Narayanan, the momentum on the Kashmir initiative was lost. It picked up again when Musharraf visited India in April 2005. The opening up of the Srinagar–Muzaffarabad bus service was a major confidence-building exercise that unfolded the PM's vision of a 'naya Kashmir'. A key idea was free travel across the so-called Line of Control. But, despite this initiative, Dr Singh was not able to make a breakthrough with the Hurriyat and the separatists in Kashmir. He needed an instrument through which he could open an internal dialogue, just as he had by then opened dialogue with Musharraf.

I was not aware what view Narayanan was taking of Dr Singh's ideas about a 'naya Kashmir' and a 'new blueprint' until I was summoned by the PM sometime in August 2005 and asked who I thought were the 'wise men' he should consult on Kashmir. He was then preparing for his third meeting with Musharraf in September 2005.

I recalled the fact that when I was editor of the Financial Express, I had once met Dr Singh at the home of journalist Prem Shankar Jha in Delhi's Golf Links where Prem and my former colleague from the Economic Times David Devadas had brought together some Hurriyat leaders for a conversation over very high-quality Kashmiri wazwan.

So I first suggested Prem's name and then went on to add the names of all those who I knew had either some knowledge or interest in the subject. This list included strategic affairs guru K. Subrahmanyam, former home secretary and the government's special representative on J&K N.N. Vohra, journalists B.G. Verghese, Manoj Joshi (who had published a book on Kashmir) and Bharat Bhushan, Kashmiri economist Haseeb Drabhu, who was then adviser to the chief minister of J&K, and Amitabh Mattoo.

Dr Singh asked me to arrange a meeting with all of them. It was decided that they would all be invited for a pre-lunch meeting on a Saturday morning and the conversation would carry on over lunch. Narayanan was miffed at the idea.

'Why does he want all these seminar-wallahs here?' he asked. 'What can they tell him that we do not already know?'

I said there was no harm in the PM hearing opinions from outside the government.

'He reads all their columns anyway!' replied an exasperated and irritated Narayanan.

Later, he sat glumly through the meeting. As he left, he asked me if I had heard one new idea. Not being a subject expert, I was not sure how much of what had been said that morning was new. But I soon realized there was a major takeaway from the meeting when Dr Singh called me and said he liked K. Subrahmanyam's suggestion that the PM should convene a 'round-table' on the future of J&K, ensuring that every single viewpoint was represented around the table.

'That is what the British did,' he added for effect. Narayanan was uncomfortable with the term 'round-table conference' for precisely that reason. As he pointed out, the British had convened a round-table conference to begin the process of granting India independence. Was that the political message the PM wanted to send? Narayanan did not like the idea at all.

Dr Singh had a different view. He believed the time had come for everyone in the state to freely express their opinion. After all, the Hurriyat and separatists did not represent the majority in the state, nor was '*azadi*' really on the cards. The separatists were a vocal and an important minority. Let them speak openly in a gathering of fellow Kashmiris and representatives of Jammu and Ladakh, he felt, and let there be an open discussion. In the end it would have to be India and Pakistan that would have to arrive at a settlement of the issue, keeping in mind the welfare of the Kashmiri people.

Invitations were sent out to every political party, to intellectuals, heads of major academic institutions, NGOs and to the Kashmiri separatists as well. On 25 February 2006, after Parliament had opened for the budget session, the First J&K Round-table was convened at 7 RCR. Invitations to the meeting were handed over personally to every important leader from the state. Intelligence officials scouted out even those who were ostensibly underground and letters of invitation were personally handed over to them. No one could claim he or she was not invited.

The round-table was a great success inasmuch as it was the first dialogue process of its kind and allowed a wide cross-section of opinion to be freely expressed. The Hurriyat boycotted the meeting but they seemed impressed by the PM's sincerity, because soon after, they agreed to meet him for a direct dialogue. He opened the day-long round-table saying:

A round-table is a dialogue. No one preaches and no one just listens. This is a dialogue of equals who promise to work together. Today's meeting is a significant event. It will, however, achieve historical importance if we are able to unleash a process by which we can arrive at a workable blueprint that can help to create a new chapter in Kashmir's history. Not by compromising on one's ideals, but in a spirit of mutual tolerance, understanding and accommodation.

This entire process is a good example of how Dr Singh used 'outsiders' of repute, like K. Subrahmanyam, Prem Jha, Amitabh Mattoo, Haseeb Drabhu and others to break the mould and seek an 'out-of-the-box' solution to a problem to which the governmental system was unable to find a solution. In seeking to push the idea of a civil nuclear energy agreement with the United States that would liberate

India from trade denial regimes in strategic technologies, Dr Singh invested even more time and effort into engaging the minds of India's top strategic affairs, nuclear policy and international relations experts. Over three years, from mid-2005 to mid-2008, 7 RCR played host to a large number of analysts and experts with differing views whose opinions shaped Dr Singh's own thinking and Indian official policy.

Many retired nuclear scientists came out of the woodwork wanting to be 'consulted' and to be seen as part of the historic process. One such senior scientist even sent me his biodata and urged me to get him appointed as an adviser to the PM. When this did not happen, he became a severe critic of the nuclear deal.

The only major organized effort was, not surprisingly, left to K. Subrahmanyam to lead. Dr Singh appointed a task force that was asked to study emerging trends and long-term implications of the global strategy of the United States as it had evolved during the Bush era and draw relevant lessons for Indian economic and foreign policy. The task force report titled 'The Challenge: India and the New American Global Strategy' was commissioned in 2005 and submitted to the PM in 2006. The Subrahmanyam task force had among its members scientists P. Rama Rao and M.S. Ananth, economists R.K. Pachauri and Arvind Virmani, strategic affairs analysts Uday Bhaskar and Amitabh Mattoo. Regrettably, it remains a classified document even though Subrahmanyam wanted it made public.

Social policy, however, was the one area in which the voice of the activist overpowered the voice of the specialist. There were a few experts like development economists Jean Drèze and Mihir Shah, the former a member of the NAC in UPA-1 and the latter a member of the Planning Commission in UPA-2, who combined activism with serious research. However, most others involved in making social policy, including most members of the NAC, were more activists than experts, and far removed from being administrators. Dr Singh tried to infuse rigour into the process of social-sector policymaking, and sometimes found his efforts misinterpreted. For example, Dr Singh was never opposed to the rural employment guarantee programme but sought rigorous analysis of the options available to see how the government could maximize the benefits while minimizing the expenditure. This was construed by activists as opposition to the scheme itself.

This insistence on securing an analytical underpinning for the government's policy initiatives sometimes made Dr Singh a frustrated head of government, because everything that a government does in a democracy cannot be justified by the principles of rigour and consistency. While, on the one hand, activists disparaged him for not being populist enough, on the other, many of Dr Singh's more academically oriented friends found fault with him for the intellectual compromises he had to make as a politician. This prompted the jibe that Dr Singh was in fact 'a first-rate politician but a second-rate economist'. But Dr Singh had been in public life long enough to know, as he often put it, that 'one has to first succeed as a politician before being viewed a statesman'.

For the same reason, I, too, would not overstate the role of 'expertise' and of the 'technocracy' in policymaking. In a democracy, that too with a fractious and ideologically disparate coalition like the UPA at the helm, public policy was inevitably a product of political interest and private lobbying. But subject experts and committees certainly informed Dr Singh's thinking and gave him the space he needed to negotiate his way through political hurdles in pursuit of policies dear to him, both domestic and foreign.

8

'Promises to Keep'

'We want India to shine.
But India must shine for all.'

First national press conference
4 September 2004

Even before he was named head of the UPA government, Dr Singh was asked by Sonia to address the media and calm the stock market down. The BSE Sensex had gone into a tailspin after it was announced that the Congress would form a government with the support of the Left. It was left to Dr Singh to calm investors' nerves. Fortunately, his track record in the 1990s reassured investors at home and abroad. The Vajpayee government had ended its term on a high note, with upwards of 8 per cent growth in the final year, fuelled by a massive expansion of investment in infrastructure, and bequeathed to its successor an economy in reasonably good shape. It was economic optimism that prompted the NDA finance minister Jaswant Singh's famous 'India Shining' campaign, aimed at promoting India internationally as an investment destination. Growth rates were going up, inflation was low, a surplus in the capital account was being registered for the first time in years. The last indicator was a vote of confidence from a global community that viewed the BJP with scepticism when it conducted nuclear tests in 1998. The challenge for the UPA was to address the grievances of farmers, especially in southern India, reassure investors and make the growth process socially 'inclusive'.

In setting out the new government's agenda through his first Independence Day address, Dr Singh emphasized that the government's 'plans and priorities' had been defined by three statements—the NCMP, the President's address to Parliament and the finance minister's budget speech. The reference to all three statements was significant. It was meant to emphasize the fact that the policy agenda of the government was not defined by the NCMP alone, but also by what the President said in Parliament (this was a speech written by the PMO, which in this case meant me) and what the finance minister said in his budget speech.

What the PM was implicitly telling the nation was that the NCMP would not become a straitjacket but would be interpreted through the government's policy statements. The NCMP had been hurriedly drafted by Sitaram Yechury and Jairam Ramesh to enable the Left to work with the Congress. It was not a carefully thought through manifesto. Dr Singh was, understandably, not fully satisfied with the NCMP. He thought the Congress had made too many concessions to the Left in its desperation to secure support. He was concerned that both the Left and many in the Congress would expect delivery on all promises, and that this might be a tough task for the government. The party seemed to have taken the easy way out, saying 'yes' to words in print and imagining that the government would not be constrained by them in action.

Having lived through the nightmare of 1991–92, namely the economic mess that confronted the Narasimha Rao government, and having handled earlier economic crises, one of Dr Singh's favourite English proverbs was 'money does not grow on trees'. He believed the NCMP's fiscal commitments, and there were many promises of subsidies and new schemes, would prove to be unsustainable. This belief lay behind the more cautious tone of what was possible and doable in the President's address and the finance minister's budget speech. Also, by emphasizing the relevance of the budget speech to government policy he was giving the government the option to define policy from time to time, rather than be constrained by commitments made on paper on an eager night.

This did not mean Dr Singh did not believe in the fundamental principles underlining the NCMP. Indeed he did. He had long conceded that as finance minister he had not done enough for health and education and that these would be his priorities as PM. He also recognized that the NDA's defeat, especially that of Chandrababu Naidu and his Telugu Desam Party in Andhra Pradesh, was because of the neglect of agriculture and rural development, and that the UPA had to focus on this. He was among the first to criticize the BJP's 'India Shining' campaign when it was rolled out in the run-up to the 2004 elections. For several months before that Sonia and he sat through long discussions with social scientists and civil-society activists to try and understand the issues they saw as priorities for policy action.

The view often purveyed by Dr Singh's critics and Sonia's admirers that he was a late convert to her way of thinking about social policy was just not true. The concerns expressed in the NCMP were uppermost in Dr Singh's mind and were reflected in his first Independence Day address where he spoke of a 'New Deal for Rural India' and the 'Saat Sutra' (seven priorities) of the UPA, namely agriculture, water, education, health care, employment, urban renewal and infrastructure. This address was crafted entirely by him.

'These seven priorities are the pillars of the development bridge we must cross to ensure higher economic growth and more equitable social and economic development,' Dr Singh told the country from the ramparts of the Red Fort.

The 'Saat Sutra' set the policy framework for the government and yielded what came to be known as the UPA's 'flagship programmes'— Bharat Nirman, Mahatma Gandhi National Rural Employment Guarantee Act, Jawaharlal Nehru National Urban Renewal Mission, National Rural Health Mission, Sarva Shiksha Abhiyan, the expanded Midday Meal Programme.

While the NAC played an important role in developing the government's thinking on some of these programmes, the PMO too played a key role in drawing up the required legislation and in working out how these programmes would be implemented. The perception that all the UPA's progressive social policies came out of the NAC, while the PMO was only preoccupied with economic growth and liberalization was false. This was a caricature that many in the Congress party, the Left and in the media liked to draw. Much as I wanted him to, Dr Singh was never keen on politically challenging such propaganda. His usual response, whenever I suggested we should respond to such comments, would be, 'Let my actions speak for me.'

Bharat Nirman, the flagship rural infrastructure development programme, for example, was entirely conceived in the PMO at the initiative of the late R. Gopalakrishnan, a joint secretary in the PMO. Gopalakrishnan had ground-level experience in development from his tenure in Madhya Pradesh where he had served as secretary to Digvijaya Singh through his two terms as chief minister of the state. A highly motivated, intellectually curious and energetic civil servant, he would never allow himself to be constrained by bureaucratic red tape and rigidity.

He was inspired by business guru C.K. Prahalad's thesis about the business potential of those at the 'bottom of the pyramid'. He believed that public investment in rural development would generate a virtuous cycle of win–win outcomes, provided such spending generated new incomes and new employment. Bharat Nirman was conceptualized as a 'business plan for rural infrastructure' rather than as a new subsidy programme. The programme sought to bring together existing schemes for rural housing, rural roads, rural electrification, drinking water and irrigation, and rural telecommunications.

When Gopalakrishnan made his initial PowerPoint presentations to the PM on the scheme, there was enormous excitement in the room. This was the kind of growth-oriented and employment-generating programme that Dr Singh liked. When Gopalakrishnan suggested the name Bharat Nirman for this clutch of programmes, Dr Singh readily agreed with a smile.

Young officers in the PMO like V. Vidyavathi and Amit Agarwal were also equally committed to the UPA's development agenda. The PM's PS, Subbu, had also worked with Digvijaya Singh's government in Madhya Pradesh, before opting for Chhattisgarh when the state was divided, and had taken keen interest in the work of NGOs in rural development in both states, as well as in Manipur where he had briefly served. Vidyavathi belonged to the Karnataka cadre of the IAS and Agarwal to the Chhattisgarh cadre. This was the core team that monitored the implementation of the NCMP.

When the idea of a rural employment guarantee scheme travelled to the PMO from the NAC and the rural development ministry, it was received enthusiastically by Dr Singh, who was familiar with Maharashtra's early initiatives in this regard. Maharashtra had, from the time of Sharad Pawar's tenure as chief minister, implemented the Maharashtra Employment Guarantee Scheme (MEGS). Though conceptualized in 1977, during Vasantdada Patil's tenure as chief minister, MEGS was launched by Pawar in 1979. As the deputy chairman of the Planning Commission in the 1980s, Dr Singh had studied this scheme and had been impressed by it. Hence, he was in favour of implementing this programme at the national level and the Mahatma Gandhi National Rural Employment Guarantee Act (MGNREGA) was nothing more than a variant of MEGS.

The so-called differences on the MGNREGA between the PMO and the finance ministry on the one hand, and the NAC on the other, related mainly to the financial implications of the programme with estimates of how much it would cost the exchequer varying from 1 to 3 per cent of national income. Neither Dr Singh nor Chidambaram wanted an open-ended fiscal commitment, since the benefits of the programme were to be based on self-selection. That is, only a person seeking employment under the MGNREGA would be offered it for the number of days and at a wage rate specified. This would mean that at the beginning of the year the government would not know how many would come forward to seek the benefit.

The minister for rural development Dr Raghuvansh Prasad Singh, a one-time physics professor and a genial grassroots politician for whom Dr Singh had high regard and great affection, played an important role as a bridge between the fiscal conservatives and the populists. Raghuvansh Prasad looked rustic, with a scraggy unshaven appearance, always sporting a well-worn dhoti and not the starched, crisp white dhotis that most politicians normally wear. His English was scratchy;

but his knowledge of the subject he was handling was superb.

Unlike many other Cabinet ministers who left it to their secretaries to brief the PM on policy issues concerning their ministries, Raghuvansh Prasad would make his own presentations. He understood the PM's fiscal concerns and worked towards a fiscally responsible programme. Raghuvansh Prasad was one person Dr Singh would have loved to induct into his council of ministers in 2009, but could not because of the parting of ways between the Congress and Lalu Prasad's RJD, of which Raghuvansh Prasad was a senior leader. On several occasions I could sense his irritation with Congress party propagandists who claimed credit for the MGNREGA in the name of Sonia and later Rahul, but would never give Raghuvansh Prasad credit for his stellar work on it.

The Congress party's obsession with giving the entire credit for the MGNREGA to the Gandhi family reached a point where it may have actually embarrassed the family. When I tried to correct that impression, I found myself in a spot of trouble. On 26 September 2007, shortly after he was appointed one of the party's general secretaries, Rahul Gandhi led a delegation of all the party general secretaries to greet Dr Singh on his birthday. After the courtesies and tea and dhokla were done with, the delegation settled down to a discussion on policy issues. At the end of the meeting, Sonia's political secretary, Ahmed Patel, handed over a statement about the meeting, requesting me to release it to the press.

The statement claimed that Rahul Gandhi had urged the PM to extend the scope of NREGA (this was before it was named after Mahatma Gandhi and consequently became MGNREGA) to all the 500-odd rural districts in the country. Until then, it was being implemented only in 200 of the most backward districts. I told Patel that it was not the practice of the PMO to issue press statements on behalf of those who visited the PM, and that I would draft a statement of my own stating that a delegation of party general secretaries led by

Rahul had come to greet the PM on his birthday. As for the political content of the statement, it was better, I suggested, that it came in a separate statement from the party office.

Later that evening, Shishir Gupta, a senior political journalist at the *Indian Express*, called me to find out if Dr Singh had accepted Rahul's suggestion and whether NREGA would now be extended to the entire country. I reminded Shishir that the prime minister had already stated his commitment to doing so in his Independence Day speech the previous month, and that the PMO was in discussions on this very point with the ministries of rural development and finance.

That evening, all TV channels dutifully reported the Congress party's statement that Rahul had asked the PM to extend NREGA to the entire country, and the next morning's papers did the same. Only the *Indian Express* made the additional remark in its dispatch the next day that 'Sources said that this issue had been on the PMO radar even before Rahul's elevation to the party post. The Principal Secretary to the PM had already discussed the issue with officials from the Finance Ministry, Rural Development Ministry and Planning Commission almost two weeks ago.'

Raghuvansh Prasad had, in fact, been the original enthusiast in favour of extending the employment programme to the entire country and he was amused when he found himself upstaged by a Congress party now claiming this was Rahul's idea. But he sportingly went along with the Congress party's spin, confining himself to telling a few reporters from his home state, Bihar, that it was he who had been pushing the finance ministry and the Planning Commission to extend the programme.

I sent an SMS, half in jest, to a journalist who wanted to know more about the programme's national roll-out, that this announcement was the PM's birthday gift to the country. After all, if Sonia or Rahul had been PM, that is precisely how the party's strategists would have spun out such an announcement on a leader's birthday.

It later transpired that this SMS had made the rounds and reached the party leadership. One senior leader told a senior editor, 'What does Baru think? He thinks Doctor Saheb [Dr Singh] can win us elections?

We have to project Rahulji's image and this kind of SMS does not help.'

When I heard this, I knew I was in trouble. Sure enough, I was summoned by the PM for a dressing-down. As I entered the ante-chamber of his room, Nair, Narayanan and Pulok were walking out. Noting that all three scrupulously avoided eye contact with me, I realized this was going to be serious. When I went in, Dr Singh was seated, arms folded and wearing an angry look.

'Did you send an SMS to journalists that the expansion of the NREGA is my birthday gift?'

I said I did, but half in jest. I pointed out that the Independence Day speech had already reiterated the government's commitment to expanding it. But even conceding that Rahul had taken things forward by demanding an early roll-out, the decision had indeed been taken on the PM's birthday.

The PM sat stiff in stony silence. I broke the silence by adding, 'The party wants to give the entire credit for this decision to Rahul. But both you and Raghuvansh Prasad deserve as much credit.'

'I do not want any credit for myself,' he snapped. He was still red with anger.

'Sir, it is my job to project your image and secure the political credit due to you. Let the party do that for Sonia and Rahul. I have to do this for you.'

'No!' he snapped again. 'I do not want you to project my image.'

There was dead silence in the room after this. I just sat there, in that still room. After several minutes of silence, Dr Singh's tense face and body relaxed.

In an almost paternal tone, he admonished me, 'Why do you do these things?'

I did not respond and, after many seconds of deafening silence, the PM said, 'Let them take all the credit. I don't need it. I am only doing my work. You just write my speeches for me. I do not want any media projection.'

He then stood up and I left the room. It was the second time I had got a scolding from him, a decade and a half after being pulled up for those editing mistakes in the '*ET* at 30' special edition, but this time it was serious. I was told, in essence, to stop doing the work I had been hired to do. Clearly, the blowback from the party and its 'first family' must have been serious enough to warrant this. I did not actually stop projecting the prime minister after this. Events themselves demanded it, like his successes in negotiating and delivering the nuclear deal. However, this episode left me with a depressing awareness of the limitations of my job as Dr Singh's spin doctor. I felt less free after this than I had been before.

———

One 'populist' initiative for which Dr Singh was happy to take credit was the farm loan waiver of 2008. Finance Minister Chidambaram had in his budget speech of February 2008 announced a plan to write off loans taken by small and marginal farmers across the country. A great deal of thinking and homework had gone into that announcement. All through 2007 and the early part of 2008, Dr Singh had wrestled with the issue. He understood only too well that the Congress party had come to power on the back of farmers' distress. Several measures had already been taken to provide support to cotton farmers in Andhra Pradesh and Maharashtra, states that had seen a distressingly large number of suicides by farmers. The farmers who had committed suicide were, for the most part, not the most impoverished, or the landless. They were landowning farmers who had been crushed by debt. On the other hand, mainstream economists have always viewed loan waivers as fraught with moral hazard. Periodic waivers encourage debtors to default on payments in the hope that such defaults are regularized.

However, Dr Singh was not just an academic economist. His understanding of Indian farm economics was profoundly shaped both by the historical experience of Punjab, by the macroeconomics of Keynes and Keynesians in India, such as K.N. Raj and his own involvement in policymaking through the Green Revolution years of the 1970s. It was about Punjab that Malcolm Darling, a distinguished British civil servant in the undivided Punjab of British India, had said, in 1925, on the eve of a period of great distress in Indian agriculture:

'The Indian peasant is born in debt, lives in debt and dies in debt.'

One evening in late 2007 after sitting through a long inconclusive discussion on the subject of loan waivers with senior officials and ministers, Dr Singh walked back to his private working space at 7 RCR. There, in that quiet corner, looking out into the patch of green where a peacock or two would always be walking around, pecking at food, he sat and gave me a long lecture on the history of loan waivers in India. It was the British, he explained, who first understood the nature of rural indebtedness and the importance of keeping the farmer alive. Rural credit, he recalled K.N. Raj telling him, is a 'public good'. Economists define a 'public good' as any good or service that, once provided, does not discriminate between beneficiaries and non-beneficiaries. A street light is a common example of a public good. Government spends money on street lighting and everyone who uses the street, irrespective of whether she is a taxpayer or not, a citizen or a visitor, benefits from it. A loan waived by a bank may appear to be a private good since the primary beneficiary is the debtor. However, in keeping farmers alive, in sustaining the livelihood of farmers and in ensuring rural social stability, a loan waiver in the case of an impoverished and highly indebted farmer would have wider social benefits. Many countries, including developed market economies, justified farm subsidies on such social grounds. A debt waiver was a subsidy, and a public good.

Dr Singh recalled how every thirty years or so there had been a farm loan waiver in India and the last one had been sanctioned by Charan Singh in 1979. The cycle of mounting debts and accumulating farmers' grievances would end with an across-the-board loan waiver. By 2007, he felt, the time had come for another loan waiver.

The policy debate within government went on for several months after that. It was possible that the party was not just mulling the decision, but had also decided to wait for the right political time. In Dr Singh's mind, though, it seemed to me that afternoon, the decision had already been taken. He understood the political significance of a farm loan waiver, he had respectable policy precedents and an acceptable theoretical justification for what would be criticized by many as a populist measure. Above all, four years of high economic growth had generated the optimistic view that the country could afford to splurge on such schemes.

After several months of deliberation and after taking stock of the views of an expert committee chaired by economist R. Radhakrishna, Dr Singh approved the loan waiver scheme. Chidambaram unveiled the scheme through his budget speech in February 2008, including under it all agricultural loans disbursed by scheduled commercial banks, regional rural banks and cooperative credit institutions up to 31 March 2007 and overdue as on 31 December 2007, with the benefit to small and marginal farmers, those with holdings up to 2 hectares, being larger than for other farmers. The scheme would benefit 4 crore, that is, 40 million, farmers and would cost the government about Rs 72,000 crore, that is Rs 720 billion.

Despite the high cost, Dr Singh viewed the farm loan waiver as 'his' contribution to 'inclusive growth'. It was set apart in his mind from the 'flagship' schemes for which his party gave all the credit to Sonia Gandhi, the NAC and the NCMP. Still lurking within the Oxbridge economist was a bit of the Punjab farmer, and he knew that this initiative would resonate well in rural India. After Chidambaram's budget presentation, Dr Singh took ownership of the initiative through a fervent reply to the debate on the motion of thanks to the President, in March 2008, and recited from memory Oliver Goldsmith's lines from *The Deserted Village*, 'Ill fares the land, to hastening ill a prey, / Where wealth accumulates, and men decay; / Princes and Lords may flourish, or may fade; / But a bold peasantry, their country's pride; / When once destroyed can never be supplied.'

In 2008, at the end of five years of unprecedented 8 to 9 per cent economic growth, with the economy and government revenues buoyant, such expenditure was seen as affordable, despite the reservations of bankers and professional economists. There was growing concern that the government was committing itself to too many new subsidies and fiscal giveaways. Even the rural employment programme was not explicitly tied to the creation of assets and an income stream that would help pay for the programme on a sustainable basis. Even though he was enthusiastic about the loan waiver, Dr Singh recognized there would be a fiscal price to pay. But his eyes, as indeed of the entire UPA leadership, were now on the next election, not on the government's fiscal bottom line.

The loan waiver came on the back of a massive investment in rural infrastructure and development through the Bharat Nirman, NREGA and other programmes. It was also coupled with steep increases in the statutory minimum price paid for rice and wheat. Taken together, this was the New Deal for Rural India that Dr Singh had promised in his 2004 Independence Day speech. It now remained for the Congress party to derive the electoral benefits of these initiatives, and the party did so in the summer of 2009.

While rural development and the farm economy was a priority imposed by larger social, economic and political considerations, the subject closest to Dr Singh's heart was education. It was, therefore, particularly unfortunate that the human resources development (HRD) portfolio went to a political adversary who neither shared Dr Singh's interest in education nor his liberal values. Arjun Singh was given the HRD portfolio because, for some reason, that came to be seen as the most important ministry politically, below Raisina Hill.

Senior politicians left out of Raisina Hill, home to the ministries of defence, finance, home and external affairs, were traditionally accommodated in the ministries of agriculture, railways and education. Rajiv Gandhi elevated the importance of the education ministry by combining all aspects of education—primary, secondary and tertiary—into one super-HRD ministry. Narasimha Rao, Rajiv's first HRD minister, had a genuine interest in the subject, having started his political career as a minister for education in Andhra Pradesh. But some of Rao's successors used the ministry for their own ends, especially the BJP's senior leader Murali Manohar Joshi, who used it to push his Hindutva agenda, and Arjun Singh, who took upon himself the task of not just 'cleansing' the ministry and its vast bureaucratic empire of Joshi's RSS legacy but also of promoting left-wing academics and causes.

In his own inclinations, Arjun Singh was no leftist. His political career, so far, had not reflected any such ideological leanings. He had worked his way up the political food chain in Madhya Pradesh politics, becoming the state's chief minister. Leaving behind a string of allegations of corruption and the mismanagement of the 1984 Bhopal gas leak tragedy, he moved to Delhi and positioned himself as a rebel, opposing Narasimha Rao's economic policies and ingratiating himself to representatives of the Muslim community by demanding Rao's resignation over the handling of the Babri Masjid demolition in 1992. This was a political ploy—his secularism was as deep as that of the average Congressman. With respect to Dr Singh, too, Arjun Singh's game was no different from that of the prime minister's other political rivals, namely to appear more pro-Left than the PM in the hope of ousting Dr Singh with Left support.

While political analysts in the media focused more attention on Pranab Mukherjee's desire to be PM, his links with the Left and his political moves, Arjun Singh was far more active than Pranab ever was in seeking to undermine the PM. Among the four senior ministers in the Union Cabinet (the other two were Natwar Singh and A.K. Antony), Arjun Singh took the longest time to adjust to Dr Singh's elevation.

Arjun Singh used his perch at the HRD ministry to reinforce his image as a 'left-wing secular' politician, favouring and funding scholars and activities that helped him project this image. Whenever a journalist asked Dr Singh what he thought of Arjun Singh's political games at the HRD ministry, the PM's stock reply would be that India needed an educational system that promoted excellence and merit rather than any particular ideology. By favouring pro-Left and Muslim academics in various ways, he created a constituency of support among those who tended to be critical of the PM for following a foreign policy aimed, as they saw it, at 'cosying up' to the US—a country at odds with the Muslim world. Such was the sycophancy he encouraged that the Jamia Millia University even named a street on its campus after Arjun Singh when he was still in office.

Understandably, Dr Singh remained wary of Arjun Singh and

took a long time to focus his energies on education even though the subject was so close to his heart. On the eve of a Cabinet reshuffle in 2006, he seriously considered moving Arjun Singh out. I reported what Narasimha Rao had said to me when I had once suggested the idea of sacking Arjun Singh to him. Rao had recalled the American President Lyndon Johnson's response when asked why he did not sack his FBI chief, J. Edgar Hoover, even though the latter was known to spy on the President and his colleagues. Johnson's frank response to the question had been: 'It's better to have him inside the tent pissing out, than outside the tent pissing in.'

Dr Singh chuckled and Arjun Singh stayed on.

More than a year into my tenure I had my own little encounter with Arjun Singh's mind games. One day he saw me in the corridor as he came out of a meeting with Dr Singh in the PMO, and stopped and smiled. I greeted him with a namaste.

'You should come and see me sometime,' he said.

I told Dr Singh what had happened and he suggested, with a smile, that I should go call on the minister. The next day I landed up at his office in Shastri Bhavan. He ordered a cup of tea, sat back in his chair and said nothing. I didn't know what to say or do, so I broke the silence with small talk. Since the meeting was going nowhere, I thought I should use the opportunity to draw the minister's attention to an important policy issue. The Singapore government had invited India to locate a campus of the IIM, India's premier network of management institutions, in that country, but the HRD ministry was opposed to the idea. The management guru Rama Bijapurkar had briefed me on the issue and I was not clear why the ministry was opposed to the idea.

Arjun Singh explained to me that the IIMs were prestigious Indian institutions and if students from Singapore or elsewhere wanted to study at an IIM they should come to India. Why should the IIM go to Singapore, he asked. I saw his point but offered the counterargument that locating an IIM in Singapore would only enhance the institution's brand name rather than divert students away from it. I explained to him the concept of 'brand' and 'branding'. I also pointed out that the demand for places at IIMs was far in excess of the availability, so the

IIMs would never have to face the prospect of empty seats. Moreover, there might be many Indian-origin management gurus in the US and elsewhere willing to move to Singapore and teach there, rather than move to India.

Arjun Singh heard me out with a bored and disinterested expression. I decided it was time to go. I returned to South Block and briefed the PM about my meeting. He heard me, without comment, and went back to his work.

Two days later, my attention was drawn to a news report in an English daily published from Madhya Pradesh, with the headline, 'PM Reaches Out to Arjun Singh'.

The report alleged that I had been sent as an 'emissary' by Dr Singh to reach out to him and seek his support, and the assurance of his confidence in the leadership of the PM. It said Dr Singh wanted to make sure that Arjun Singh was on his side. The report added that Arjun Singh had conveyed to the PM through his media adviser that news reports suggesting the HRD minister had policy differences with the PM were untrue, and had assured him of his support.

I took the clipping to the PM and we had a good laugh.

———

Dr Singh did go on to pay attention to education in UPA-2, dubbing the Twelfth Five-Year Plan the 'national education plan', ensuring the highest ever financial allocation to this sector, and appointing the high-profile lawyer and Congressman Kapil Sibal as his HRD minister, in place of Arjun Singh, who was finally dropped from the Cabinet. However, in UPA-1, his hopes of breathing fresh air into a ministry made moribund by Murali Manohar Joshi's whimsical leadership could not be realized, with the equally whimsical Arjun Singh at the helm.

Despite this limitation, the government managed to push some good programmes, including Sarva Shiksha Abhiyan, a universal literacy programme originally launched by the Vajpayee government but for which Dr Singh ensured a tenfold increase in budgetary allocation from around Rs 2000 crore in 2004 to around Rs 20,000 crore by

2012. He insisted on funding several new central universities, IITs, IIMs and institutes of science education and research. My colleague Sanjay Mitra, who dealt with HRD in the PMO, was an enthusiastic promoter of these initiatives. Mitra was from the West Bengal cadre and had worked closely with Jyoti Basu. But, unable to get a firm grip on Arjun Singh's HRD ministry, he could not ensure the effective follow-up of these projects.

However, the South Asian University (SAU), a project dear to Dr Singh, was poorly conceived and executed and will remain a blot on Dr Singh's record in the field of education. While preparing for the Dhaka Summit of the South Asian Association for Regional Cooperation (SAARC), Dr Singh came up with the idea of starting a regional university that would enable bright young minds from South Asia to spend their formative student years together. He envisioned SAU as a centre of excellence and the best university in the region. But for that vision to be realized, the university needed to attract a top-notch South Asian faculty. Imagine if the Nobel Prize-winning Amartya Sen or the Abel Prize-winning mathematician Srinivasa Vardhan had been encouraged to be its founding vice chancellor. Imagine that eminent Indian, Pakistani, Bangladeshi, Sri Lankan and other South Asian scholars constituted its founding faculty. That was Dr Singh's dream, but it was never translated into reality. SAU's first vice chancellor, G.K. Chaddha, had earned the reputation of being a good administrator as the vice chancellor of JNU but he was not an internationally known scholar. He was just another friend of the PM from Punjab. SAU not only had enormous teething troubles, it also never managed to establish itself as an institution of regional, not to mention international, excellence. A weak start may well have killed a fine idea.

———

One initiative in the field of education that Dr Singh felt truly passionate about was his effort to increase and widen scholarships given out by the government. The biggest ever expansion of government-funded scholarships in India has happened during Dr Singh's tenure.

The government instituted new and better-funded scholarships for students from scheduled caste and scheduled tribe families. There was a threefold increase in scholarships for Muslim students. There was a severalfold increase in scholarships for girls and a new scheme of merit-cum-means scholarships was introduced for post-matric students, with twenty million students benefitting by the end of UPA-1.

It is telling that the only initiative Dr Singh was willing to lend his name to, as prime minister, was a student scholarship instituted at his alma mater St John's College, Cambridge. The Manmohan Singh Scholarships are awarded for both undergraduate and doctoral studies. Every year, the awardees get to meet the PM and he is always very happy on such occasions.

The PM's personal passion for scholarships came from the fact that his life, as he once put it, was made by scholarships. Given his modest background, he would never have secured the kind of college and post-graduate education he did without scholarships. It was scholarships that enabled him to study both in India and then at Cambridge and Oxford.

Some of Dr Singh's warmest smiles have been captured at events where he is handing out a scholarship certificate or an award for excellence in education to bright young students. Nothing made him happier than to see himself in the eager face of a young middle-class student.

Dr Singh was always conscious of the fact that what enabled UPA-1 to step up spending was the unprecedented growth of economic activity in the period 2003–09. For fifty years before Independence, from 1890 to 1940, the national income of British India grew by just a little over 0 per cent. Between 1950 and 1980, national income grew at 3.5 per cent per year. Between 1980 and 2000 the rate of growth picked up to roughly an average of 5.5 per cent per year. The near 9 per cent rate of growth recorded in 2003–08 was unprecedented. Many explanations have been offered for this sharp improvement in India's growth performance. Clearly, the global economic and strategic environment was favourable to India. At home, the national savings and investment rates went up sharply and so did agricultural output and income generated by a buoyant services sector. Finally, the stability of UPA-1 and the fact that Dr Singh's team of economic policymakers, including P. Chidambaram, Montek Singh Ahluwalia and C. Rangarajan, inspired investor confidence at home and abroad combined to generate positive expectations that further fuelled growth.

This acceleration of economic growth generated the revenues required to finance the government's social development programmes, including Bharat Nirman, NREGA and spending on health and education. Without the 8 to 9 per cent growth during this period the government could not have sustained its spending programmes. It is this fiscal foundation that sustained the strategy of 'inclusive growth' in UPA-1. What if the rate of economic growth were to slow down? What if the fiscal situation got out of hand? This always worried the PM. But as long as the going was good, and in UPA-1 it was, no one really worried about the return of the fiscal constraint on growth. Thanks to high growth, UPA-1 managed to adhere to the timetable of deficit reduction imposed by the Fiscal Responsibility and Budget Management Act until 2009. Some of the PM's advisers, like Rangarajan, worried that this period of rising income growth was not being used to improve government finances on a more sustainable basis and feared the consequences of such 'fiscal irresponsibility', but in UPA-1 there were few takers for such caution.

When I left the PMO in August 2008, the performance of the economy was not a matter of any great worry, with five years of unprecedented high growth behind us, though a high fiscal deficit and inflation rate remained important concerns. The big picture gave confidence. India's national income, Chidambaram proudly claimed, had crossed the one-trillion-dollar mark in 2008. With high investment rates India was seen as catching up with the Asian 'Tigers' and on its way to match China's impressive performance.

International conferences in New Delhi and Mumbai would discuss India's emergence as a global power, and Dr Singh could get away with sermonizing to business billionaires about the need for a social conscience. At the annual meeting of the Confederation of Indian Industry in May 2007 he made bold to suggest a ten-point 'Social Charter' for business, including affirmative action in employment, attention to workers' health and shunning of conspicuous consumption and excessively high remuneration for top management. While the business media chided Dr Singh for this socialist advice, business leaders took it sportingly since their overall mood, driven by healthy corporate bottom lines, was still positive.

Against this background, when the Lehmann Brothers crisis hit Wall Street in mid-September 2008 and the transatlantic economies went into panic mode, the Indian government acted fast to boost investor confidence. Despite setbacks like the terror attack on 26 November 2008 in Mumbai, in which 160-plus people were killed at hotels, restaurants and the railway station, the government was able to boost confidence in India's relative insularity from the global financial crisis. The PMO's quick response to the Satyam scandal, in which a major software services company admitted to cooking its books, enabled India to protect the company from collapse and boosted investor confidence in government policy. Even though Chidambaram had moved from finance to home in the aftermath of the terror attack in Mumbai, which led to the departure of the much-criticized incumbent, Shivraj Patil, the finance ministry was still alert to international developments and responded calmly. A new governor at the Reserve Bank of India was still cutting his teeth but was able to work closely with Delhi and manage the fallout.

India's capable handling of the global crisis was positively commented upon around the world and Dr Singh's interventions at the meeting of the newly constituted Group of 20 (G-20) heads of government in Washington DC in November 2008 were much appreciated. These developments raised India's global profile and also the PM's. The UPA, therefore, ended its term with a satisfactory record of performance on the economic front. If there was one area of concern, it was fiscal. The government's many welfare and development programmes, the various subsidy schemes and the farm loan waiver imposed a huge financial burden on the government that would increase with time.

For someone whose favourite aphorism was 'money does not grow on trees', Dr Singh presided over a government that had begun to spend money as if it was growing on trees.

This became the Achilles' heel of economic management in UPA-1 that came to haunt the government in UPA-2. For all his talk about fiscal rectitude, and despite his record as finance minister in 1991–93 when he did manage to sharply bring the deficit down, as PM, he presided over a regime of fiscal irresponsibility, given the pressure on the government to spend on a variety of programmes.

This despite the fact that he not only shared a good working equation with Finance Minister Chidambaram in UPA-1, compared to the very formal relationship he had with Pranab Mukherjee in UPA-2, but also took much keener interest in budget-making. He would insist Chidambaram sit with him and finalize the finance minister's annual budget speech. Pranab, on the other hand, would not even show him the draft of the speech till he had finished writing it.

While Chidambaram and he shared a common worldview on economic policy, the two did have their differences and some were important ones. At a meeting convened to discuss a reduction in energy subsidies in 2007 the PM assumed he would have the finance minister on his side. While he had no problem getting Petroleum and Natural Gas Minister Murli Deora on to his side (a sharp contrast to the argumentative Mani Shankar Aiyar who preceded Deora in that ministry), he was surprised to hear a lecture from Chidambaram on middle-class sensitivity to the price of cooking gas.

The fiscal irresponsibility of UPA-1 was to eventually hit investor sentiment. It also contributed to inflation during the UPA's second term. Clearly, in UPA-1, while Dr Singh had delivered on his promise of boosting growth and making it more inclusive, he failed to deliver on ensuring the fiscal sustainability of growth. It is this fiscal overreach that came to haunt UPA-2 as growth slowed down. It was a slowdown that nobody anticipated.

The psychological impact of the slowdown on market sentiment was even greater because investors, at home and abroad, had come to take India's economic rise during 2003–08 for granted. Even though the

Congress party rubbished the BJP's 'India Shining' campaign and sought to compensate for it with its spending schemes, it too assumed that the Indian economy was on a roll. The rising rates of investment and savings and rising exports were seen as drivers of sustainable growth. So much so that some of the early signs of the 'policy paralysis' that came to haunt UPA-2 were not taken too seriously. One of them was the slowdown in the national highways construction programme. The Vajpayee government ensured speedy implementation of the programme. However, some in the UPA, influenced by the Left and a few NAC activists, came to view road construction as an elitist activity meant to please automobile owners, and work on the highways slowed to a crawl. Moreover, the BJP's disinvestment programme aimed at selling off, or reducing, the government's stake in public sector enterprises, was halted, and despite creating a new Investment Commission headed by industrialist Ratan Tata, there was no consistent strategy to increase capital expenditure by the government.

None of this made much of a difference to investor perceptions about India's growth prospects as long as the economy was on a roll. Even the transatlantic financial crisis of 2008–09 had limited impact, initially, on growth. Economist Shankar Acharya, who joined Dr Singh's team at the finance ministry as chief economic adviser in the early 1990s, was one of the few consistent critics of the government's fiscal and economic policies. Even before the transatlantic crisis hit the economy in 2008, Shankar would keep warning the government that many of its spending and other policy decisions would cost the economy dear. Each time Shankar's column appeared in the *Business Standard* I would mark it to the PM. But for a long time Shankar was viewed as a pessimist who was needlessly ringing the alarm bells. In the end, and not just due to the global economic slowdown, Shankar was proved right.

When the UPA-2 government became paralysed by a political storm in 2010–11 over explosive financial scandals, many of the inherent weaknesses of the economy, built up due to the creeping populism of UPA-1, surfaced and took their toll. By then Dr Singh had lost control over fiscal policy and much else. In March 2012 he was not even aware till the day before the budget was to be presented that his finance minister Pranab Mukherjee was going to introduce a new corporate tax policy, with retrospective effect, that would have disastrous consequences for investor sentiment.

For a man whose professional reputation was built by his role in battling the hyper-inflation of the mid-1970s, reining in the fiscal deficit in the early 1990s and restoring growth momentum to the economy around 2005–06, Dr Singh, by the end of UPA-2, was still battling inflation, still trying to get the fiscal deficit down and still pushing for a revival of the growth momentum.

9

The Manmohan Singh Doctrine

'India is destined to recover its due status in the world,
but this process will be speeded up if we do what we must at home
and build bridges of mutual interdependence with the world.'

Manmohan Singh at the India Today Conclave
February 2005

Whenever he wanted to draw attention to the limits of Central government, in particular prime ministerial power, Dr Singh would quote Telugu Desam founder-leader N.T. Rama Rao's famous remark that 'the Centre is a conceptual myth'. The Indian Constitution defines the powers of the Centre and the states but the balance between them has shifted from time to time depending on the nature of the political dispensation. India has gone through both centralizing and decentralizing phases with prime ministerial power waxing and waning.

While in times of a crisis or an emergency—including economic crises, war and natural disasters—the Central government can mobilize and deploy its power in ways that override the power of the states, in normal times the Centre's real power derives only from its control over fiscal resources, and the security and intelligence apparatus. Even then, a prime minister is constrained by the Cabinet form of government in which he is, at best, a 'first among equals'. Coalition governments impose further restrictions on prime ministerial authority. In the case of the UPA, the PM's authority was further curbed by the nature of powersharing between the Congress party president and the PM.

For all these reasons, and given that the economy was in reasonably good shape in 2004, and there was no major challenge on the military side, Dr Singh decided to focus his attention on foreign policy. This was one area in which prime ministerial prerogative was paramount. The external affairs minister does not have the kind of freedom of action that a finance, home or defence minister can hope to enjoy, even in normal times. That is in part because most foreign policy initiatives flower at the level of the head of government or head of state.

Dr Singh's only problem in choosing foreign policy as the area where he would put his stamp was that his external affairs minister was a retired diplomat with a mind of his own. Natwar Singh not only had clear views on major foreign policy issues but also believed that Dr Singh was a political greenhorn and a novice in foreign affairs. He also probably assumed that his long-standing proximity to the Nehru–Gandhi family placed him a peg above Dr Singh in the dynasty-based Congress party's nebulous hierarchy. However, Sonia Gandhi never allowed any one person to assume he or she was the last word on any issue. During her journey to power, she turned to a range of partymen, including Karan Singh, Mani Shankar Aiyar and Mani Dixit, for foreign policy advice, even though it was Natwar Singh, and sometimes Dr Singh, who would accompany her to meetings with visiting heads of government. Similarly, on the economic policy side, her key aide was always Dr Singh but she would lend her ear to Pranab Mukherjee and P. Chidambaram, among others.

In the end, Natwar Singh, who lasted about eighteen months as external affairs minister, proved to be more supportive of the PM than we had assumed he would be. But the PM also had to make a conscious and determined effort to befriend Natwar and at the same time exert his authority. The episode, reported earlier, in which Natwar Singh exceeded his brief on the matter of India sending troops to Iraq, offered Mani Dixit a good opportunity to assert the PMO's role in foreign policy. A second, if less important, opportunity for the PM to assert his individual authority overruling diplomatic advice was provided a few days later when Ronald Reagan died. Dr Singh wanted to go to

Roosevelt House, home of the US ambassador, and sign the condolence book as a gesture of regard to the late President and goodwill towards the US. Reagan was generous in his dealings with both Indira Gandhi and Rajiv Gandhi. But the foreign service officers in the PMO advised him against going to the ambassador's home and said the condolence book would be brought to him.

Noticing that Dr Singh was torn about whether he should follow his own instincts or the advice of his diplomats, I reminded him how Jawaharlal Nehru would at times drive down to see John Kenneth Galbraith at Roosevelt House just for a cup of coffee and quiet conversation. In fact, when Robert Blackwill was the US ambassador in Delhi, he would sit his visitors down for coffee in the far right corner of his living room, saying, 'Let's have coffee where Nehru and Galbraith used to.' Dr Singh decided he would go to Roosevelt House and sign the condolence book. On his way home for lunch from Parliament, his carcade took a detour and drove there at short notice, surprising everyone.

Slowly but steadily, Dr Singh began to assert himself in the field of foreign affairs and policy. He mostly conceded limits to his authority in shaping domestic policy, given that his council of ministers had loyalties to other centres of political power. But he zealously guarded the foreign policy turf and ensured his writ would run at least in this sphere. By September 2004, when he travelled to New York to address the UN General Assembly, he was firmly in the saddle.

Dr Singh was, of course, not a novice in foreign affairs. As secretary general of the South Commission based in Geneva, he had the opportunity to deal with world leaders and familiarize himself with world affairs. As finance minister in the early 1990s, he engaged actively in economic diplomacy to strengthen India's external economic profile. Taking charge as India's finance minister in the midst of a major external payments crisis and at the end of the Cold War, Dr Singh was forced to grapple with the challenge of handling an external crisis in the midst of a rapidly changing geo-political and geo-economic environment. His experience in dealing with the US, Japan and Singapore in particular, and with the Europeans, was firmly etched in his memory and he would often recall events from that period. He had closely bonded with his counterparts in countries belonging to the Organization for Economic Cooperation and Development, and many of them, now in retirement, would seek appointments to meet him either in Delhi or in their home capitals whenever Dr Singh visited them.

In his very first budget speech in Parliament in July 1991, Dr Singh linked India's global standing to the country's economic performance. In doing so, he enunciated a new approach to Indian foreign policy for the post-Cold War era. After spelling out his strategy to deal with an immediate crisis—a balance of payments and fiscal crisis—Singh firmly anchored his economic initiatives in a wider strategic setting, viewing them as the foundation for 'the emergence of India as a major economic power in the world'.

Six years later, recalling this speech in an interview published in the inaugural edition of a new international affairs journal, *World Affairs*, Dr Singh underlined the foreign policy implications of the 'new economic policies' unveiled by the Narasimha Rao government. There was no doubt in Dr Singh's mind that the liberalization of the Indian economy was part of a new orientation taken in the context of the collapse of the Soviet Union, the rise of China and East Asian economies and India's own economic rise in the 1980s.

Indeed, Narasimha Rao himself viewed his foreign policy initiatives in those terms. In one of his first media interviews, Rao told *Sunday* magazine in September 1991, 'Now the Cold War is over. There is an element of cooperation instead of confrontation. It is a new situation. And we have to respond to that. So certain policy orientations will take place to ensure that our national interest does not suffer.'

In 1991, this 'national interest' was defined essentially in economic terms, given the crisis at hand and the need to pull India back from the brink of bankruptcy. However, it was not merely the compulsions of crisis management that forced a rethink on foreign policy priorities. Many economists had anticipated the crisis and there was a long period of rethinking on economic policy priorities preceding the 1990–91 crisis. This rethinking was triggered by the development experience of East and Southeast Asian economies and that of China, which had launched its own 'Four Modernizations' policy a decade earlier.

In the interview he gave me for the *Economic Times* in February 1991, three months before he assumed charge as India's finance minister, Dr Singh did speak about the relevance of the East Asian growth experience for India and the need to reorient domestic economic policies. He returned to this theme in his last budget speech in February 1995 when he said, 'It is this vision of a resurgent India taking her rightful place as an economic powerhouse in Asia, which has inspired our economic policies.'

In relating India's economic capabilities to its global profile and influence, Dr Singh was in fact drawing on early 'Nehruvian realism'. In his first major speech on foreign policy, Jawaharlal Nehru told the Constituent Assembly in December 1947:

> Talking about foreign policies, the House must remember that these are not just empty struggles on a chessboard. Behind them lie all manner of things. Ultimately, foreign policy is the outcome of economic policy, and until India has properly evolved her economic policy, her foreign policy will be rather vague, rather inchoate, and will be groping . . . A vague statement that we stand for peace and freedom by itself has no particular meaning, because every country is prepared to say the same thing, whether it means it or not. What then do we stand for? Well, you have to develop this argument in the economic field. As it happens today, in spite of the fact that we have been for some time in authority as a government, I regret that we have not produced any constructive economic scheme or economic policy so far . . . When we do so, that will govern our foreign policy more than all the speeches in this House.

He then went on to add what can be regarded as an early exposition of 'Nehruvian realism' and said, 'Whatever policy we may lay down, the art of conducting the foreign affairs of a country lies in finding out what is most advantageous to the country.'

Dr Singh was guided by this perspective in defining his own worldview. That was the worldview he chose to express publicly when he addressed the Hindustan Times Leadership Initiative Conference on 5 November 2004. He repeated many of the ideas in that speech at the India Today Conclave on 25 February 2005. Taken together, the two were seminal speeches that defined Dr Singh's view of Indian foreign policy. Much thought went into their drafting. I had several sessions with Dr Singh and he devoted considerable time to reworking successive drafts.

These speeches made six significant statements:

First, that India's relations with the world—both major powers and Asian neighbours—would be shaped by its own developmental priorities. The single most important objective of Indian foreign policy has to be to 'create a global environment conducive to her economic development and the well-being of the people of India'.

Second, that India would benefit from greater integration with the world economy—'the world wants India to do well ... our challenges are at home'—and that India should be more closely integrated with other Asian economies as an active member of a future 'Asian Economic Community'.

Third, that India's relations with 'major powers, especially the United States, and more recently China, have increasingly been shaped by economic factors', and that 'our concern for energy security has become an important element of our diplomacy'.

Fourth, that South Asia's shared destiny required greater regional cooperation and that this would be facilitated by better physical 'connectivity' across the region.

Fifth, that India's experiment of pursuing economic development within the framework of a plural, secular and liberal democracy held lessons for the world. As the prime minister put it, 'Economists quantify our engagement with the world in terms of our share of world trade and capital flows; strategic analysts look at military and political alliances. I submit to you for your consideration the idea that the most enduring engagement of a people with the world is in the realm of ideas and the idea we must engage the world through is the "idea of India"—the idea of *Vasudhaiva Kutumbakam.*The idea that even as nations may clash, cultures and civilizations can coexist.'

Finally, that as a democracy India had a global responsibility to assist 'societies in transition'—'Just as many developed industrial economies assisted the so-called "economies in transition" to make the transition from centrally planned economies to open market economies, the experience of a democracy like India can be of some help in enabling "societies in transition" to evolve into open, inclusive, plural, democratic societies.'

In an early comment on Dr Singh's foreign policy initiatives, the strategic affairs analyst C. Raja Mohan picked these elements and dubbed them the 'Manmohan Singh Doctrine'.[1]

Each of these 'early thoughts' began to shape Dr Singh's foreign policy in the months to come. He was probably the first Indian prime minister to unabashedly hold up India's plural, secular and democratic credentials as worthy foreign policy principles for India's international engagement. In the early post-colonial and the long Cold War years India was more comfortable touting its anti-colonial and 'non-aligned' and 'socialist' credentials rather than its democratic credentials. Dr Singh took the UPA's idea of 'inclusive growth' at home to global forums where he spoke of 'inclusive globalization'. This too was new. Rather than fulminate against globalization, as Indian leaders were wont to do, he chose to demand more inclusive structures, arguing that globalization could be a 'win–win' process.

His interest in regional economic integration with South and Southeast Asia found expression in the movement forward on the South Asian Free Trade Agreement (SAFTA) and the ASEAN-India FTA, while the focus on energy security opened the door to the discussion on the nuclear deal. His foreign policy priorities, driven by the emphasis on India's own economic development and regional security, were defined fairly clearly. He sought to improve India's

---

[1] C. Raja Mohan, 'Rethinking India's Grand Strategy', in N.S. Sisodia and C. Uday Bhaskar (eds.) *Emerging India: Security and Foreign Policy Perspectives*, IDSA and Bibliophile South Asia, New Delhi and Chicago, 2005.

relations with all major powers, especially the US and China, with all of India's economic partners, especially East and Southeast Asian economies, and with India's neighbours.

Draft speeches for the PM's foreign visits coming from the ministry of external affairs invariably had a reference to India's aspiration for UNSC membership. But Dr Singh's view was that India's economic rise and its regional and global profile would make it impossible for the world community to ignore its legitimate claim when the time would come for UNSC expansion. There was no need, he felt, for India to make a repeated claim each time the PM spoke somewhere. During the first three years of UPA-1 Dr Singh referred to the UNSC membership issue only on three occasions—when he addressed the UN General Assembly in 2004 and 2005, and when he addressed the US Congress in 2005. It became my job to delete any reference to India's claim for membership of the UNSC each time a draft speech came to the PMO from the MEA.

Another phrase that never appeared in Dr Singh's early foreign policy speeches was non-alignment. In fact, in September 2006, he actively considered skipping the Havana Summit of the Non-Aligned Movement (NAM) but came under pressure from his party not to do so. His reason for wanting to stay away from NAM jamborees was not what the Left and old-world Congressmen accused him of, namely a pro-US bias. The truth was that it was not in Manmohan Singh's nature to be hypocritical. He was convinced by K. Subrahmanyam's view that India's 'non-alignment' was a tactical move by Nehru to avoid getting into Cold War alliances, while maintaining good relations with both sides, rather than a pillar of Indian 'grand strategy', as it came to be viewed after Indira Gandhi's time. At critical moments when India's own security was threatened, neither Nehru nor Indira hesitated to ally with one side or another. Nehru tilted towards the US to deal with China in 1962 and Indira entered into a formal alliance with the Soviet Union at the time of the Bangladesh war.

So India's non-alignment was tactical, not strategic.

The best realist interpretation of non-alignment came from a distinguished Polish Marxist economist, Michal Kalecki, who worked briefly at the Planning Commission in the 1960s and wrote extensively on Third-World development. In his famous essay 'Observations on Social and Economic Aspects of Intermediate Regimes',[2] an essay that spawned a most fascinating debate between Dr Singh's friend and mentor Professor K.N. Raj, and the communist party leader E.M.S. Namboodiripad in the columns of the *Economic and Political Weekly*,[3] Kalecki called the non-aligned countries 'the proverbial clever calves that suck two cows'. The simultaneous suckling of two udders, the US and the USSR, was a tactical response to an opportunity that presented itself. Given the existing geo-political environment, a group of countries that Kalecki called 'intermediate regimes'—neither capitalist nor socialist in a bipolar world—grabbed this opportunity to further their own developmental possibilities.

In response to criticism at home that Dr Singh's strategic initiatives with the US constituted a departure from the 'national consensus' on foreign policy, and in an effort to outline how India should respond to American overtures, the PM invited K. Subrahmanyam to head a multidisciplinary task force on US Global Strategy: Emerging Trends and Long-Term Implications. The task force submitted its report in June 2006. Among the many issues his report considered was the question of how India should respond to the dynamics of post-Cold War balance of power politics. The report's message was simple: the time had come for India to advance its interests through greater integration with the global economy, making the best use of economic opportunities provided by developed economies, especially the US.

At a ceremony where he laid the foundation stone of the Jawaharlal

---

[2] Michal Kalecki, *Selected Essays on the Economic Growth of the Socialist and the Mixed Economy*, Cambridge University Press, 1972.
[3] K.N. Raj, 'Politics and Economics of Intermediate Regimes', *Economic and Political Weekly*, vol.VIII, no. 27, 7 July 1973, p. 1191. E.M.S. Namboodiripad, 'More on Intermediate Regimes', *Economic and Political Weekly*, vol.VIII, no. 45, 1 December 1973.

Nehru Bhavan, the new home of the external affairs ministry, in February 2006, Dr Singh stated the core principle of his foreign policy outlook when he said the objective of Indian foreign policy was to 'create the space needed to have the freedom to make policy choices in an increasingly interdependent world' and that policy must evolve from time to time 'in response to the changing realities of an ever-changing world'. The emphasis on India's economic interests, its economic relations with other Asian economies, other developing and developed economies, in shaping Indian foreign policy became the leitmotif of the 'Manmohan Singh Doctrine'.

In October 2005 he told the Combined Commanders' Conference,

> Our strategy has to be based on three broad pillars: First, to strengthen ourselves economically and technologically; second, to acquire adequate defence capability to counter and rebut threats to our security; and, third, to seek partnerships, both on the strategic front and on the economic and technological front, that widen our policy and developmental options.

The following year, he returned to the Combined Commanders' Conference with a formulation relating his thinking on defence policy to this grand strategy:

> Our lines of communication which need to be protected are today not just the maritime links that carry our foreign trade and vital imports, but include our other forms of connectivity with the world. None of this is possible without an active process of security cooperation with like-minded nations and littoral countries. When we look at our extended neighbourhood we cannot but be struck by the fact that India is the only open pluralistic democratic society and rapidly modernizing market economy between the Mediterranean and the Pacific. This places a special responsibility upon us not only in the defence of our values but also in the search for a peaceful periphery. We have traditionally conceived our security in extending circles of engagement. Today, whether it is West Asia, the Gulf, Central Asia or

the Indian Ocean region, there is increasing demand for our political, economic and defence engagement.

Dr Singh consistently defined India's maritime strategy in terms of growing economic links with its major trading partners spanning the rim countries of the Indian and Pacific oceans. The idea that the Indian and Pacific oceans, and the region connecting them, was an important strategic space for India, given the flow of goods and energy, was implicit in Dr Singh's view of Indian maritime strategy. India had, after all, created the Andaman and Nicobar naval command to keep an eye on this region and to police it. This thinking, which Dr Singh strongly endorsed, predated the talk of the 'Indo-Pacific' as a region in US strategic discourse. The idea's clearest exposition was, however, made by Japan's prime minister Shinzo Abe, in an address to the Indian Parliament in 2007, when he spoke of 'the confluence of the two seas'.

Abe's short-lived tenure delayed the launch of a new strategic engagement with Japan that Dr Singh wanted to pursue even in UPA-1. Abe's return to power in 2012 revived that agenda and the building of closer economic and defence ties with Japan became the only significant foreign policy achievement of UPA-2.

It is within this framework of thinking that Dr Singh situated his initiatives towards India's key partners—the United States, Russia, Japan, the European Union and ASEAN—and its important neighbours—China, Pakistan and the South Asian countries. The civil nuclear energy cooperation agreement was not just about India's nuclear weapons status but was equally importantly about access to high technology and nuclear energy. On the other hand, the India-ASEAN free trade agreement and the South Asian Free Trade Agreement were not just about accessing new markets or opening up one's own markets but about building strategic partnerships and relationships of interdependence, as he told Sonia Gandhi in his letter of April 2006.

By linking India's geo-political interests with its economic interests Dr Singh defined the new 'geo-economics' of Indian grand strategy. It was easier to explain this to his own party and the wider public in the context of India's relations with the West, especially the US and the EU, and its relations with the newly industrializing economies of Asia and the global South. Of course, even in the case of the US there was the baggage of Cold War attitudes, both within India and the US, that had to be overcome. The resistance of many in the US State Department and in the Washington DC think-tank community to President Bush's radical restructuring of India–US relations based on a recognition of India's nuclear status came from those still living in the past, as did the criticism in India that Dr Singh was taking India into the 'US camp'.

However, the real problem in seeking to define Indian foreign policy within this geo-economic perspective arose in defining India's relations with Pakistan and China. India had 'border' problems with both. With Pakistan the problems were more deep-rooted. Admittedly there was no simplistic 'geo-economic' solution to either relationship. The point, however, was that increased economic interdependence could open up new spaces for diplomacy and high politics. Such interdependence in the case of South Asia had a 'people-to-people' dimension.

Dr Singh repeatedly defended his initiatives with the US, with China and with Pakistan within this perspective of people-to-people and business-to-business relations and not just government-to-government relations. India, he always emphasized, is destined to play a larger role in world affairs, but it must first stabilize its own neighbourhood, secure its own borders and create new interdependencies with countries that matter. He saw a 'stable' South Asian neighbourhood as an important basis for India's development. It was in India's interests to resolve long-standing border disputes and the problem of Kashmir. India was doing no one but itself a favour by seeking to resolve these issues.

But the 'Manmohan Singh Doctrine' was not just about 'interests' devoid of any 'values'. On the contrary, Dr Singh made bold to impart to Indian foreign policy new values based on India's own civilizational inheritance. Rejecting Samuel Huntington's 'clash of civilizations' theory he repeatedly spoke of India as a symbol of the 'confluence of civilizations' and the 'coexistence of civilizations'. His repeated use of the idea of *Vasudhaiva Kutumbakam*—'the whole world is one family'— sought to link this value to India's ancient heritage.

But he did not stop with mouthing phrases. He readily agreed to sign on to the United Nations Democracy Fund launched by UN Secretary General Kofi Annan in 2005, sitting alongside President Bush, and offered Indian professional expertise in conducting elections, and in the use of electronic voting machines developed by India, to countries that sought such assistance. India had rarely identified itself with such democracy-related foreign policy initiatives in the Cold War era for fear of offending many Third-World potentates.

In a bold assertion of these values, he declared in the Lok Sabha, in his May 2005 speech:

> Our steadfast commitment to democracy, to building a multiethnic, multireligious, multilingual, multicultural democracy based on respect for fundamental human rights and the rule of law gives us a unique place in our era. All nations of the world, I believe, will one day function on these very principles of liberal and pluralistic democracy. This enjoins upon us the obligation to nurture these roots of our nationhood. I commit our government to work earnestly to realize this vision of India's tryst with destiny.

He went to the ASEAN Summit, the SAARC Summit, the IBSA (India, Brazil, South Africa) and even the summit of the Non-Aligned Movement with proposals for economic cooperation, defending greater interdependence between nations. Dr Singh recognized that the single most important exception to this worldview on foreign policy is Pakistan. The India–Pakistan relationship stands on a completely different footing, unlike even the India–Bangladesh relationship. He recognized there were limits to the role economic interdependence could play in altering this one relationship. However, even here he was convinced greater interdependence would widen the policy space for normalization of relations.

On major policy issues, including relations with the US, China and Pakistan, Dr Singh and Natwar came to have similar views and Natwar increasingly became a source of support for the PM in dealing with critics within the Congress party. When Natwar had to resign after the Paul Volcker Committee's report alleged that both the Congress party and he had benefitted monetarily through deals struck with Iraq's Saddam Hussein, Dr Singh was genuinely sorry to see him go. He then took his own time to choose a successor, retaining the portfolio from December 2005 to October 2006, when he handed it over to Pranab Mukherjee.

Pranab Mukherjee proved to be a more difficult customer. While Natwar was transparent in his dealings, Pranab was difficult to fathom. For me, two incidents captured this difference. At the end of Dr Singh's first visit to the UN General Assembly in September 2004, he was to address a press conference. Minutes before the conference began I received a call from Natwar.

'Baru, I am told you have not placed a chair for me at the press conference?'

I told him that earlier that month Dr Singh had addressed a press conference at Vigyan Bhavan where he sat alone on the dais and his colleagues sat in the front row, along with the media. That is what I had proposed for the New York press conference too.

'This is preposterous. You are new, Baru, so you should know this. From the days of Panditji whenever the prime minister of India has met the press at the UN he has done so with the foreign minister next to him. Tell that to the PM and please let him know that I expect to sit next to him.'

I promptly conveyed this to Dr Singh. Mani Dixit, who was present at the time, interjected and said, 'Tell Natwar that the PM will sit alone.'

Dr Singh waved to Mani as if to say 'let it be' and turned to me and smiled, nodding his head as if to signal his approval for Natwar to be on the dais with him. Natwar reciprocated the gesture by letting the media know that the PM had excellent meetings with President Bush and President Musharraf, even though he was not privy to what happened in either meeting. Natwar's public support had its uses.

Pranab was never so transparent either in expressing his disagreement or support. After returning from an important visit to Washington DC, Pranab chose not to brief the PM for three days. He had gone to see Sonia Gandhi but had not sought an appointment with Dr Singh. On the third day, I asked Dr Singh what had transpired at Pranab's meetings with President Bush and Condoleezza Rice. 'I don't know,' was his plaintive reply.

I was taken aback. How could the foreign minister not have briefed the PM immediately on return? I suggested to him that he should summon the foreign minister and demand a briefing. I am not aware if Pranab was actually summoned or himself found time to drop in, but in any event, he visited the PM the next day. Similarly, Pranab would 'forget' to brief the PM on his meetings with the Left. Another curious aspect of his personality was his reluctance to delegate much work to his minister of state Anand Sharma. Sharma would sit in his room in South Block with a clean table in front of him, a diary with no appointments and bemoan his marginalization. Pranab routinely declined permission for Sharma to travel abroad, deputing junior officials to go for some of these meetings.

'Tell PM that the external affairs ministry is not even allowing me to reply to questions in Parliament,' Anand would complain to me. During the debate in Parliament on the nuclear deal, Anand had to lobby to get a speaking opportunity and got one only when the PM intervened to suggest that he be allowed to speak. The PM would try to compensate him for this neglect by his immediate boss by occasionally taking him abroad on his visits.

When the nuclear deal became a political hot potato for the Congress, some in the party would brief journalists on the Congress party beat that the party was not as keen as the PM on taking this forward. Almost always, the reason given would be the so-called 'minority vote', minority being a euphemism in India for 'Muslim'. When the Left and the BJP started raising their pitch, and the Congress party remained diffident in extending its support to Dr Singh, it was finally left to him to defend himself.

In fact, fairly early in the game, on his flight to the US in July 2005, the mild-mannered Dr Singh lost his cool when a journalist asked for his response to the criticism that he was deviating from the 'national consensus on foreign policy' by seeking closer relations with the US. He retorted: 'Can you imagine any prime minister consciously or unconsciously selling India? Nobody can sell India. India is not on sale. Nobody has to teach us lessons on patriotism.'

While he had to battle it out pretty much on his own when it came to defending the government's engagement with the US, Dr Singh found wider support within his party on his initiatives with China and Pakistan. Everyone welcomed 'normalization of relations' with both neighbours and a resolution of the border problem. What very few recognized was that any success on those two fronts was linked to success on the Western front. Improved relations with the US were the key to better relations with China, Pakistan and much of the rest of the world. This simple fact, one that Subrahmanyam ingrained in Dr Singh, escaped most of Dr Singh's critics.

———

While the key security and foreign policy challenge that Dr Singh had to deal with in the last months of his first term was the fallout from the Mumbai terror attack of November 2008, it was only fitting that the second major challenge was in a field that he was truly interested in—international economic diplomacy.

India's entry into the newly created leaders' summit of the G-20 was a tribute to Indian diplomacy in UPA-1. The G-20 was created to offer a portmanteau platform of major economies within which the US and the EU could deal with China. When the USSR disintegrated and Russia made peace with the West, the G-7 expanded to include Russia and became the G-8. Something similar could have happened in 2008 when the US and the EU discovered they would need Chinese cooperation to handle the fallout of the post-Lehmann 'transatlantic' financial crisis.

Indeed, Fred Bergsten, at the Peterson Institute for International Economics in Washington DC, even wrote an essay suggesting that the US and China come together into a 'G-2' and manage the global economic slowdown and crisis. President Nicholas Sarkozy of France was horrified. He flew down to Camp David to meet President Bush and suggested that the G-20 finance ministers group should meet at the heads of government / state level and discuss the global crisis.

Over the previous decade, from 2000 onwards, the G-8 would invite several 'emerging economy' leaders to their summit meetings for an 'outreach' meet. This group came to include Brazil, China, India, Mexico and South Africa. Sarkozy convinced Bush that instead of a G-8 plus 5 summit, it might be best to create a new platform under the G-20. Bush readily accepted the idea since it was appealing to him that the US could deal with China in a larger group that would include Mexico, India, Indonesia, Australia, Saudi Arabia and other economies.

Dr Singh played an active role in the first two G-20 summits, in November 2008 and April 2009. The impressive performance of the Indian economy in the 2004–08 period and its ability to withstand the immediate impact of the Lehmann collapse contributed to India's global standing and to Dr Singh's global image. Leaving the London G-20 summit in April 2009, President Barack Obama went to Germany where a young school student asked him which politician he admired. Obama's instant reply was that among existing world leaders he admired Dr Singh of India the most.

The robust performance of the economy during UPA-1 provided the policy space within which Dr Singh could push his ideas on economic interdependence, the irrelevance of borders and the importance of strategic partnerships defined by economic interests. The Subrahmanyam task force also drew pointed attention to the strategic importance of sustained economic growth.

The keys to India's 'tryst with destiny' were, first, overcoming the challenge of wiping out 'poverty, ignorance and disease', as Nehru reminded the nation in 1947, and, second, creating a competitive economy that would enable India to rebuild the 'bridges of mutual interdependence' with the world, as Dr Singh reminded the India Today

Conclave. In short, 'India must do what it must at home' for it to be able to deal more confidently with the world.

That, the world believed, India was doing in UPA-1. Once the economy began to falter and the government became wobbly, India and its PM lost their sheen, underscoring the fact that the 'Manmohan Singh Doctrine' requires as its foundation a rapidly growing and dynamic economy capable of overcoming domestic challenges, facing international competition and being engaged with the global economy.

10

Making Borders Irrelevant

'I dream of a day when, while retaining our respective national identities,
one can have breakfast in Amritsar, lunch in Lahore and dinner in Kabul.
That is how my forefathers lived. That is how I want our grandchildren to live.'

Manmohan Singh, FICCI annual general meeting
8 January 2007

The Indian subcontinent was always a crossroads between Asia to its east and Asia to its west. Conquerors, travellers, traders and teachers set foot or set sail and moved across Asia through India. The Indian cultural and economic footprint extended from the banks of the Mediterranean to the Pacific, from the coasts of East Africa and the Arab/Persian Gulf to the coasts of Vietnam and Indonesia. India was both enriched and impoverished by such flows of people across the Indus and the Gangetic plains.

It was this vision of India that shaped Dr Singh's approach to India's relations with its neighbours, including Pakistan, the land of his birth. Partition in 1947, and the creation of Pakistan, could never be reversed but why should political boundaries now come in the way of free movement of today's travellers, traders and teachers when they had not done so over centuries? He spoke about a subcontinent without borders or, as he put it to Pakistani President Pervez Musharraf, 'where borders are mere lines on paper'.

The state of India–Pakistan relations and the need to find a lasting solution to the problem of Jammu and Kashmir, had occupied Dr Singh's attention for years. His interest in it predated his prime ministership and he kept himself informed on what was happening in J&K. So it was not surprising that while preparing for his first visit as PM to the UN General Assembly, in September 2004, Dr Singh devoted considerable time to his planned meeting with President Pervez Musharraf.

To create a favourable environment for the meeting, India took the initiative to announce unilateral liberalization of the visa regime for Pakistani academics, businessmen and senior citizens. That some back-channel discussions had already taken place on Kashmir was evident from the fact that President Musharraf made no reference to the troubled issue in his speech. Singh reciprocated the gesture by telling the UN General Assembly that he 'reaffirmed' India's determination to carry forward the dialogue with Pakistan initiated by his predecessor, Atal Bihari Vajpayee, in January 2004, 'to a purposeful and mutually acceptable conclusion'.

Those statements set the tone for the meeting of the two leaders at New York's Roosevelt Hotel on 24 September 2004. While Dr Singh drove to the hotel with a delegation that included External Affairs Minister Natwar Singh, the two leaders chose to meet without aides and talked for over an hour. Earlier it had been decided that the two would not meet the media and only a spokesperson would brief journalists. But as the meeting came to an end, they announced that they would like to jointly address the media.

Almost fifty to sixty waiting journalists from both countries had to be security checked and allowed into the hotel lobby within minutes. The hotel did not have a suitable conference room, so it was decided that the two leaders would stand in a wide corridor outside the room where they met and make a statement. As TV crews set up their cameras, it was left to MEA spokesperson Navtej Sarna to get a hotel staffer to unscrew the 'Exit' sign on the wall so that the two leaders would not be caught on camera standing below it.

The two then issued a bland joint statement, hurriedly drafted by their aides, that said they had 'agreed that confidence-building measures of all categories under discussion between the two governments should be implemented keeping in mind practical possibilities'. It became clear that the two had a more wide-ranging conversation when, about a month after Musharraf returned home, the Pakistan correspondent of the *Tribune* reported from Islamabad, on 27 October 2004, that, 'In a new formulation to resolve the vexed Kashmir issue, President Pervez Musharraf last night suggested that India and Pakistan consider the option of identifying some "regions" of Kashmir on both sides of Line of Control, demilitarize them and grant them the status of independence or joint control or under UN mandate.' The report quoted Pakistan's government-run TV channel, PTV, to say that Musharraf had said that 'a solution to the lingering Kashmir problem cannot be found either by insisting on plebiscite or making the LoC (Line of Control) into a permanent border'.

Even though the Indian government rejected this interpretation of the New York conversation, it encouraged a public debate on the pros and cons of Musharraf's thinking. After all, the idea was originally canvassed by none other than Dr Singh. On the eve of his becoming prime minister, in May 2004, Dr Singh told journalist Jonathan Power (*Statesman*, 20 May 2004) in an off-the-record conversation that Power published without his permission, 'Short of secession, short of re-drawing boundaries, the Indian establishment can live with anything. Meanwhile, we need soft borders—then borders are not so important.'

Enough had happened in backroom talks between September 2004 and February 2005 for Musharraf to want to carry the conversation forward. He chose to speed up things by publicly expressing his desire to watch the India–Pakistan one-day cricket matches scheduled for that spring. Musharraf's public solicitation of an invitation from India was met with stunning silence from New Delhi.

After waiting for a couple of days, the Indian media became restive and sought a response. Several journalists called me to find out if the PM was aware of Musharraf's stated desire and whether he would invite the Pakistan President to come watch a match. I walked into the PM's room in South Block and sought an answer.

'I have been advised that this is not a good time for a visit because the budget session is going on,' the PM told me. 'The foreign ministry will inform Pakistan that the visit can take place sometime later.'

I asked the PM if he and his diplomatic advisers had considered what headline they would get the next morning: 'Musharraf wants to go to India to watch a cricket match. India says no!'

The PM laughed and asked, 'So what do you think we should do? You realize if he visits India, it will not be just to watch a cricket match but for formal discussions.'

True, I said, but for now Musharraf was only seeking an invitation to watch a cricket match. It was clear from the PM's demeanour that he was quite willing to invite Musharraf and continue their conversation from where they had left it in September 2004. In fact, while we were speaking, he summoned Foreign Secretary Shyam Saran and national security adviser Narayanan. Within minutes they joined us. 'Sanjaya says I must invite Musharraf,' he told his two nonplussed senior aides, who already appeared unhappy to find me present at such a hurriedly convened meeting with the PM. This was, of course, his old tactic of putting his own views into other people's mouths. Those unfamiliar with his style would offer a counterview, thinking they were responding to a view other than the PM's own. Those who had come to know Dr Singh well would realize this was just the PM's way of expressing his own view, while retaining an exit route. Perhaps both Narayanan and Shyam understood this, but neither hesitated to disagree with my view. Shyam shared Dr Singh's vision on most foreign policy issues but on Pakistan he was a hawk and was as sceptical as Narayanan about Pakistan's readiness to normalize relations with India. We were soon joined by Nair and Pulok and I was pleased when they both agreed with me. The PM turned to Shyam and asked him to draft a letter of invitation to Musharraf. The meeting had ended.

I was asked not to breathe a word of this plan to the media till the diplomats had done their job of deciding the date and the venue, and getting a formal acceptance of the PM's invitation from Islamabad. For two days, I heard nothing more about this and had to fob off an eager media which kept asking me: 'Will the PM invite Musharraf?' I was told by a colleague that both Shyam and Narayanan were in discussions with state governments to figure out which match Musharraf should be invited to—the one in Visakhapatnam or the one in Kochi.

I could not believe my ears when I heard this and decided to speak to the PM. I went over to 3 RCR and told him that the media would view this as an attempt to keep Musharraf away from New Delhi. He hinted at considerable resistance within the government to the idea of a Musharraf visit at this time. The main reason, it seemed, was that it was not a good idea to have such a high-profile visit with Parliament in session. So why not downplay the visit by making it semi-official and go along with the pretence that he was only being invited to witness a cricket match and nothing else? In Europe, heads of government travel to each other's capitals without too much protocol. Why should there be a joint statement, I argued, each time two South Asian heads of government meet? I could see that Dr Singh was ready and willing to invite Musharraf and the matter was getting delayed because of the usual bureaucratic processes and diplomatic protocol. I suggested to him that he could use the opportunity provided the following morning when he was scheduled to speak in the Lok Sabha by using his intervention in a parliamentary debate to publicly extend an invitation to President Musharraf. He asked me to give him a draft statement.

Next morning, on 10 March 2005, I drove to 3 RCR and handed him a draft before he left home. He read it, folded the paper and placed it in his pocket, as was his wont, saying, 'Let me think about it.' Later that morning, I went to the Lok Sabha to hear him speak. He spoke for over half an hour, replying to all the points made by several members in the course of the debate. I waited anxiously to see what he would say when talking about foreign policy.

He went through the discussion on foreign policy as well, and finally, when he came to the very end, he put his hand in his pocket and pulled out the folded sheet of paper and read from it:

> Mr Speaker, Sir, I am happy to inform the honourable members of the House that I have decided to invite President Musharraf to come to India to watch a cricket match between our two teams. It is my earnest desire that the people in our neighbouring country and their

leaders should feel free to visit us whenever they wish to do so. Be it
to watch a cricket match; be it to do some shopping; or be it to meet
friends and family—India is proud to be an open society and an open
economy. I do hope that President Musharraf and his family will enjoy
their visit to our country.

Members of Parliament from around the hall thumped their table
in approval. Even before his officials and diplomats had got around to
placing a letter of invitation to Musharraf in front of him, the PM had
verbally issued that invitation from the floor of the Lok Sabha and
had secured instant approval from Parliament. In the officials' gallery,
everyone around me, including the NSA, was stunned. Nair turned to
me and winked. I walked out quietly and went into the PM's room to
watch TV channels splash the 'breaking news'.

———

With the visit scheduled for a little more than a month away in mid-
April, Dr Singh moved quickly to take the next steps. On 4 April he
announced the setting up of a high-level task force to prepare a plan
for the development of Jammu and Kashmir under the chairmanship of
Dr C. Rangarajan, chairman of the PM's Economic Advisory Council.
The task force members included Kashmiri economist Haseeb Drabhu,
business leaders Sunil Mittal, Sunil Munjal and Analjit Singh, public
sector CEOs Moosa Raza and T.N. Thakur, and Duvvuri Subbarao.

He then scheduled for 7 April 2005 the launch of a cross-LoC
Srinagar–Muzaffarabad bus service. On 6 April, terrorists attacked
the state tourism office in Srinagar, the place from where the new
bus service was to be launched. By the end of the day, the national
security and intelligence agencies were advising the PM to cancel
his visit the next morning to Srinagar. While two terrorists had been
killed by security forces, two had escaped. Home Minister Shivraj Patil,
Narayanan, IB chief E.S.L. Narasimhan and others advised the PM to
cancel his trip. Sonia Gandhi was to accompany the PM. She told him
that she would go along with him, whatever his decision.

It was a tiring day. The final review meeting ended at 9 p.m., with
the PM being advised to cancel his visit. Almost everyone had left the
room. Dr Singh sat pensively, with anger and concern writ large on
his face. Suddenly he came alive and said, 'I will go!'

Officers on their way out of 7 RCR were called back in. The
PM called Sonia and informed her that he had decided to travel to
Srinagar. She endorsed his decision and said she too would travel with
him. Next morning the two flew to Srinagar, amid tight security, and
flagged the first bus off.

'This is the first step,' Dr Singh told the crowd that had gathered in
the heart of Srinagar, 'on the long road of peace.'

This act of political courage gave Dr Singh a huge boost both within
the Valley and across the country. It set the stage for Musharraf's visit
the following week.

A major concern for the officials handling the visit was that
Musharraf's Delhi visit should not become a repeat of the disastrous
Agra Summit of July 2001. The general view was that Musharraf
had had the last laugh and staged a PR coup, leaving the Indian side
embarrassed by the outcome. It was too early in Dr Singh's prime
ministerial tenure for such a foreign policy disaster, officials pointed
out. While our diplomats did their bit to ensure a positive outcome, I
was instructed by the PM to manage the media and prevent an Agra-
style PR disaster. My biggest concern was that our side should speak
in one voice and that our internal differences should not come out in
the open, as those between Vajpayee and Advani did at Agra.

I convened and chaired a press briefing at South Block. Every
important journalist and writer on foreign affairs and on India–Pakistan
relations was invited. From the government side we had Narayanan,
Nair, Shyam Saran and Shivshankar Menon, India's high commissioner
in Pakistan. It was the first time in the PMO that the media adviser had
chaired a press briefing and spoken for the PM with all senior officials
present. It was a high-risk strategy. If my efforts to ensure supportive
media coverage failed and Musharraf got away with yet another media
coup, I knew all the senior officials at the table would not just blame
me but also hang me. As I offered the media the PM's perspective on

the Musharraf visit, everyone, including Narayanan, made supportive statements.

As it happened, I need not have worried. Dr Singh came out of that April 2005 Musharraf visit both politically and diplomatically stronger. It had the added benefit of making him more confident and assertive.

After watching the cricket match at Delhi's Ferozeshah Kotla grounds, Dr Singh and Musharraf went to Hyderabad House for a formal conversation. Musharraf was in a great mood because Pakistan had got off to a good start. In fact, the President, who had apparently been informed by his staff that Pakistan was set to win (which it did in the end), began the conversation saying, 'Doctor Saheb, if you and I decide, we can resolve all our disputes before lunch and then go back to watch the match.'

'General Saheb, you are a soldier and much younger,' replied Dr Singh to Musharraf, 'but you must allow for my age. I can only walk step by step.'

While Dr Singh was socially awkward and shy he always seemed to relax in the company of gregarious and outgoing personalities. They would do most of the talking and fill Dr Singh's silences with remarks that would make the PM laugh and unwind. Musharraf was certainly more talkative than Dr Singh, as were Hamid Karzai, George Bush, Tony Blair and Mahmoud Ahmedinejad. He was never too comfortable with those as reserved as he was, like Gordon Brown and Hu Jintao.

The septuagenarian economist and the sixty-one-year-old general walked their talk. Over the next two years, they outlined a roadmap for the resolution of the Kashmir issue based on Dr Singh's famous formulation that 'borders cannot be changed, but they can be made irrelevant'. Much of this conceptualization was done secretly through a diplomatic 'back channel'. On the Pakistani side Musharraf's trusted envoy was Tariq Aziz, a former income tax officer who was a personal friend of Musharraf. Musharraf had appointed him secretary to the NSC.

Aziz was the liaison between Musharraf and Vajpayee, keeping in touch with Brajesh Mishra through a mutual friend, the late R.K. Mishra of the Observer Research Foundation. During the Kargil war, R.K. Mishra and Aziz would meet secretly, exchanging messages between Musharraf and Vajpayee. Mishra also doubled up as Reliance Industries Ltd (RIL) chairman Dhirubhai Ambani's aide, seeking assurances from the Pakistanis that they would not bomb RIL's Jamnagar plant.

On the Indian side, Dr Singh's back channel was former Indian ambassador to Islamabad, Satinder Lambah. Lambah was a highly skilled diplomat who knew how to keep his mouth shut and function below the radar. His meetings at 7 RCR with Dr Singh were always secret. Any appointment scheduled on the daily programme sheet risked becoming public knowledge. Only fourteen marked copies were printed and circulated to key PMO officials, the security and intelligence staff. If the PM wished to keep a meeting secret from any one of these fourteen, then the meetings would never be listed. A further danger was that enterprising journalists would often manage to find out the PM's programme. Therefore, Lambah's meetings with the PM were rarely, if ever, listed.

Lambah would meet Aziz in Pakistan, in India and in third places, like Dubai. He was assisted by the PM's second personal secretary, Jaideep Sarkar, who was his note taker. Whenever Jaideep took leave, reporting sick or leaving word that he was helping his son prepare for exams, I knew he was away with Lambah. The Lambah–Aziz back channel helped prepare the groundwork for summit meetings and develop the framework agreement that Dr Singh hoped to sign with Musharraf.

The first step, they both agreed, would be to make the LoC just 'a line on a map'. Towards this end it was decided that cross-LoC travel and trade would be freed up. This would mean that for the people of Kashmir, now living on either side of the LoC, life would return to the pre-Partition era when they could travel to each other's villages with ease, and normal life would go on as if there was no border.

The second step would be to strengthen local self-government on both sides of the LoC, so that the people of Kashmir elected their own government, if necessary under international supervision.

The third step would be the trickiest. It would entail the creation of 'joint' or 'cooperative' institutions under the charge of Kashmiri leaders to coordinate policies on matters of common interest. Everything except foreign policy and defence would be locally and jointly administered and these two would be handled by New Delhi and Islamabad respectively. If all this worked and peace was restored, then the fourth and final element of the peace formula would be the 'agreed withdrawal' of troops on both sides.

Dr Singh followed up this meeting with a visit to the Siachen Glacier in June 2005 where he declared that Siachen would be a 'symbol of peace' rather than conflict. It was an optimistic thing to say amid the snowy wastes where India and Pakistan, both laying claim to the same territory, have fought intermittently since 1984.

Reassuring the listening men in uniform, he added that there was 'no question of redrawing borders. In search of peace, existing boundaries cannot be changed because these are for our protection and are related to our honour.'

While there has been some criticism of Dr Singh's Siachen proposal in India, the fact is that he pursued this idea only after consulting every retired army general who had actually commanded the troops at Siachen. Each one of them had been witness to the tragic deaths of soldiers and the huge expense of the operation. All of them supported Dr Singh's decision to find a final solution to the problem of Kashmir and Siachen.

Dr Singh wanted President Musharraf to own and propagate the Kashmir 'peace formula'. He was quite willing to sell this as a 'Musharraf formula' rather than a Manmohan–Musharraf formula. And that is how it has come to be known. He believed at the time that it would be tougher for Musharraf to sell the peace formula in Pakistan than for him to get majority opinion in India on his side. While the peace formula would give a special status to Kashmir, it would not alter the 'ground reality', with the Kashmir on this side of the LoC being a part of India and the region on the other side remaining a part of Pakistan.

In Pakistan, Musharraf would have to deal with political parties, religious groups and the army. Dr Singh felt that in India there would be a wider constituency of support, including large sections of the Congress, several regional parties and the Left. He thought the only real opposition would come from the BJP.

This was not the way it turned out. What Dr Singh perhaps underestimated was the likely resistance from within his own party. Pranab and Antony, as successive defence ministers in UPA-1, were reportedly not enthusiastic about a deal on Siachen, though Sonia had blessed the peace formula. The armed forces were ambivalent, with retired generals who had served in Siachen favouring a deal to end the agony of the troops serving in that inhospitable terrain, but serving generals not willing to trust Pakistan on a deal.

A warm and friendly person, Antony played straight but was a tough customer to handle. I had a good personal equation with him because he knew I had been a student of that distinguished Keralite, Professor K.N. Raj. In fact, being aware that I had got married in Thiruvananthapuram, he would always refer to me as a 'son-in-law of Kerala'. But, when it came to policy, personal warmth mattered little. Antony was politically conservative and risk averse and depended excessively on the advice of IAS officers inexperienced in strategic policy and defence. His stewardship of the defence ministry has been widely criticized for this reason.

To add to this, Dr Singh had to also contend with a declining quality of defence services leadership, which has since become all too visible. For me, the first sign of this decline was evident in the manner in which army chief General J.J. Singh dealt with the Siachen issue. In closed-door briefings, the general would say that a deal with Pakistan was doable, but in public he would back Antony when the defence minister chose not to back the PM. Even in Narasimha Rao's Cabinet Antony was a critic of that government's economic policies. With his left-of-centre background, from his time in Kerala politics, Antony was an old-style Congressman critical of both the economic and foreign policy initiatives of the Rao government and now of Dr Singh's. While he, and indeed Sonia, supported Dr Singh's initiative to normalize relations with Pakistan, Antony was sceptical about Dr Singh's Siachen initiative.

I was never sure whether Antony's hawkish stance was because he genuinely disagreed with the Siachen initiative or whether he was merely toeing a Nehru–Gandhi family line that would not allow Dr Singh to be the one finally normalizing relations with Pakistan. After all the Kashmir problem had its roots in Nehru's policies. Both Indira and Rajiv tried to solve it and failed. Would Sonia, who backed the peace initiative with Pakistan, finally allow Dr Singh to in fact resolve this legacy of history and enter the history books? I remained a sceptic. I felt she would want to wait till Rahul became PM so that he could claim credit. My scepticism did not, however, blunt Dr Singh's enthusiasm to keep trying for a breakthrough. Events on the ground did.

———

Religious extremists in both countries were opposed to this process of normalization. A key objective of the terror attacks that followed, both in Kashmir and in different parts of India, was to ignite communal passions and prevent a meeting of minds between India and Pakistan on Kashmir.

On 29 October 2005, Delhi was rocked by a series of bomb attacks. Crowded markets in Sarojini Nagar and Paharganj were made targets. Dr Singh was in Agartala during the day and was scheduled to spend the night in Kolkata, returning the next day to Delhi. Through that day he had been preoccupied with the revelations from the Volcker Committee report on the oil-for-food scam reported in *The Hindu*.

On the flight to Agartala, Dr Singh read *The Hindu* report in full and called me into his cabin to discuss the fallout. During lunch he watched a media briefing by Congress spokesperson Ambika Soni on TV. Ambika carefully defended only the Congress party and said that Natwar would speak for himself. Dr Singh viewed this as the party abandoning Natwar. Foreseeing the inevitable, on the flight back from Agartala, he asked me for names of potential foreign ministers. We shortlisted Pranab Mukherjee, Karan Singh and S.M. Krishna for the job. Even as I was putting forward the pros and cons of various names, the SPG chief Bharat Wanchoo came into the cabin with the news of bomb blasts in Delhi.

On hearing the news, Dr Singh decided that we would fly directly to Delhi, with only a technical halt at Kolkata airport. That night he made an extempore statement on television linking the blasts to a deliberate attempt to spread disaffection among communities during the forthcoming festival season. After every such terror attack the priority was to prevent communal conflict. He wanted to ensure that what had happened in Godhra in 2002 would never happen again.

On this score, the government succeeded. However, such terror attacks did manage to stall and delay the process of normalization of India–Pakistan relations. Each time the process was disrupted, Dr Singh would try and pick up the threads and move forward after a decent interval. In March 2006, a year after his initial efforts with Musharraf and after the impact of the Delhi blasts had been politically absorbed, and when many had assumed the Kashmir agenda was off the PM's table, Dr Singh tried again.

Addressing a huge public rally in Amritsar, Dr Singh spoke in Punjabi. It was intended that his speech, telecast live from Amritsar, should be heard loud and clear in Lahore. While Dr Singh was addressing the rally, I was in Delhi ensuring that all national TV channels were relaying the speech live and reporting the key messages. Delivering his boldest speech to date on the issue of Kashmir and India–Pakistan relations, and that too in Punjabi and at a mass rally, Dr Singh said that both sides should begin a dialogue with people in their respective 'areas of control to improve the quality of governance so as to give the people on both sides a greater chance of leading a life of dignity and self-respect'. He then went on to add:

I have often said that borders cannot be redrawn but we can work towards making them irrelevant—towards making them just lines on a map. People on both sides of the LoC should be able to move more freely and trade with one another. I also envisage a situation where the two parts of Jammu and Kashmir can, with the active encouragement of the governments of India and Pakistan, work out cooperative, consultative mechanisms so as to maximize the gains of cooperation in solving problems of social and economic development of the region.

This was the clearest exposition of the Manmohan–Musharraf formula ever made by Dr Singh himself. The statement was heard around the world. By the time the two leaders met again, in Havana in September 2006, on the sidelines of the summit of the Non-Aligned Movement, the bilateral engagement process had survived more terror attacks, the most recent one being in Mumbai in July 2006.

Arriving in Havana on the afternoon of 14 September 2006, both Pulok and I stepped out of the hotel in search of Cuban cigars. After walking through several narrow lanes we discovered the Havana black market for Cohibas. The price a foreigner has to pay for a cigar in a government shop in Havana was no different from what duty-free shops in Europe charge. But in the back alleys of Havana one could get the genuine stuff for a tenth of that price. We could have asked the Indian ambassador to get us a box of cigars but we chose to be adventurous. Laden with our loot of low-cost Cohibas we went to El Floridita, Ernest Hemingway's favourite bar, for mojitos. After imbibing several rounds with Indian journalists who had accompanied the PM to Cuba, Pulok and I returned to our hotel.

As I entered the lobby, an SPG officer informed me that the PM wanted to see me. I rushed to my room, brushed my teeth, dabbed some cologne and went to his suite. He was seated there with Narayanan and Shivshankar Menon.

Dr Singh showed me a draft joint statement that he and Musharraf would issue the next day after their meeting. Shivshankar had drafted the statement along with his counterparts in the Pakistan foreign office and had brought it from Islamabad to the PM for his approval. I read through the text. The draft proposed a bilateral 'anti-terrorism institutional mechanism to identify and implement counter-terrorism initiatives and investigations'.

'What do you think will be the reaction at home to this idea?' Dr Singh asked me. It seemed to me that the three had already discussed this at length and there was a difference of opinion between Narayanan and Shivshankar. Narayanan looked serious and glum, always a bad sign. Shivshankar, smooth and seasoned diplomat that he was, revealed no emotion. Clearly this was his draft and Narayanan had reservations about it. I knew I had been summoned to take sides and tilt the balance in the direction the PM wanted.

The BJP would criticize it, I told him, but the Congress party and the Left would back him. He needed their support to be able to move forward on other fronts. Senior Congress leaders remained divided on Dr Singh's policy towards Pakistan, but he seemed to still have Sonia's support. There was, however, no doubt that the Left Front fully backed his peace initiatives. Earning occasional praise from the Left was politically useful, especially since they were so critical of his policy towards the US. I assured Dr Singh that we would be able to manage the political fallout. He seemed satisfied with my intervention. He turned to Menon and instructed him to go ahead and finalize the joint statement with his Pakistani counterparts. Narayanan was by now looking very unhappy.

As we all walked out of the room Narayanan grabbed my hand firmly and said, 'You have stabbed me in the back!'

'Not true,' I said calmly and with a smile, not wanting to appear intimidated. 'I disagreed with you in your presence. You can of course accuse me of stabbing you in the front.' The mojito was still working.

———

Dr Singh met Musharraf at a villa that had been made available by the Cubans for this summit meeting. Musharraf, like so many other heads of government, usually appeared more relaxed and socially at ease than Dr Singh. In Havana, however, both seemed at ease and struck up a conversation between themselves while members of both delegations stood and watched. Suddenly, as if it was preplanned, the two walked together into an adjacent room and the SPG closed the door. Pakistan's foreign minister Khurshid Kasuri and Narayanan looked at each other in bewilderment. It was obvious that they had been kept out. While Narayanan remained standing where he was, Kasuri walked briskly to the door of the adjacent room. The SPG guard told him that he had been instructed not to let anyone in.

The two delegations then sat down for tea and biscuits. Indian and Pakistani officials get along famously in such settings. There are always many subjects to talk about. Cricket, Bollywood, the latest fancy restaurant in Lahore or Delhi that serves the best kebabs or biryani, the welfare of common friends and their children. For almost an hour Dr Singh and Musharraf were closeted in that room, while the two delegations socialized. Narayanan's discomfiture was palpable but Kasuri, who knew who the boss was, had regained his poise and now seemed utterly indifferent.

The idea of a joint terror mechanism came in for considerable criticism, especially from the BJP. I had to devote considerable time to ensuring that the media backed the PM, especially because several retired diplomats and members of India's intelligence and security agencies issued a statement criticizing the PM. Quiet conversations with a few editors and hinting to them that this was the beginning of a more substantial movement forward with Pakistan helped.

The joint statement had gone further than any until then in setting out the agenda for bilateral talks and agreements. Importantly, it called for an 'early solution of the Siachen issue' and for an agreement between 'experts' 'on coordinates for a joint survey of Sir Creek and adjoining area, without prejudice to each other's position on the issue'. It said, 'The Survey should commence in November 2006. The experts should start discussions on the maritime boundary.' Sir Creek is a disputed strip of water in the Rann of Kutch.

The two sides also agreed to 'facilitate implementation of agreements and understandings already reached' on confidence-building measures relating to the LoC between India and Pakistan in Jammu and Kashmir, 'including bus services, crossing points and truck service'.

On 20 December, Dr Singh went back to Amritsar to address yet another public meeting. He spoke again in Punjabi and explained at length how he had been trying to improve relations with Pakistan because the 'destinies of the two nations are linked'. He did not want India to be weighed down by the past but think of its future and move forward. He then made bold to talk of 'his' vision, a rare personalization of policy by the reticent Dr Singh.

> I too have a vision regarding India and Pakistan. I earnestly hope that the relations between our two countries become so friendly and that we generate such an atmosphere of trust between each other that the two nations would be able to agree on a Treaty of Peace, Security and Friendship . . . I am sure that we can overcome all hurdles in our path and realize such a Treaty. This will become the instrument for realizing our collective destiny and the basis for enduring peace and prosperity in the region.

After Indira Gandhi met Zulfiqar Ali Bhutto in Shimla in 1972, this was the first time an Indian prime minister had taken the step of offering a treaty of peace, friendship and security to Pakistan. Events, however, overtook the two leaders. Musharraf found himself embroiled in domestic political trouble. His problems with Pakistan's judiciary threw that country into turmoil by the first quarter of 2007. Musharraf's regime became weaker, making Dr Singh cautious. By mid-2007, the bilateral process he had initiated came to a grinding halt as Musharraf's political stock went down.

In September 2007, Dr Singh chose not to go to New York to attend the UN General Assembly. India waited to see what would happen to President Musharraf before reviving the dialogue process, while keeping in touch with Benazir Bhutto, who had indicated her support for the Manmohan–Musharraf formula. By the end of 2007, Benazir Bhutto had been killed by an assassin's bullet. The news of Benazir's assassination reached Dr Singh at the Raj Bhavan in Goa. He was crestfallen. Benazir was privy to his consultations with Musharraf and he was confident she would back their effort and extend the required popular support to their plans. He spent the entire evening watching television reportage on the assassination.

By the end of 2008, Musharraf's rule had ended and a new regime was elected to office. The Manmohan–Musharraf formula went out of play and has been waiting since then to be resurrected. Over the years Dr Singh has repeatedly articulated his vision of a subcontinent of peace. When he welcomed Musharraf at a banquet in his honour in April 2005, it was with an eloquent dinner speech delivered with rare emotion:

> We cannot rewrite the past, but we can build a more secure future. A future that generates people's trust and confidence in the political leadership in South Asia. We must find practical ways and means to resolve all outstanding issues between us in a reasonable, pragmatic manner, cognizant of the ground realities. Our people and our common destiny urge us to make an earnest attempt to find a lasting solution to all issues.
>
> In a globalizing and increasingly integrated world, borders have lost meaning for much of the world. The journey of peace must be based on a step-by-step approach, but the road must be travelled. As an ancient saying goes, a road is made by walking.

Dr Singh was convinced that destiny was on India's side and India's rise as the world's largest democracy and an economic power would only be slowed down by an unsettled neighbourhood. The subcontinent had to rise together, he felt. He wanted India's rise to be viewed as a win–win game rather than a zero–sum game by its neighbours. He felt they too should benefit from it, recognizing that they might be able to slow India down with their tactics, but would never be able to stop India's resurgence.

That is why he persisted with his efforts against all odds and sought to pick up the threads with Musharraf's successors, President Asif Zardari and Prime Minister Syed Yousaf Raza Gilani, in the face of the gravest of provocations India had faced—the terror attacks in Mumbai in November 2008.

After his impressive victory in the 2009 elections Dr Singh assumed he had the political space to take forward his dialogue with Pakistan and wrap up the deal he was on the verge of striking with Musharraf with the general's democratically elected successors. After all, he had got Benazir's support before her death, and now her husband was President. His meeting with Zardari in June 2009, on the sidelines of a Shanghai Cooperation Organization (SCO) meeting in Yekaterinburg, Russia, was a non-starter, since this was the first meeting with a Pakistani leader after the November 2008 terror attack in Mumbai. He was, however, better prepared for his dialogue a month later with Prime Minister Gilani at Sharm el-Sheikh, on the sidelines of a summit meeting of the Non-Aligned Movement.

I met Dr Singh two days before he was due to fly to Sharm el-Sheikh. After we discussed my plans to return to India from Singapore, where I was then living, he asked me what I thought he should say to Prime Minister Gilani. I felt he ought not to have started his second term with a focus on Pakistan. Let the Zardari–Gilani team settle down I suggested, feeling he should focus on the economy at least for the first six months. The global economy was still in choppy waters. While the G-20 initiatives had calmed the markets and restored some stability, the outlook was still negative. I felt he should use his impressive victory to push for reforms at home while bringing the fiscal deficit down. But he seemed keen on taking the dialogue with Pakistan forward. With the nuclear deal done, normalizing relations with Pakistan remained his second major policy preoccupation. Speculation about a change of leadership midway through the second term, with Rahul taking charge, may have also lent some urgency to this agenda. Who knew how long he would remain PM.

In the event, that keenness seemed to have been responsible for his agreeing to refer to Baluchistan, in an apparent concession to Pakistan, in the joint statement he hurriedly issued with Gilani. The Congress party quickly rubbished the controversial statement, even though Dr Singh defended it twice in Parliament during the course of the month. Despite criticism from his own party, he never gave up hope of using the Thimphu SAARC Summit, in April 2010, to impart momentum to the dialogue process. Within months he was enveloped by political problems at home and never recovered from them to be able to return to the historic agenda he had so eagerly set for himself and so passionately pursued. He could not even manage to visit his birthplace at Gah.

Not completing the process he began will surely remain his greatest regret. However, whenever the two countries do find a lasting solution to their disputes, I have little doubt it will be along the lines that Dr Singh had envisioned with Musharraf.

11

Ending Nuclear Apartheid

'I am aware of the risks that I do incur.
Mr T.T. Krishnamachari once told me that
there are tigers on the prowl on the streets of Delhi.
I am aware of the risks, but for India's sake, I am willing to take those risks.'

Manmohan Singh in the Rajya Sabha
17 August 2006

In January 2004, it was Atal Bihari Vajpayee who had initiated a new round of dialogue with President Musharraf, aimed at resolving the Kashmir dispute, but it fell to Dr Singh to take that initiative forward. In the same month, Vajpayee also initiated a new strategic dialogue with the United States, dubbed the Next Steps in Strategic Partnership, aimed at ending what many in India believed was a nuclear 'apartheid' that discriminated against India. That process too was destined to be taken forward by Dr Singh.

After the Pokhran nuclear test of 1974, and for refusing to sign the NPT, India had been subjected to US restrictions on the export of 'dual-use' and 'high' technology, that is technology that could be used for both civilian and military, and strategic purposes. India's grouse was that China managed to become a nuclear power under the terms of the NPT only because it tested before the treaty was signed while India missed the bus by a few years. The NPT thus, from the Indian perspective, divided the world into nuclear 'haves' and 'have-nots' and

198

India, along with Israel, North Korea and Pakistan, was a 'have-not'.

The 1998 'Shakti tests' at Pokhran had invited a fresh round of sanctions. By 2004, India had managed to secure a whittling down of the post-1998 sanctions, but the post-1974 restrictions (which prohibited US nuclear trade with India) were still in place. Removing these restrictions required amendments to US law.

President George Bush was the first US President to recognize, publicly at least, that this was unfair discrimination against India. He appreciated the fact that it was incongruous for the US to be doing more business in high-technology areas with communist China than democratic India. China managed to avert restrictions because it was an NPT signatory as a 'weapons power'.

As the world entered the twenty-first century, several factors encouraged the US to seek closer relations with India. First, India's own improved economic performance and the opening up of the economy to foreign capital and trade in the 1990s. Second, India's proven capability in the new information and knowledge economy as demonstrated in its ability to help the US manage the Y2K problem, also known as the Millennium Bug. Third, growing US concern about the rise of China and Islamic radicalism, and the US view that India could be a partner in tackling these challenges because India too was concerned about these developments. Finally, the favourable impression made in the US by the Indian American community, which had emerged as a prosperous, vocal and cooperative interest group capable of influencing US lawmakers.

All this was reflected in Condoleezza Rice's influential essay on 'Promoting the National Interest' (*Foreign Affairs*, January–February 2000) in which she urged the US to 'pay closer attention to India's role in the regional balance' in Asia, 'de-hyphenating' India from Pakistan (the US tendency to couple the two countries had long infuriated India) and, instead, thinking of 'India as an element in China's calculation'. India, suggested Condoleezza, who was already an influential adviser to President Bush and was to later become his national security adviser and secretary of state, 'is not a great power yet, but it has the potential to emerge as one'. The US, she suggested, must help India so emerge.

It was against this backdrop that the first Bush administration launched the NSSP, to enable cooperation in civilian nuclear activities, civilian space programmes and high-technology trade. While India had addressed US nuclear proliferation concerns, the US had addressed some export-control issues, easing trade in dual-use technologies required by India's space programme and civil nuclear programme. But enough progress had not been made by the time the government changed in New Delhi.

Dr Singh decided to pursue this dialogue. In his very first address to the nation on 24 June 2004 he specifically said that he would 'welcome the expansion of cooperation between the two governments to include new and mutually beneficial areas, particularly high technology'. High technology was the euphemism for nuclear technology, but also referred to space, defence and advanced computer technology. These words reflected a conversation that had already been initiated by Mani Dixit on the NSSP with the Bush administration during the visit to New Delhi of Ken Juster, the US co-chair of the US–India High Technology Cooperation Group, and Richard Armitage, then US assistant secretary of defence. Dixit instructed S. Jaishankar, who took charge as the joint secretary dealing with the US, to end the impasse on the NSSP and bring the process to fruition. Jaishankar travelled to Washington DC and between him and India's ambassador, Ronen Sen, they were able to get an agreement on the NSSP by mid-September. This paved the way for the official announcement of a Bush–PM meeting later that month in New York on the sidelines of the UN General Assembly.

The meeting in New York between Dr Singh and President Bush went off better than expected. The two were able to have a one-on-one conversation with Mani Dixit discreetly holding Foreign Minister Natwar Singh back in the anteroom. At the time I thought it was Mani's way of keeping Natwar out of that conversation for political, perhaps ideological, reasons, assuming Natwar would not be enthusiastic about improving relations with the US. Only later did I come to understand the intense nature of the 'turf war' between the two and their battle to be the real architects of the UPA's foreign policy. After Mani's death, and before Narayanan became more familiar with the US account,

Natwar in fact played a constructive role, as it became clear by the time the PM went to Washington DC in July 2005. Bush was extremely deferential towards the older Singh, repeatedly calling him 'Sir', and the two seemed relaxed in each other's company.

On 29 September 2004, days after Dr Singh's meeting with President Bush, the US government announced further movement on the NSSP. Dubbing this 'Phase One of the NSSP', the 29 September announcement said the US and India would work towards closer cooperation in these areas in phase two of the NSSP. The visit to India in December 2004 of US defence secretary Donald Rumsfeld was the next milestone. It showed that a key Bush aide had joined the President in wanting to pursue closer strategic relations with India, overruling the traditional India sceptics in the State Department. Close on the heels of Rumsfeld's visit, the tsunami that hit the Indian coast on Christmas Eve offered an unexpected early opportunity for cooperation between the two navies.

Mani Dixit's death in January 2005 briefly disrupted the process because Narayanan was relatively new to the nitty-gritty issues relating to India's nuclear programme. Among senior officials, the person best informed was Ronen Sen, at the time India's ambassador to the US. He had served as secretary to the Atomic Energy Commission and was *au fait* with nuclear policy. But given that the Indian bureaucracy functions in silos, and given the PMO's obsession about remaining in command, the ambassador in a distant capital was not easily drawn into the dialogue process. Moreover, there was considerable resistance to working with the US, leave alone trusting the US, within India's diplomatic and scientific establishment, dating back to the dark days of the Cold War.

After a bout of cooperation in the aftermath of China's attack on India in 1962, Indo-US relations went through a turbulent, often contentious, phase with the events around the liberation and creation of Bangladesh marking the nadir. Nowhere in the Indian system was the hostility towards the US more palpable, and with good reason, than in its nuclear establishment. Not only had the US, through the NPT, helped legitimize China's status as a nuclear weapons power, but it also looked the other way when China actively collaborated with Pakistan to help the latter emerge as a nuclear power.

On the other hand, the US continued to impose draconian controls on high-technology and defence-equipment sales to India in the name of non-proliferation. More than one generation of Indian nuclear scientists had worked hard, in the face of US sanctions, to develop India's nuclear capability and they deeply resented US official attitude towards India's nuclear aspirations. Even within the Indian foreign service many egos had been bruised because of the rough manner in which US diplomats would deal with what they often regarded as 'sanctimonious' Indian diplomats.

The turning point came in March 2005 when the newly appointed US secretary of state Condoleezza Rice chose to make New Delhi her first port of call on a whistle-stop tour of Asia. Rice laid out a broad new agenda of bilateral cooperation, including on the defence and energy fronts. New Delhi woke up to the potential of a new phase in relations with the US and, in April 2005, Dr Singh sent Natwar Singh and Montek to Washington DC. After an unexpected audience with President Bush in the White House, Natwar returned home with the message that Bush was 'extremely excited' about the state of India–US relations.

Condoleezza's outreach on cooperation in the field of energy security became the talking point for Bush and Dr Singh when they met again on the ramparts of the Kremlin on 9 May 2005, the sixtieth anniversary of World War II's Victory Day. Dr Singh and Mrs Kaur were witnessing the parade when President Bush walked up to them, holding his wife Laura's hand.

'Laura, you must meet the Indian prime minister,' Bush said to his wife. 'You know India is a democracy of over a billion people, with so many religions and languages and their economy is on the rise, and this man is leading it.'

He then turned to Dr Singh and said that he thought if India had to sustain its growth it needed assured energy. He suggested they talk about it during Dr Singh's visit to the US that summer and added, 'We can do great things together.'

Dr Singh returned to Delhi convinced that the US was ready to take a big step forward to help India develop nuclear energy as part of the 'next steps'. On 4 June he went to the Bhabha Atomic Research Centre in Mumbai and delivered an important address on taking forward the dialogue on nuclear energy development. Praising India's nuclear scientists for their contribution, Dr Singh said the time had come for the country to benefit from an expansion of its energy programme, so that by the year 2020 India could generate 20,000 megawatts of nuclear power. Towards this end, he pointed out, India needed access to nuclear fuel and technology, and an end to the sanctions that impeded trade in this field. Emphasizing India's record as a 'responsible nuclear power', Dr Singh added, 'While we are determined to utilize fully the advanced technologies in our possession—both civilian and strategic—we are also prepared for a constructive dialogue with the international community to remove hindrances to a free flow of nuclear materials, technology and knowhow.'

This was a clear signal to the world, in particular the US, that India would like to do business. Dr Singh's problem was to convince sceptics on his side. Apart from the residual anti-Americanism in the Indian policy establishment, many in the Congress party were also not keen on closer ties with an administration that was being viewed with great animosity in the Muslim world. Even though opinion polls showed that both the US, as a country, and President Bush, as a leader, were very popular in India, neither enjoyed that popularity within the Muslim minority.

The other, even more pressing, political problem was that the UPA government was dependent for its survival on the Left Front, and the Indian Left was still very anti-US. In short, the wider political context was not favourable to the pursuit of closer ties with the US. If India was unwilling to signal a new warmth in the relationship, it was unlikely that even a friendly administration would go out of its way to grant India the huge favour of ending its nuclear isolation.

Robert Blackwill, the American ambassador in Delhi during Bush's first term, put it pithily at one of his famous 'round-table dinners' in Roosevelt House, the US ambassador's home in Delhi: 'India wants US support for Security Council membership, for its case on Kashmir, for recognition of its nuclear power status, for modernizing its economy and its defence capability. So what will India give the US in return?'

Indian politicians and diplomats were not yet attuned to such a transactional relationship with the US, but they knew that the Bush administration would expect something, and they were not yet prepared to offer anything substantial. Aware of the wariness not just towards America, but the West as a whole, Dr Singh decided to bring some intellectual heft to the discussion. He chose the subject of India's relations with the West as the broad theme for his special convocation address at Oxford University in July 2005, days before his US visit.

Speaking in Oxford's imposing seventeenth-century convocation hall, Dr Singh quoted Rabindranath Tagore in support of his worldview. Tagore had written in his Nobel Prize-winning collection of poems, *Gitanjali*, 'The West has today opened its door. / There are treasures for us to take. / We will take and we will also give, / From the open shores of India's immense humanity.'

So saying, Dr Singh added, 'To see the India–British relationship as one of "give and take", at the time when he first did so, was an act of courage and statesmanship. It was, however, also an act of great foresight. As we look back and also look ahead, it is clear that the Indo-British relationship is one of "give and take". The challenge before us today is to see how we can take this mutually beneficial relationship forward in the increasingly interdependent and globalized world that we live in.'

Many in the audience, including *The Hindu*'s chief editor N. Ram, walked up to Dr Singh and complimented him for his 'visionary' speech. However, a misreading of his speech by the London-based *Times of India* reporter, who was not even present in Oxford, resulted in a front-page story accusing Dr Singh of 'genuflecting before the Empire'. Both the BJP and the communists instantly attacked him. Since Ram had praised the PM, I urged him to write an editorial explaining why he thought the PM's speech was 'visionary' and he agreed to do so. However, the next day he called to say that Irfan Habib, the Marxist historian, and Prabhat Patnaik, the Marxist economist, had penned a strong attack against the PM and it would be difficult for him to editorially defend him. Ram, like Irfan and Prabhat, was a member of the CPI(M). For that matter, even Congress party spokespersons told beat reporters that Dr Singh should not have said what he did, even though the PM had quoted Mahatma Gandhi, Jawaharlal Nehru and Rabindranath Tagore in support of his views!

This setback did not deter Dr Singh from persisting with his view that the time had come for India to renegotiate its relations with the West. He continued to believe that the ending of what K. Subrahmanyam famously dubbed as 'nuclear apartheid' against India, was an important step in that process. Ties with the US got a boost when India and the US agreed to cooperate in the field of defence procurement and exercises that year. The initiatives taken during Condoleezza's visit to India in March that year were pursued by Defence Minister Pranab Mukherjee during his visit to Washington DC in June. He signed a defence framework agreement with the US, setting the stage for the PM's visit in July.

However, on the nuclear deal, the Indian establishment remained deeply divided. There were two sources of dissent. The DAE was, understandably, suspicious of US intentions in befriending India after years of keeping India out of the nuclear club. Subrahmanyam dubbed US critics of India's nuclear programme the 'Ayatollahs of nuclear non-proliferation'. While Subrahmanyam himself had come around to accepting President Bush's sincerity in ending this regime and encouraged Dr Singh to trust the US, the 'hawks' in the DAE remained deeply suspicious, arguing that the US was seeking to trap India into technological dependency aimed at ending India's strategic autonomy. On our flight to Washington DC in July 2005, DAE secretary Anil Kakodkar gave me a lecture on US perfidy and declared emphatically, 'I will never trust the Americans.' While his anger and suspicion were understandable, Dr Singh wanted to seize the opportunity being provided and end India's isolation so that India's nuclear energy programme would develop, without its strategic programme being impacted. This was the deal on offer. A second source of dissent came from old Cold War ideologues who were unwilling to accept that in the post-Cold War world the US was looking for new partnerships and India would benefit from such a partnership. They held the view that the US would never allow India to emerge as an independent strategic power. Both strands of opinion within the government were used by the Left Front and the BJP to constantly attack the PM in public. When I told some journalists that the DAE scientists and some MEA diplomats were overstepping their brief, and that in a democracy policy is made by the political leadership and not by officials, I was criticized by some of them for, as they put it in complaints to the PM, speaking out of turn.

While negotiations between officials of the DAE, the ministry of external affairs and the PMO on the Indian side, and State Department and White House officials on the US side, carried on through this period, Dr Singh and Bush had another round of conversation on the sidelines of the G-8 plus 5 summit at Gleneagles in Scotland in early July. Even as back-channel talks continued and there was another round of conversation between Dr Singh and Bush in the G-8 plus 5 summit in Scotland, there was no meeting of minds on the Indian side. Heated arguments between MEA and DEA officials continued even on board the prime minister's special flight, Air India One, as we flew from Delhi to DC for the PM's US visit.

During the stopover in Frankfurt, Dr Singh, pondering over the challenges that lay ahead, appeared preoccupied. If he was unable to get his own people to agree to a common position, how would he negotiate with the US when the other side was rife with India-baiters and non-proliferationists. However, when he landed in DC he was pleasantly surprised to find Natwar Singh appearing optimistic and willing to help him strike a deal. After a meeting with Condoleezza, Natwar went across to Blair House, the US President's guest house, where Dr Singh was staying, to brief the PM. He brought good news—the US was willing to address some of India's concerns. More importantly, President Bush had let it be known to his staff that he wanted Dr Singh's visit to bear fruit. The Indian delegation discussed issues late into the night but their differences with their US interlocutors remained.

Early next morning, Condoleezza came over to meet the PM, in an effort to break the impasse, and then went back to the White House to have breakfast with President Bush. Her efforts did not bear fruit, as naysayers on both sides held up an agreement. Even as the President and the PM met in the Oval Room, and had a substantial conversation on a wide variety of issues, their officials had still not come up with an agreed text. A press briefing had been arranged at noon to catch Indian newspaper deadlines.

Briefing the PM in the Oval Room before he came out to face the media, the only advice I could give him was that his body language should exude confidence and suggest that he had achieved what he had wanted. Keep smiling and look confident, that will do for now, I said. After that, the PM was to go to the State Department for a lunch in his honour. With no agreement reached as yet, a bland press statement had to be issued. It was read by the media as a clear sign that the expected breakthrough had not happened.

Just as we left the White House for Foggy Bottom, the home of the State Department, Jaishankar came hurriedly to me, showed a thumbs-up and said, 'It's done!'

The negotiations had gone down to the wire. Both leaders had virtually commanded their aides to iron out their differences and produce a mutually acceptable joint statement before the day was out. The assertion of political leadership over bureaucratic and technocratic objections, in both camps, made all the difference.

It was decided that the joint statement would be made public only after another round of talks between the officials after lunch. Till then, mum was the word. But I was worried about newspaper deadlines in India. It was already approaching midnight back home and newspapers would soon be put to bed. We had to get the headline out in time for readers to see it when they opened their newspapers the next morning. I took the PM's permission to brief a couple of senior journalists, N. Ravi of The Hindu and C. Raja Mohan of the Indian Express, who could be relied upon to keep their stories ready, ask their editors in India to delay printing but not reveal the news till they got the green signal.

This arrangement proved to be useful, since by the time the joint statement was released, it was too late for most newspapers to carry it.

News channels were able to report it in their early morning bulletins on 19 July. While *The Hindu*'s conservative desk staff gave the story a bland headline that said 'Manmohan Expresses Satisfaction over Talks', Ravi's 'informed' report said it all:

> In a significant development after the meeting that Prime Minister Manmohan Singh had with American President George Bush at the White House, the United States, acknowledging India as a nuclear weapons power, agreed to cooperate with it in the area of civilian nuclear energy. This formulation was part of the joint statement to be issued following the talks, according to a highly-placed official source.

What exactly had Dr Singh achieved? In the joint statement, the US had recognized that 'as a responsible state with advanced nuclear technology', a phrase devised to recognize India's nuclear capability without declaring it a nuclear weapons power, India 'should acquire the same benefits and advantages as other such states'.

The US had agreed to help develop India's nuclear power industry and, to this end, would seek Congressional approval of the required changes to US laws that would enable US companies to export nuclear fuel and technology to India. Apart from easing restrictions on the sale of fuel for the Tarapur atomic power station, the US also agreed to work with other countries to help India get access to uranium. This meant changing the existing restrictions imposed by the Nuclear Suppliers Group (NSG).

In return for this, India agreed to 'assume the same responsibilities and practices and acquire the same benefits and advantages as other leading countries with advanced nuclear technology, such as the United States'. An important Indian commitment was to separate civilian and military nuclear facilities and programmes, and place civilian facilities under the IAEA safeguards regime. India also renewed its commitment, made unilaterally by the Vajpayee government in May 1998, that it would not conduct any more nuclear tests.

The subsidiary commitments included working towards a multilateral Fissile Material Cut-Off Treaty and refraining from transfer of enrichment and reprocessing technologies to countries that do not have them. India also agreed to sign up to the Missile Technology Control Regime and NSG guidelines. All this was nothing more than an assurance that India would adhere to its already existing stellar record as a non-proliferator of nuclear technology.

The critical next step was for the US to secure Congressional approval of changes to its laws that would enable the US President to offer India access to high- and dual-use technologies. Once India signed what was called the 123 Agreement, the US Congress would be able to change the relevant laws.

The 18 July joint statement opened the door for these negotiations. Dr Singh had made history. In the midst of our euphoria, however, we little imagined that the process would finally end only thirty-nine months later, after hundreds of heated hours of debate in Parliament, many days of excruciating negotiations around the world, and the reconstitution of the UPA alliance.

The summit meeting at the White House was followed the next day by the PM's address to the joint session of the US Congress. It was a speech written with care and deliberation by Montek and myself, with important inputs from Jaishankar. Dr Singh rehearsed his delivery diligently. Since US audiences like to applaud well-crafted sentences, the punchlines were underlined so that he knew which sentences to emphasize and when to pause, in case there was applause.

Dr Singh entered the hall to a standing ovation and, as he made his way down the aisle, he was repeatedly stopped for handshakes, the longest stop being with Senator Hillary Clinton. Usually, Dr Singh was a weak orator. The only occasion on which he made an effort to speak clearly and loudly, emphasizing key phrases, was when he delivered the Independence Day address. However, he knew the US Congress speech was a historic foreign policy statement to an important audience. His listeners were the very Congressmen and women who would have to give their vote of approval to the nuclear deal that he was seeking to strike with President Bush. The purpose of this speech was to win over their hearts and minds. He rose to the occasion.

As Jaishankar and I sat with copies of the speech, pen in hand to mark statements that were applauded, we found him being applauded for every minute of speaking time. The prime minister, we later noted, had been interrupted no less than thirty-three times. It was a 3000-word speech. In his early days in office, Dr Singh would read 100 words in a minute. As he aged, his pace slowed down to seventy-five to eighty words per minute. At this rate, the address should normally have taken him a little over thirty minutes. It, in fact, took close to forty-five minutes, because of the frequent ovations—some brief, about five to ten seconds, some long and some standing.

Sure, there were many India sceptics in that audience and some would later actively try to block the nuclear deal. But that morning, the halls of the US Congress reverberated to unending applause for a man who spoke candidly and honestly, and presented India in a new light to a new world.

'Partnerships can be of two kinds,' he said as he ended his address. 'There are partnerships based on principle and there are partnerships based on pragmatism. I believe we are at a juncture where we can embark on a partnership that can draw both on principle as well as pragmatism.'

With each round of applause, we could see Dr Singh's confidence grow, his voice rise and his articulation become clearer. It was very moving to see and feel the palpable admiration for this shy, diminutive turbaned man trying to alter the destiny of the world's biggest democracy.

———

In another era, with a different prime minister, like Indira Gandhi or Rajiv Gandhi, the Congress party would have had its members lining the streets of Delhi to welcome the PM back after such a historic visit. That was not to be. Not only did the Left Front and the BJP manage to put the Congress on the defensive with their knee-jerk condemnation of the agreement even before the PM explained its details to them, there were also internal worries that the PM's bonhomie with President Bush would alienate the party's Muslim vote base and encourage the traditionally anti-US Left to destabilize the minority government.

Within ten days of returning home, Dr Singh made a statement in Parliament allaying fears that there was a 'secret deal' behind the public one, and denying that India was entering into a military alliance with the US against China. He also assured the Parliament that the negotiations with the US to work out the separation plan and other details would not hurt India's strategic nuclear programme. The media believed the PM, but the BJP and the Left refused to do so. The Left's opposition was ideological, given its traditional anti-US stance. The BJP's was expedient, given that it was the Vajpayee government that had initiated a dialogue with the US to get this very result.

As the negotiations progressed, Dr Singh discovered that he had to handle far too many egos at home. The debate on the nuclear deal got enmeshed, on the one hand, with domestic political battles both within the ruling Congress party and with the Opposition, and on the other, with inter-ministerial turf battles, especially between the DAE and the ministry of external affairs.

A considerable part of Dr Singh's time was taken up explaining the deal to his party leadership and the Opposition, and handling critics and opponents within the government, especially the DAE. The DAE had to not only overcome its trust deficit with the US, created by years of US sanctions, but also its lack of trust in the PM. He was seen as a pacifist who was opposed to nuclear weaponization and, therefore, likely to sell India cheap.

Some of Dr Singh's critics spread the word that he had not only cut the DAE's budget as finance minister, but had also opposed a plan to conduct nuclear tests in the winter of 1995. This was only half-true. Narasimha Rao did consider the option of testing in 1995 but chose not to do so because the ministry of finance had estimated that the economy would not be able to bear the burden of the sanctions that developed countries would impose on India. Later, in 1998, the Vajpayee government, too, calculated the economic cost of testing, and took several steps to neutralize the likely impact of sanctions, which in the end turned out to be much less than feared. This was partly because, in 1998, the economy was stronger than it had been in 1995. But India's nuclear hawks preferred to see the issue in simplistic terms.

Dr Singh realized that he had to build a wider constituency of support for his initiative within the government and not allow the DAE to have a veto. Towards this end, he created the ECC in July 2005, including in it ministers from all energy-related ministries, which brought in Finance Minister Chidambaram and Power Minister Sushil Kumar Shinde, politically influential and supportive of the PM; the DAE was just one of the many departments dealing with energy policy represented here. This omnibus group was tasked to create a wider energy policy framework within which, it was hoped, negotiations with the US could be explained to the domestic political audience. It is a different matter that over time the DAE secured a veto over the deal mainly by using the political opposition to bolster its own position as a reluctant party to the deal.

After the ECC's first meeting on 6 August 2005, a PMO press release said:

> The Prime Minister said that India must invest in nuclear energy and the recent steps he has taken to end India's global isolation in this regard should help the country increase the share of nuclear energy in the overall energy mix of the economy. Dr Anil Kakodkar, Secretary, Department of Atomic Energy, also emphasized the need for India to import uranium and invest in uranium mining to meet the requirements of nuclear power generation. He drew attention to the fact that the price of domestically mined uranium is 4 to 5 times that of imported uranium. Several participants complimented the Prime Minister for successfully concluding a deal with the United States that would enable India to import uranium for nuclear power projects.

The PMO spared no effort to educate public and political opinion on the agreement and Dr Singh spoke at length in both Houses of Parliament. Diplomats Jayant Prasad and S. Jaishankar, both of whom had intimate knowledge of the nuclear deal, helped me prepare a booklet, 'Facts about India's Initiative for Seeking International Cooperation in Civil Nuclear Energy', that was then translated into all Indian languages and published by the Directorate of Advertising and Visual Publicity (DAVP) of the ministry of information and broadcasting. While the essence of the deal was a strategic gain for India, in that India's isolation within the international nuclear regime would end, the gains were projected to the general public as an easing of the domestic energy supply situation. Ordinary people across the country would easily understand that, deprived as they are of assured electricity.

Between August 2005 and February 2006, the negotiations focused on the separation plan. India had a total of twenty-two nuclear power plants in 2005. The US side suggested that India could classify four of these as required for its strategic programme. The Indian side wanted eight of the twenty-two, including two research reactors, classified as part of its strategic programme, with fourteen separated out as civilian facilities that would be brought under IAEA safeguards. For seven months these negotiations went on with no agreement.

———

President Bush was scheduled to visit India on 2 March and even a fortnight ahead of his visit, there was no agreement on a separation plan. Without a separation plan the Bush administration would not be able to go to the Congress to secure its approval of the deal. If the two sides were unable to arrive at an agreement, the Bush visit would be long on rhetoric and short on substance.

On Wednesday, 22 February, Rama and I went to Andhra Bhavan for dinner. We were in 'mid-thaali' when my mobile phone rang. It was a 3 RCR number. It was the PM himself, summoning me. I forced Rama to forgo dessert and we drove straight to the PM's house.

While noting the urgency in the PM's voice, I thought I was being summoned for a discussion on his reply the next morning to the debate in the Lok Sabha on the motion of thanks for the President's address to the Parliament. I had drafted his reply and felt he might want to go over some points I had made. At RCR, Rama chose to wait in the car park assuming I would be back soon.

When I reached 3 RCR, Dr Singh was seated in his living room looking distraught. 'We do not have an agreement as yet and President Bush is coming in a week's time. I don't think this nuclear agreement will go through,' he said.

I was not prepared for this. I had not been in the loop on the ongoing negotiations and was unaware that they were on the verge of breaking down. The Indian side still wanted a 14:8 division between civilian and military reactors, while the American side had not budged from its position of 18:4. Moreover, the Indian side was particularly keen on keeping the two research reactors out of IAEA safeguards. The PM was clear in his mind that his government had made its best offer and would not back down. It was up to the American side to agree, or close the negotiations and walk away. The latter would be disastrous, given the political capital the PM had already expended on this matter. Clearly, he was worried.

He also believed that the deadlock was only at the level of the negotiators and if President Bush were made aware of this, he would get the American negotiators to back off and accept Indian terms. 'When I explained to President Bush what we would be able to accept, he was okay with that,' he said. 'He kept repeating to me that it was not his intention to hurt India's strategic capability. So I do not think this US insistence on eighteen has his approval. He needs to be made aware of the deadlock so that he can intervene with his people.'

I realized Dr Singh was wondering if there was any way I could help. I imagined he must have reached out to other interlocutors as well. I knew my friend Ashley Tellis, who had access to people in the White House, was already in Delhi. Maybe he could convey a message to the White House. Offering to try, I went back to the car park and called Ashley. We agreed to meet for breakfast at his hotel the next morning.

I first met Ashley as a member of an India–US 'track two' group sponsored by the Confederation of Indian Industry and the Aspen Strategy Group, a high-powered US think tank. An Indian American from Goa, Ashley had made his mark as a bright spark on the foreign policy and strategic affairs think tank circuit in the US. After the Pokhran-II nuclear tests, he wrote an authoritative book on India's nuclear strategy. He came to be noticed in India's policymaking circles when US ambassador Robert Blackwill inducted Ashley as his adviser in the US embassy in Delhi. Ashley was the perfect interlocutor between India and the US. He understood both systems well and was committed to good relations between the two democracies. He had acquired impeccable professional credentials as an 'American' analyst, while developing friendships in India based on trust. I certainly knew I could trust him.

Over breakfast, we discussed all the options and the offers the two sides had made to each other on the separation plan. I conveyed Dr Singh's view that a 14:8 separation plan was India's bottom line and that Dr Singh felt President Bush would approve the Indian offer, if only he were made aware of it. Ashley said this would be difficult to sell with the anti-deal 'non-proliferation lobby' in the US Congress. He felt the second-best deal possible would be one where India committed to 14 in the first round and agreed to go up to 18 by a specified date, like 2014 or 2016 at the latest. He was also not sure if the US side would agree to the Indian demand to keep fast breeder research reactors outside the civilian category.

Having offered his own views, Ashley agreed to convey Dr Singh's message to his contacts in the White House. When I drove to 3 RCR and told the PM what had transpired with Ashley, he was disappointed. 'This will not work,' he mumbled. It seemed as if he had not slept through the night.

Later that morning, he drove to Parliament to reply to the debate on the motion of thanks to the President's address. He spoke at length about almost every issue that was raised in the debate but, surprisingly, made no reference at all to the state of the negotiations on the Indo-US nuclear agreement, or what he expected from the Bush visit a few days later. He ended his lengthy, mostly extempore statement by defending his vision of Indian foreign policy and concluded:

Sir, this House has my solemn assurance that in pursuing our foreign policy, in ensuring our national security, and in promoting our economic development, our government will always have the nation's interest uppermost in our mind. I do believe we have the trust and confidence of the people of India.

Four days later, on 27 February, Dr Singh made a lengthy suo moto statement in Parliament, virtually setting out India's terms for an agreement. This statement was aimed partly at reassuring domestic critics of the deal and partly at drawing public red lines on what was on offer to the US. His lengthy statement pressed all the right buttons for various constituencies at home and abroad. On the key issue of the separation plan it said:

> ...our proposed Separation Plan entails identifying in phases, a number of our thermal nuclear reactors as civilian facilities to be placed under IAEA safeguards, amounting to roughly 65% of the total installed thermal nuclear power capacity, by the end of the Separation Plan. A list of some other DAE facilities may be added to the list of facilities within the civilian domain. The Separation Plan will create a clearly defined civilian domain, where IAEA safeguards apply. On our part, we are committed not to divert any nuclear material intended for the civilian domain from designated civilian use or for export to third countries without safeguards.

The percentage specified indicated that only fourteen plants would be on offer for separation. The DAE had obviously rejected Ashley's 'second option' and forced the PM to state India's bottom line in Parliament, thus closing any window for negotiation. It was a take-it-or-leave-it stand. US negotiators were reportedly livid. Till the very last minute, they did not relent.

On the evening of 1 March, President Bush was received at

Palam airport by Dr Singh. As he got into his car, Bush turned to M.K. Narayanan and, placing his hands on Narayanan's shoulder and making direct eye contact with him, he said, loud enough for others around to hear, 'I want that deal!'

The negotiating teams on both sides got the message. President Bush was making it clear to everyone, on his side and ours, that whatever differences were still holding up an agreement should be resolved overnight so that by the next morning, when he sat down with Dr Singh for the formal summit meeting, the agreement would be ready for the two leaders' signatures.

Indian and US negotiators burnt the midnight oil narrowing their differences so that they could report back to their leaders the next morning that they now had a deal. At 8.30 a.m. on the morning of 2 March, I arrived at the forecourt of Rashtrapati Bhavan for the ceremonial welcome of the President. Soldiers from the army, navy and air force were smartly lined up for the guard of honour. As senior ministers and officials arrived one by one and took their allotted seats, Ronen Sen walked up to me and indicated that most differences had been ironed out and things should fall into place in time for the two leaders to make an announcement.

Referring to a conversation he had with Pranab Mukherjee, at the time defence minister (referred to in official parlance as raksha mantri, and therefore RM), whose support for the nuclear deal was not fully assured till then, Ronen added, 'I spoke to RM. He is now supportive. He understands the importance of getting the deal and the dangers of it falling through. We have him on our side.'

Pranab's support for the deal was in some doubt mainly because, according to some political observers, it was felt he may want to remain in the good books of the CPI(M) given his dependence on the Left to get re-elected to the Lok Sabha from West Bengal. Ronen's outreach to Pranab and the reassuring reply was, therefore, helpful.

I saw the PM's motorcade arrive at the forecourt and walked up to Dr Singh. He looked preoccupied. After he finished greeting his ministerial colleagues, he turned to me, saying, 'So?' in a matter-of-fact way. That was always my cue to offer him the latest news or gossip. I briefed him on what Ronen had just mentioned to me.

'Can I trust him?' he asked, referring to the defence minister. I said there was no reason why Pranab would lie to Ronen. If he had assured Ronen of his cooperation, then we should trust him. But, I added that there was no harm in Dr Singh having another word with Pranab before the formal meetings at Hyderabad House.

President Abdul Kalam's motorcade arrived and soon we heard the guns boom, announcing the entry of President Bush's carcade into the Rashtrapati Bhavan forecourt. After the twenty-one-gun salute, the guard of honour and other formalities, the two heads of state went their separate ways. Dr Singh walked up to Pranab and the two drove down together to South Block.

At Hyderabad House, Dr Singh and President Bush were closeted together for thirty minutes, with officials on both sides still discussing the fine print of the joint statement in another room. When the two delegations finally met, it was Condoleezza Rice who spoke first and informed President Bush, 'We have an agreement.' All the tension in the air evaporated. President Bush was his warm and jovial self and Dr Singh wouldn't stop smiling.

The 2 March 2006 agreement accepted the Indian red lines, as specified by the PM and conveyed to Ashley a week earlier. India was required to place under IAEA safeguards only fourteen power reactors, with an installed thermal power capacity that would amount to 65 per cent of the total capacity by 2014. The US side also agreed that India would not accept safeguards on the two fast breeder research reactors at Kalpakkam. Finally, it was agreed that the Indian government would determine which of the twenty-two plants would be classified as civilian and which would be set aside for the strategic programme. Bush and the PM had satisfied the DAE.

The Bush visit was a great success and a shot in the arm for Dr Singh. Whatever his political image, at a personal level Bush was warm and friendly. Being shy and a poor conversationalist, Dr Singh always relaxed in the company of men who were gregarious, and took an instant liking to Bush. When the two first met in New York in September 2004, Bush was deferential and, rather surprisingly for an American President, kept addressing Dr Singh as 'Sir'. By the time they met in Delhi in March 2006, the two had become buddies. Bush's gesture of placing his arm around Dr Singh's shoulder as the two walked towards the media was frowned upon by some Indian diplomats and journalists, who read it as a patronizing one. But to me, watching from close quarters, he seemed to be treating Dr Singh like a 'buddy' in a natural sort of way. They clearly had good personal chemistry and that played a key role in bringing the nuclear deal to fruition.

In the months that followed, Indian officials had to present their separation plan to the US to enable the US government to secure Congressional approval. Amendments to US law, namely the US Atomic Energy Act, were made through the Henry J. Hyde Act of December 2006. This enabled the US government to then conclude the 123 Agreement with India that would enable the two countries to resume trade in nuclear fuel and technology. All these processes were long drawn-out and full of controversy. Naysayers on both sides tried their best, at every stage, to sabotage the deal.

The legislative process in the US was as contentious as it was in India. Many US lawmakers were not convinced by President Bush's arguments in favour of an India-specific exemption and argued that this would encourage nuclear proliferation by other powers. In India, both the BJP and the Left parties ganged up against Dr Singh. Many tried to fish in these troubled waters.

Every now and then someone or the other would come and tell me that a plot was afoot to unseat Dr Singh since his insistence on the deal had become an embarrassment for the Congress. Sometimes, even senior Cabinet ministers would walk into my room whispering conspiracy theories and advising me to carry them to the PM.

What complicated the politics of the nuclear deal was the US's insistence that India too demonstrate its willingness to address US security concerns. This was the 'Blackwill Question'—what was India prepared to do for the US in exchange for what India expected the US to do for it? Rahul Gandhi had captured the idea well when he paraphrased John Kennedy's famous line—'ask not what your country can do for you, ask what you can do for your country'—and said in the Lok Sabha during the debate on the vote of confidence sought by Dr Singh in July 2008: 'What is important is that we stop worrying about how the world will impact us . . . and we step out and worry about how we will impact the world.' That was the question the US was posing at the time. How did India intend to impact the world around it? Would this accord well with the interests of the United States?

It was clear that the test of true love would be India's position on Iran's nuclear programme. Dr Singh had already stated in interviews to the US media that India's stance was clear. Iran should adhere to its commitments as a signatory to the NPT. Since Iran was an NPT beneficiary as a non-weapons power, it should adhere to the terms of NPT which, among other things, required Iran to be transparent about its civilian nuclear programme and committed it to full adherence to IAEA inspections and protocols.

This was not an anti-Iran position. It merely stated the obvious. However, US lawmakers and the media sought even more explicit statements and Dr Singh finally gave one when he told the media in the US that India did not wish to see any more nuclear weapons powers in its neighbourhood. By asserting that it was in India's interest to see no new nuclear powers emerging in its neighbourhood, Dr Singh defined his government's stance on Iran's nuclear programme in terms of India's national interest and not as a gesture to the US. It was a view that no Indian political party could have objected to. Yet, there were critics in India, especially in the Left. They interpreted the PM's categorical statement as 'kowtowing' to the US.

It was against this background that Dr Singh was required to take a view on a resolution that Germany, France and Britain (EU-3) put up for vote at the IAEA. The resolution stated that Iran had breached its IAEA commitments and called on Iran to adhere to these while stating that the matter be resolved at the IAEA itself. While supporting the resolution in principle, India disagreed with parts of the resolution to demonstrate its independent position.

The politics of how this position was arrived at was important. Dr Singh was in Chandigarh on 24 September when the EU-3 resolution came up for voting. Natwar Singh called him late in the evening to seek his guidance on how India should vote. Natwar was in New York at the UN. His own view was that India should be on the side of the majority. Dr Singh agreed and suggested that he seek the views of Sonia Gandhi and the members of the CSS, which meant Pranab, Chidambaram and Shivraj Patil. Once Natwar ensured that they were all on board, Dr Singh asked him to convey the government's view to the Indian ambassador to the IAEA.

Twenty-two countries voted in support of the EU-3 resolution, twelve abstained and only Venezuela voted against it. India went along with the majority. The important thing was that the CCS took a unanimous view on this. Yet, stories were planted in the media that the decision on the Iran vote at the IAEA was that of Dr Singh alone. This appealed to the Left and suited its interpretation of what was happening. Months later, when the IAEA voted to take the matter to the UN Security Council, Russia and China, which had abstained in September, voted with the majority, vindicating India's stance.

The politics of the Iran vote had less to do with India's foreign policy than with domestic concerns about the voting preferences of India's Shia community, on the grounds that they felt an affiliation with Shia-majority Iran. Dr Singh refused to accept the view that the Shia community would not support an initiative that was in the interest of the country. They were Indians first and as patriotic as any other community, he pointed out to those who raised these issues. Dr Singh held steadfastly to that view, refusing to do what he accused Karat of doing, namely of 'communalizing India's foreign policy'.

———

Progress on the India–US negotiations was slow through 2006. On 17 August 2006, Dr Singh put up one of his best performances in Parliament when, at the end of a lengthy debate on the nuclear deal, he presented his case. He listed out the assurances that the Left had sought, popularly referred to as Sitaram Yechury's 'red lines', and assured the Lok Sabha that the final agreement would adhere to these principles. He assured Parliament that India was not giving up its strategic autonomy. But, he pointed out, in order to secure what was India's due, the government had to enter into negotiations that involved some 'give and take', which is what negotiations are all about.

He quoted Machiavelli's *The Prince*, a book I had gifted him on his birthday in September 2004, to say:

> It must be considered that there is nothing more difficult to carry out, nor more doubtful of success, nor more dangerous to handle, than to initiate a new order of things. For the reformer has enemies in all those who profit by the old order, and only lukewarm defenders in all those who would profit from the new order. This lukewarmness arises partly from the fear of their adversaries, who have the laws in their favour; and partly from the incredulity of mankind, who do not truly believe in anything new until they have the experience of it. Thus it arises that on every opportunity for attacking the reformer, his opponents do so with the zeal of partisans, the others only defend him half-heartedly, so that between them he runs a great danger.

Dr Singh admitted that the negotiations he had authorized entailed taking some risk in the hope of making important gains and reassured the House, 'I am aware of the risks, but for India's sake, I am willing to take those risks.'

It was a rare act of courage and political grandstanding that won him applause in Parliament and from across the country. The media finally came to accept that the PM knew what he was doing and that this was an important project that deserved support. A series of public-opinion polls conducted by TV channels and newsmagazines showed overwhelming support for the PM, for the deal and for good Indo-US relations. In the weeks to come, negotiations proceeded apace.

In late 2006, there were two important changes of personnel in the ministry of external affairs. Shivshankar Menon, then India's high commissioner to Pakistan, took charge as foreign secretary and, a month later, Jaishankar was appointed India's high commissioner to Singapore. Shivshankar's appointment happened amidst much drama.

Till the eleventh hour, I thought Shyam Saran would get an extension.

I got an inkling it was otherwise when, just before lunch on 31 August 2006, Pulok Chatterjee walked into my room and asked how much time it would take for an official announcement to be made public.

I said, 'Two minutes.'

He was not convinced. I then explained to him that if I were to send a statement as an SMS text message to any TV channel it would appear as 'breaking news' within a minute. He seemed satisfied and said he might have an important announcement to make once the PM signed the relevant file, and that I should let him know in case I was going out for lunch. After lunch, Pulok walked in again and told me that the PM had cleared the appointment of Shivshankar Menon as foreign secretary.

I sent a text message to editors at three English news channels, namely Rajdeep Sardesai of CNN-IBN, Barkha Dutt of NDTV and Navika Kumar of Times Now. The three channels flashed the news immediately. Minutes later, the MEA's spokesperson, Navtej Sarna, called to check if the news report was correct. I confirmed it. I did not know why the announcement was made in this manner. Some speculated that the secrecy was meant to prevent officers superceded by Menon going to court and securing a stay order on the grounds that due procedure had not been followed. Normally, such an announcement is only made after members of the Appointments Committee of the Cabinet sign the file. In this case, it was made before the file was signed. Perhaps the PMO did not want a controversy before the announcement.

However, the manner of Shivshankar's appointment did become the subject of controversy when an IFS officer complained that her seniority had been overlooked in appointing him and demanded an explanation from the government by appealing to the Central Administrative Tribunal. She also questioned 'the unprecedented manner and timing of the announcement of his [Shivshankar's] appointment by the Prime Minister's Office on Aug 31, 2006, well before the approval of the Appointments Committee of the Cabinet on Sept 4, 2006'. The Central Information Commission accepted the officer's plea that the government owed the officer an explanation for its decision but ultimately dismissed the petition, taking the view that all of this was the PM's prerogative.

Perhaps Dr Singh's mindfulness of the Left's concerns over the India–US nuclear agreement may have led him to give up the idea of giving an extension to Foreign Secretary Shyam Saran, who was handling the negotiations, and overlook the claims of over a dozen foreign service officials, to appoint Shivshankar Menon. On account of Shivshankar's long-standing personal equations and family connections with Left leaders, the Left regarded him as a 'friend'.

These changes of personnel in the MEA coincided with the slowing down of the process of negotiation. Indeed, right through the first half of 2007, negotiations between Indian and US officials proceeded at a slow pace. Officials of the DAE, christened by the media as 'scientists' and therefore somehow given a superior status than the ordinary 'bureaucrats' of other ministries, played their own games.

Once elections to the state assembly in Uttar Pradesh were announced, in early 2007, some DAE officials began to deliberately drag their feet, assuming a victory for Mulayam Singh Yadav and his Samajwadi Party—at the time a critic of the nuclear deal—would weaken Dr Singh. They miscalculated in assuming that Mulayam's public criticism of the nuclear deal was as 'ideological' as that of the Left, rather than just a bargaining chip with which he would eventually seek to strike a deal with the government, for whatever end. One senior DAE scientist–administrator had the audacity to suggest that Mulayam's victory would mean the end of the nuclear deal, if not of Dr Singh himself.

All these were pipe dreams of technocrats nervous about what the impending transformation of India's civil nuclear programme would mean for their own turf. It took a long time for Narayanan to get a grip over the DAE establishment. At one stage, Dr Singh had to prod him to speed up the process by saying to him, 'MK, this agreement should be more important for you than me. I have already made my mark with the economic reforms we launched in 1991. Even if I do not achieve anything as prime minister, I will still be remembered for what I did as finance minister. What about you? Who knows what you have done all your life as an intelligence officer? If you get this agreement done you can publicly claim you have also achieved something.'

When I tried to expose some of these games of DAE officials, a campaign was launched against me in the media by a nuclear scientist who had, in fact, come to me more than once seeking an advisory role in the PMO. By June 2007, impediments had also arisen on the US side and Dr Singh had to raise the issue with President Bush at the G-8 summit at Heiligendamm in Germany. Bush summoned his national security adviser and instructed him to bang heads together in Washington and get the deal done. Worried that on his side the PMO was not able control the negotiations, Dr Singh took the unusual step of redrafting Jaishankar, by then posted in Singapore as high commissioner, into the negotiating process.

Finally, on 3 August 2007, the government was able to make public the 123 Agreement. After a careful reading of the agreement, N. Ram, chief editor of *The Hindu* and a sceptic on the deal, wrote a full-page editorial comment under the headline 'A Sound and Honourable 123'. He wrote enthusiastically.

'It is a sound and honourable agreement and the assurances provided to Parliament by Prime Minister Manmohan Singh in 2006 have been fulfilled virtually in their entirety,' said the editorial. The editorial criticized the BJP for raising ill-informed objections. 'The Manmohan Singh government has won for India the keys to unshackle its nuclear programme from the unfair restrictions it has been subjected to for the past 33 years.'

On reading the editorial, I called Ram and thanked him on Dr Singh's behalf. He sounded ecstatic and was full of praise for the PM. 'Tell the prime minister he has made history!'

I suggested that he should tell that to him personally. Ram agreed to fly down the same day from Chennai. After checking with Dr Singh, I invited Ram to have breakfast with the prime minister the next day. For more than an hour over breakfast, Ram waxed eloquent on the deal, calling it a great achievement for India and a great political coup for the PM.

When Ram left, Dr Singh sat back in his chair looking completely satisfied. He had crossed the rubicon, he thought. Ram was a close friend of Prakash Karat, and himself a long-standing member of the CPM. Dr Singh took Ram's endorsement as a signal from the Left that it would not attack the deal. Rarely had I seen Dr Singh so pleased, so at peace, so content as he was that morning.

An hour or so later Ram called me at my office in South Block. Right after his breakfast meeting with the PM, he had gone off to meet Karat.

'Sanjaya, I have bad news. The Left will not support the 123 Agreement. They will ask the government to put the negotiations on hold.'

This came as a shock. Ram agreed it was so, and said he, too, was surprised. He had spent some time explaining the benefits of the deal to Karat but the latter, he said, was not interested.

'He has taken a political decision,' said Ram. 'It is not about the merits of the deal, but the politics. You have to tell the PM that he should put the deal on hold. Karat will be making a statement asking the government not to operationalize the deal.'

I rushed to RCR to deliver the message to the PM. While driving down I called Sitaram Yechury to seek an explanation. He confirmed Ram's account and said this was Karat's decision and would have to be ratified by the politburo. Yechury sounded displeased and helpless. It was he who had read out in the Rajya Sabha the famous 'red lines' to the government on what would be acceptable to the Left. He agreed now that the 123 Agreement had offered reassurance on every one of the issues raised by the Left and DAE officials. Neither Ram's friendship nor Shivshankar's equations, nor indeed Yechury's best efforts, would come in the way of Karat's decision.

It was clear that Yechury was not happy with Karat's decision. On reaching 7 RCR I conveyed Ram's message and Yechury's remarks to the PM. He was furious. He had been let down by the Left.

Before publicly responding to the Left's rejection of the 123 Agreement, Dr Singh invited its leaders to a briefing and a discussion a couple of days later. All the details of the agreement were presented to them by officials from the DAE and PMO. Shortly after they left the meeting, the Left leaders addressed a press conference rejecting the agreement.

As Dr Singh watched Karat address the press on television, I was struck by the contemptuous manner in which the CPI(M) leader spoke, as he charged the government of giving up India's 'independent foreign policy' and becoming an ally of an imperialist power.

'It is this same "independent foreign policy" that they opposed when they attacked Panditji and Indiraji,' Dr Singh said mockingly as he watched Karat fume and fulminate. When the press conference ended, he became glum and angry.

After several minutes of silence, he got up to go home for dinner, making one last comment, 'The Left have always opposed the Congress on foreign policy when it suited them. They criticized Panditji, they criticized Indiraji, they attacked Narasimha Raoji. Whatever I did as finance minister, they criticized. They criticized non-alignment when it suited them, they supported it when it suited them. As long as I am prime minister, I will not allow these communists to dictate our foreign policy.'

———

A couple of days later, Dr Singh met Manini Chatterjee of the *Telegraph* (Kolkata) in his room in Parliament. She had just taken charge as the *Telegraph*'s Delhi bureau chief and wanted to meet the PM. It was a courtesy call, not an interview, but it turned into one. The prime minister, still angry, was in a talkative mood and was willing to be candid while replying to her questions on the Left's demand. As his remarks became more and more interesting and newsy, Manini realized she had a front-page story. She sought the PM's permission to quote him and report his views. He looked at me. I told him that if he truly felt this way, he owed it to the nation to make his views known. This was an important issue on which his critics were freely offering their criticism. He should not remain silent, I said.

Dr Singh agreed to allow Manini to report what he said. He only insisted that since she had not recorded his remarks on tape she should clear the text of her report with me before its publication. Manini and I sat in an anteroom and shared our notes. She then went to her office, typed out her story and emailed it to me. It was an accurate report and I gave her the green signal.

Next morning, on Saturday 11 August, the *Telegraph* ran the headline 'Anguished PM to Left: If You Want to Withdraw, So Be It'.

The report said, 'Tired of the Left parties' constant bark, Prime Minister Manmohan Singh dared them to bite after their latest diatribe against the Indo–US nuclear deal.' It quoted Dr Singh as saying, 'I told them it is not possible to renegotiate the deal. It is an honourable deal, the Cabinet has approved it, we cannot go back on it. I told them to do whatever they want to do. If they want to withdraw support, so be it.'

The news report sent shock waves around Delhi. Narayanan and Nair called me to find out if the report was accurate. They were not aware of the PM's meeting with Manini, which had taken place in Parliament House while they themselves were in South Block. It is also possible that neither was as aware of the PM's anger and anguish as I had been. They reported that the Congress party's leadership was unhappy with the interview and might want the PM to issue a denial. Since the PM's statements were not taped, felt Narayanan, it should be possible to issue a denial. I was appalled by that line of argument, but kept silent. It occurred to me that they, along with Congress party functionaries, might have already decided to get the PM to issue a denial and to put the blame on me for what Manini had written. I realized that the prime minister might come under pressure from his party, and was not sure what he would do. I returned to my room, read through my own notes of what exactly the PM had said and waited for the summons.

Several journalists called to say that the Congress party was planning to deny the story, saying Dr Singh never issued any such ultimatum to the Left. One senior journalist called to tell me that Ahmed Patel had said to him, 'How can Doctor Saheb issue any such ultimatum to the Left? He did not bring them into an alliance with us, so he cannot ask them to go.'

I waited the whole day for a call from Dr Singh. Would he regret having said what he said? Would he disclaim his remarks and ask me to issue a denial? The phone never rang through the weekend, but there was no official denial either. Meanwhile, Delhi's political circles buzzed with speculation.

On Tuesday, 14 August, a day before Independence Day, Subbu told me, to my surprise, that Dr Singh had decided to drop all references to the 123 Agreement from his address to the nation from the ramparts of the Red Fort. The approved draft had a powerful paragraph taking credit for an achievement for which he had been hailed widely. It was dropped at the eleventh hour. Standing on the ramparts, the PM could have proudly claimed that he had done the nation proud. He had secured for India a new status as a nuclear power. But while he spoke at length about everything else the government had done during the year, his one great achievement that year found no mention at all.

As they walked down the stairs from the ramparts of the Red Fort, leaving the function, ministers, officials and diplomats were puzzled by this omission. Those who knew that I was Dr Singh's speech-writer asked me why there was no reference to the 123 Agreement in the PM's address. I had no answer.

———

While the diplomats had done India proud, negotiating a historic agreement, India's politicians let the country down. The hypocrisy of the Left was exposed by the somersault Ram had to perform on the editorial pages of *The Hindu*. After proclaiming the 123 Agreement 'sound and honourable', he followed up with an editorial a few days later, toeing Karat's line and advising the government to put the deal on hold. And Yechury, who had privately agreed that the PM had done what he had promised to, publicly criticized him.

The Left's opposition evolved from being purely ideological into becoming a political ploy by Karat aimed at marginalizing all the pro-PM elements within his own party. Surjeet, Jyoti Basu, Buddhadeb and Yechury were the moderates. Having upstaged Surjeet, Karat used the issue of opposition to the nuclear deal as a way of consolidating his own position within the CPM. The CPI was uncomfortable with Karat's rigid opposition. CPI leaders D. Raja and S. Sudhakar Reddy knew me well, especially the latter, whom I had known from my student days in Hyderabad. He was a disciple of Mohit Sen. He came home to see me and let me know that the CPI was not happy with Karat's rigid anti-deal line, but felt helpless. The CPI, he admitted, did not want to destabilize the government but was unable to get Karat to alter his line.

The BJP too was a divided house. Moderate leaders like Vajpayee and even younger ones like Arun Jaitley were not resolutely opposed to the deal. It was clear that just as Karat had used his opposition to the deal as a way of rallying his own party's cadres behind him, L.K. Advani, too, chose to adopt a rigid stance to force his party to abandon the Vajpayee line and accept him as the new leader.

Divisions within the BJP came to the fore even at Dr Singh's briefing of the party's leaders on the 123 Agreement. Advani was not in Delhi, but the meeting, at 7 RCR, was attended by Vajpayee, Jaswant Singh, Yashwant Sinha, Arun Shourie and Brajesh Mishra. Sinha and Shourie asked the scientists, diplomats and PMO officials many searching questions, expressing their scepticism about what had been secured. Jaswant Singh, on the other hand, complimented the officers with his usual gravitas, saying, 'Gentlemen, you have done the nation proud!' Vajpayee remained silent.

At one point Brajesh Mishra walked around the table and handed over a piece of paper to Vajpayee. He looked at the paper, folded it and put it in his pocket. Dr Singh turned to Vajpayee and asked him if he wished to say anything. Vajpayee smiled and remained silent. Yashwant Sinha, Shourie and Brajesh looked eagerly at Vajpayee, obviously hoping he would say something. He still did not oblige. The meeting ended. Everyone stood up and one by one walked out of the room through a door opening into a corridor. Vajpayee took his own time to stand up. Then, Dr Singh walked his predecessor out through an adjacent door with a shorter route close to where his car was parked. I was a step behind Dr Singh. Standing at the door of his car, Vajpayee gave Dr Singh a warm smile and the two shook hands. Vajpayee nodded his head and smiled, as if to suggest the PM had done a good job and he was satisfied.

'I have only completed what you began,' Dr Singh said, breaking the silence. Vajpayee smiled, nodded his head again, got into the car and drove away.

What followed, over the next few weeks, was a period of political suspense. It was not clear what would happen next, even though the government kept up the pretence of carrying on negotiations with the Left. Every now and then, rumours would circulate that Dr Singh was contemplating resignation. When a senior political journalist with a major national daily asked a senior Congress leader known to be close to Sonia how true these rumours were, the leader retorted, 'Let him resign. We have so many others ready to become PM. Any one of them can do an equally good job.'

———

On 12 October 2007, both Sonia Gandhi and Dr Singh spoke at the Hindustan Times Summit. In response to pre-approved questions that Vir Sanghvi posed to Sonia, she said the survival of the government took precedence over the nuclear deal and while the Congress would continue to try and win over the Left it would do nothing to force the issue and risk a break with the Left.

Dr Singh watched her remarks live on television at 7 RCR. As soon as her session was over, the PM's carcade left for Taj Palace Hotel where Dr Singh was scheduled as the second speaker.

In a pointed question, the newspaper's editorial director, Vir Sanghvi, asked him, 'You made a statement to a newspaper which was a bit out of sync with your persona and that started all the controversy. Do you think you overstepped a bit?'

Dr Singh responded with uncharacteristic firmness, 'I don't think I overstepped. I was responding to a public statement issued by the four Left parties and I don't think I overstepped. I am quite conscious of my responsibilities and what I should say and what I should not say.'

However, fully aware of what Sonia had said before him, the PM parried questions on the nuclear deal, saying his government was not a 'one-issue government' and 'one has to live with certain disappointments . . . If the deal does not come through, that is not the end of life.'

He returned home deeply disappointed. As I took leave of him he asked me, 'Who are the wise men around whom I can turn to for advice?'

I said I knew only two wise men. One was my father, who happened to be in Delhi that day, and the other my guru, K. Subrahmanyam. He asked to see them both and met each of them separately. Both advised him to stand firm. He had done what he had done with full Cabinet approval. Backing off now under pressure from the communists would show India in a bad light. If the party was not prepared to back him, he should quit.

'She has let me down,' he said to both in the separate meetings he had with them, in a voice tinged more with sadness than anger.

The next day, Dr Singh flew on a state visit to Nigeria. As I settled down in my hotel room, my phone rang. Subbu was on the line. 'PM wants to see you, can you come immediately to his room?'

I sensed a rare urgency in his tone and left my room as I was, without footwear, in shirtsleeves and trousers. When I entered the PM's suite, I found Dr Singh seated in the middle, with Mrs Kaur on one side and Subbu on the other. Subbu got up and offered me his chair. Dr Singh looked grim.

'What did you tell the US ambassador?' Dr Singh asked.

I was surprised by the question and the tone. What did I tell the US ambassador? I could not recall talking to him. I asked what the context was.

'I am told you made some remark to him on the nuclear deal. What did you say?'

It came back to me in a flash. Just as I was packing up to leave my office room in South Block the day before we left for Nigeria, I had a call from Ted Osius, a diplomat at the US embassy. He called to say that he had a copy of the PM's speech at the Hindustan Times Summit but that copy did not contain the remarks that the PM had made on the fate of the nuclear deal. So where did he say what he was quoted in the press as saying?

I told the diplomat that those were extempore remarks made by the PM in response to questions posed by Vir Sanghvi and he would find the transcript on the PMO website. He then went on to say that the US ambassador David Mulford was keen on reading the PM's statement to understand what exactly he had said. Could I explain to him the PM's remarks?

I was in a hurry to wind up for the day and was not sure what else I could offer by way of explanation. Whatever the PM had said was out there. I had nothing more to add. The diplomat persisted, asking me what I thought the PM meant by what he said. I then offered an explanation. The PM was saying, 'Que sera sera.'

As I recalled this, Dr Singh said, 'Exactly. What is the meaning of que sera sera?'

I couldn't help laughing out loudly. 'Oh,' I said to Dr Singh, 'You mean someone reported to you that I may have spoken in some secret code?!' I continued to laugh. Maybe those eavesdropping on my conversation could not decode the phrase for the PM. Mrs Kaur smiled. She knew what the words meant.

Que sera sera, I told Dr Singh, was Spanish for 'whatever will be, will be'.

He had not seen Hitchcock's movie, *The Man Who Knew Too Much*. Mrs Kaur, who had seen it, said, 'Yes, I remember that movie and that song.'

Doris Day sang it, I pointed out. Yes, agreed Mrs Kaur, it was Doris Day. As I hummed the tune, Subbu was amused. Dr Singh was not. He heard me with a sombre expression.

What else could I say, I asked him. It is not just the US ambassador, the entire media and many in government have been asking the same question. What exactly did the PM mean when he said his was not a 'one-issue government' and that 'one has to live with certain disappointments . . . If the deal does not come through, that is not the end of life.'

Was the deal dead? I did not know, I explained to him, so I felt the best answer to give the US diplomat was: 'Que sera sera!'

Finally, Dr Singh smiled. He said he had a call from Pranab Mukherjee who told him that Mulford had called on him and sought an explanation of both Sonia's and the PM's statements at the Hindustan Times Summit and wanted to know if the government had decided to shelve the negotiations and the deal. Pranab tried to offer an explanation. Mulford then told him that when his colleague asked the PMO for an explanation, he was told 'Que sera sera'. What did he think the PMO guy meant, Mulford asked Pranab.

Several days later, back in Delhi, I found myself seated at the banquet table in Rashtrapati Bhavan at a dinner in honour of the visiting President of Switzerland. The President's banquets usually have a live band playing music. The tunes being played that evening are listed on a card and placed in front of every guest along with the menu card. As I glanced through the card, my eyes caught the name of the second number, which was yet to be played. It was Doris Day's *Que sera sera*.

I circled the name of the tune on my card and passed it down the table to Dr Singh. He looked at the card and then looked at me. I pointed him in the direction of the band and made a gesture with my forefinger, as if it was a conductor's wand. Dr Singh smiled. For the first time in his life, he was hearing that lovely tune from a fantastic Hitchcock movie.

It seemed that evening that as with so many other issues, he would take the fatalistic view that 'whatever will be, will be' on this signature initiative. At times I would be frustrated by this fatalism—even more so by some of his aides justifying it in the name of political survival. At other times I would step back and wonder if there was something to be learnt from his approach. On the nuclear deal, at least, he proved to be more a strategist than a fatalist. In the weeks that followed he began to reveal the cards he had held so close to his chest. Slowly but surely, he began to make his moves, before finally using the threat of resignation to get Sonia on his side.

12

Singh Is King

*'It is very important for us to move forward to end this
nuclear apartheid that the world has sought to impose on India.'*

Manmohan Singh to IFS probationers
11 June 2008

After Sonia Gandhi's rebuff at the Hindustan Times Summit in September 2007, Dr Singh went silent on the nuclear deal. The Congress party and the Left kept up a show of continuing to discuss the deal in a fifteen-member UPA–Left committee. Senior Congress ministers, including Pranab Mukherjee, Kapil Sibal and Prithviraj Chavan would sit with Karat, Yechury, A.B. Bardhan, D. Raja and others and come out of these meetings with inane statements about how the government was clarifying the doubts raised by the Left.

Even after six meetings during September–November 2007, Left spokespersons would continue to claim that they were only offering the government an 'honourable exit route' and that the Left did not want the deal 'operationalized' till the scheduled General Elections in 2009, and certainly not as long as George Bush remained US President.

Despite the Left's rigid stance, the government managed to get the Left's permission to proceed to the IAEA to negotiate an 'India-specific safeguards agreement', adding the proviso that the Left would have to approve of such an agreement before the government took the next step, which would be to sign on to the 123 Agreement, so that the US

President could secure Congressional approval for the deal with India.

In his first public reference to the nuclear deal after the Hindustan Times Summit, Dr Singh told the AICC on 17 November 2007, referring to the problem of power shortage at home and the need to increase power generation capacity:

> We are in the process of finalizing a historic agreement with the United States which will enhance our prospects of increasing the production of nuclear power. There are doubts and misgivings in many minds about this agreement. . . . The Civil Nuclear Agreement is an effort to open closed doors so that we can obtain nuclear fuel and technology from other countries, such as USA, Russia and France . . .

Having explained it thus for the nth time from a written text, he then chose to add extempore:

> The agreement concerns only the civil side of the nuclear energy programme and will have no bearing on our strategic programme. It remains intact without international interference and won't affect our sense of judgement on foreign policy. You need to understand this reality and explain it to our people.

Coming after him, Sonia too referred in positive terms to the nuclear deal and added, 'Working in a coalition does not mean that the Congress should lose its political space forever.' This enthused the votaries of the deal. Journalists following the issue would ask me if the deal was 'not yet dead'. Some would even sit in my room and take bets on the topic. But, at the time I was still not sure if what Sonia had said signalled a change in her own position, or whether this was her way of not letting the PM down in public, even while pressing him to give up in private. That Dr Singh went once again into prolonged silence on the issue suggested to me that it might be the latter.

It was only four months later, in his reply to the debate on the motion of thanks to the President for her address to Parliament, on 5 March 2008, that he made a reference to the deal. This time, however,

I knew he was once again serious about moving forward because we had just crossed an important turning point in the interminable discussions on the deal.

On 20 February 2008, John Kerry, a US senator and chairman, at the time, of the US Senate Committee on Foreign Relations, landed in New Delhi along with his Congressional colleagues Joseph Biden (later to become the US vice president) and Chuck Hagel. They were in India to discuss the situation in Afghanistan but the conversation quickly moved on to the fate of the nuclear deal. Dr Singh briefed them on the state of play and said he was still trying to evolve a domestic political consensus that would enable him to complete the negotiations with the US. The three offered some candid advice.

They stressed that it was imperative that India complete all necessary steps to conclude the nuclear deal by end-July to ensure that the US Congress approved it before the presidential election. 'Otherwise,' warned Kerry, 'it will be very difficult for Congress to ratify it. If it is not ratified by Congress by July-end, there is no prospect.' In order to be able to have time for the agreement to be passed in the senate, said Kerry, it should be brought to it by end-May. 'So I think,' he added, 'somewhere in the next few weeks the decision has got to happen.'

Kerry advised that the agreement process should be completed in the US Congress with a Republican President still in office and a Republican majority in the senate. The forthcoming US elections, he predicted, would bring the Democratic party to power and the Democrats, all three agreed, would find it very difficult to support the nuclear deal. Interestingly, Kerry and Biden were Democrats and Hagel was then a Republican. In late February 2008, it was still not clear whether Barack Obama or Hillary Clinton would get the Democratic party nomination. They were still competing in the primaries. The US media had been reporting that if Barack Obama won the candidacy, Biden would be his secretary of state and if Clinton came out on top then Kerry would be her secretary of state. Of course, in the end, Biden became Obama's vice president, Kerry succeeded Clinton as Obama's secretary of state and Hagel became secretary of defence in Obama's second term.

While all three focused on the requirements of the US legislative timetable, Kerry went a step further and drew Dr Singh's attention to the enormous influence exerted within the Democratic party by non-proliferationists (K. Subrahmanyam had famously dubbed them 'the Ayatollahs of nuclear non-proliferation'). Kerry warned Dr Singh that a future Democratic President would not be able to do for India what President George Bush was clearly willing and ready to do. He made it clear that neither Obama nor Hillary Clinton would challenge the anti-deal non-proliferation lobby and its rigid anti-India stance in their party. In the event, neither Obama nor Clinton voted in favour of the 123 Agreement in the senate.

The three senior American leaders were only confirming what Dr Singh always knew, that if there was any chance of India getting the nuclear deal, it was only because President Bush wanted to do this for India. It was not because Bush had any special love for India. After the 9/11 terrorist attacks on the US the spectre of jihadi terrorism had come to haunt the US, and led American leaders to understand what their Indian counterparts had been telling them about the need to fight this threat. Moreover, the inexorable rise of China was beginning to alter not just the Asian balance of power but also the global balance of power. Helping a democracy like India become stronger would enable it to deal both with the threat of Islamic radicalism and the rise of China. The US had a stake in this outcome. And, critically, Bush was willing to ignore the non-proliferationists' objections. Other US leaders were not as willing.

It was crystal clear to everyone involved in the negotiations that without President Bush's personal commitment, they would not even have reached this stage. Securing a 'sound and honourable 123 Agreement' was as much a tribute to Indian negotiating skills as it was to President's Bush's desire to be fair in his dealings with India, a country he saw as being on 'his side'. When critics of Bush in India poked fun at him saying he had an American cowboy's view of the world—that there are 'good guys' and 'bad guys' ('axis of evil' as he called them), I would ask why one should criticize a man who thought we, Indians, were the good guys.

As Biden, Hagel and Kerry walked out of their meeting with Dr Singh, I suggested to Kerry that he brief the media waiting outside 7 RCR and let them know what the PM had been told. He readily agreed and did just that. Biden chipped in and added, 'A number of senators are prepared to vote [for the 123 Agreement] though they don't think it is as good as it should have been.' Their reluctance on substance, said Biden, 'was overcome by their belief in the India–US relationship.' Kerry went to the extent of certifying to the media that he did not think India was a 'proliferator'.

That conversation set Dr Singh thinking. After September 2007, when negotiations appeared to be on a policy treadmill—only motion but no movement forward—Dr Singh gave the impression of having given up hope of concluding the deal. In March 2008 when he once again initiated a dialogue with supporters of the deal he was pleasantly surprised to find Brajesh Mishra finally willing to back him.

Mishra had been the first to jump the gun, so to speak, and attack the deal on the very day it was unveiled, 18 July 2005. His initial opposition cost the government dear because he was the national security adviser who had initiated the NSSP, the precursor to the agreement that Dr Singh was seeking. Many in the foreign service took their cue from him and became internal saboteurs of the deal. Several interlocutors spoke to Mishra on the PM's behalf and finally Dr Singh himself reached out to Mishra. Until February 2008 Mishra was not ready to publicly endorse the deal. After the Kerry visit, it would seem, he finally came on board, endorsing the deal as being in India's national interest. I encouraged Karan Thapar to interview him and make this public.

Mishra told Thapar that if the government were to now back off and not clinch the deal with the US it would be a 'serious loss of face' for India. He said that he had been briefed by 'various representatives of the Government of India at a fairly high level and some scientists' and he was now 'convinced that there is not going to be any major impact on the strategic programme through the deal . . . this deal doesn't stop us from continuing our strategic programme.' When asked by Thapar if the time was opportune for India to sign on, Mishra said 'Now, now, now.'

Dr Singh was pleased and made a point of raising the matter in Parliament. He told the Lok Sabha, 'Sir, I was very happy some days ago that the former national security adviser Shri Brajesh Mishra came out openly in defence of the nuclear cooperation agreement.'

The second shot was fired by Subrahmanyam. He wrote a column that the India Abroad News Service (IANS) put out on 16 March 2008 titled 'Will the Nuclear Deal Finally Go Ahead?' In fact, Subrahmanyam challenged the Congress party to pursue an 'independent foreign policy', one that was independent of the Left! Resorting, uncharacteristically, to political commentary, he remarked that 'the strategy of the Left' was to denigrate the Congress, and make it less acceptable to the Left's potential 'third front' allies so as to revive the non-Congress, non-BJP experiment that the Left had backed in the mid-1990s.

Many journalists followed his line of argument, with the result that the media overwhelmingly came out in support of Dr Singh taking further steps to pursue the nuclear deal. With the exception of *The Hindu* and the *Asian Age/Deccan Chronicle* (two interlinked newspapers with a common editor) and a few Urdu newspapers, most major English, Hindi and other Indian-language newspapers and television channels supported the prime minister. Public-opinion polls conducted by *India Today*, *Outlook*, CNN-IBN and the *Times of India* showed a clear majority supporting the PM and the nuclear deal.

With the media's backing, the PM gained confidence and began pushing the envelope. On 24 March, while laying the foundation stone of the Bawana power project in Delhi, he once again spoke publicly of the need to develop India's nuclear energy potential. At the PMO, we were busy collecting data from the Nuclear Power Corporation to show that capacity utilization in all nuclear power plants was gradually declining because of the shortage of uranium. This was even threatening the functioning of a few nuclear power plants. The DAE had claimed in the past that India need not worry about imported uranium because of the availability of domestic supply in the North-East. However, environmental groups had been blocking uranium mining in that region. With no domestic production of uranium worth the name, the lack of imports was starving nuclear plants.

Such hard facts helped the government win public opinion, but the Left continued to resist allowing the government to go to the IAEA to negotiate a safeguards agreement. It even threatened to boycott the meetings of the UPA–Left committee and some Left leaders began issuing statements that they might have to reconsider their support to the UPA. Not surprisingly, this curbed Dr Singh's enthusiasm and led to a few telltale silences on his part. He did not bring up the subject when he spoke at the UPA's annual anniversary celebration, on 22 May 2008, when presenting the annual *Report to the People*. With Left leaders present in full strength at the anniversary dinner at 7 RCR, journalists attending the event assumed that the deal was once again dead, drawing attention to the fact that the PM made no reference to it in his speech.

But the prime minister was not, in fact, giving up on the deal. A fortnight later, a sharp rise in oil prices forced the government to effect a steep hike in petrol, diesel, kerosene and LPG prices. Dr Singh decided to address the nation on 4 June. In a televised address he explained in detail why the government was being forced to undertake an across-the-board hike in energy prices and then boldly ended his address saying, 'We have to develop alternative sources of energy, whatever be the source. We cannot remain captive to uncertain markets and unsure sources of supply. We have to develop renewable sources of energy, including nuclear energy.'

The next day, the Left Front threatened to quit if the government did not roll back the price hike and announced that it would meet on 23 June to 'evaluate the political situation and the relations with the UPA government'.

On 9 June, Dr Singh inaugurated an international conference on disarmament on the theme 'Towards a World Free of Nuclear Weapons', to mark the twentieth anniversary of Rajiv Gandhi's address on that subject to the UN General Assembly. His speech, written by a PMO official, repeated the government's stock views on the subject. It seemed to me that Dr Singh was paying ritual obeisance to disarmament before making one last-ditch attempt at securing India's status as a nuclear weapons power.

Two days later, on 11 June, Dr Singh spoke from the heart. In an extempore address lasting almost an hour to a group of Indian Foreign Service probationers, he spoke eloquently about his views on Indian foreign and strategic policy. Since we had installed a recording system at Panchavati, the meeting rooms at 7 RCR, it was possible to record and transcribe the full text of the PM's speech and place it on the PMO's website. He spoke about every major issue confronting Indian foreign policy, including climate change, a relatively recent challenge, hard power and soft power, non-alignment and coalition-building, relations with neighbours and big powers.

'The world is not a morality play,' Dr Singh told the young diplomats. 'The world's political and economic system is a power play and those who have greater power use it to their advantage. Our effort has been, through collective strategies, to work with various coalitions of developing countries, sometimes with coalitions of like-minded developed countries, to create an environment where (the) power factor does not work to our disadvantage.'

It was a masterful survey of Indian foreign policy and offered a group of young diplomats a panoramic view from a prime minister's vantage point. Then, at the very end of a long survey, he finally touched a subject that he had not spoken much about in recent weeks. Highlighting the significance of the nuclear deal for national security and India's global standing, he boldly claimed:

> It protects our national interest, it protects our capacity to use nuclear power to protect our strategic interests. At the same time it opens up new opportunities for civilian cooperation and without that, I think, the trade in dual technologies—sensitive advanced technologies— cannot become a reality. But our domestic politics has prevented us from going ahead. I still continue to hope that we will make progress in the months that lie ahead. But it is very important for us to move forward to end this nuclear apartheid that the world has sought to impose on India. This agreement, if it materializes, if it sees the light of day, will open up new possibilities of cooperation, not only with the US but all other nuclear powers like Russia, France, who are

very keen that once we have this deal through, India should become eligible for civil nuclear cooperation.

It was clear that the PM was going to make one last effort. Interestingly, a day after Dr Singh's remarks appeared in the media, Sonia Gandhi too spoke about the importance of nuclear energy while addressing a farmers' rally in Assam, and located it in the context of rising oil prices. It seemed that something was bubbling below the surface.

On Wednesday, 18 June, I was being driven to office around half past nine in the morning when I saw a couple of cars parked in the 7 RCR compound and police escort cars parked on the road outside. This was normal whenever the PM was having a meeting with anyone entitled to a police escort. The escort cars would always be parked outside the RCR compound. However, since I knew the PM's official schedule that day, I wondered who he was with so early in the morning, and why the meeting was not shown on his daily programme sheet.

I called Subbu on my mobile to ask what was happening. He told me that Sonia Gandhi had come calling on the PM and the two had later been joined by Pranab Mukherjee. The two of us agreed that something very important was being discussed, and Subbu promised to call and let me know when he found out what was going on. I sat in my room at South Block waiting for a call. I was jolted when Subbu finally called to say that Dr Singh was unwell and had cancelled all his appointments for the day. In Telugu, he mumbled to me that I should drive down to RCR.

When I met him there, Subbu told me he did not know what had transpired at the meeting. But he did know that Dr Singh had spoken to Sonia the previous night, prior to her visit this morning. Given our knowledge of the tensions around the nuclear deal, we immediately assumed that the fat was finally in the fire. The boss had given his quit notice.

There was no way anything could be confirmed because not only had the PM cancelled all his appointments, he was not even available to meet his own staff. Narayanan, Nair and I were told that the PM would not meet anyone in the PMO. I returned to South Block and spent the next few hours dealing with phone calls from the media. I blandly told suspicious reporters, who had heard the news of the day's appointments being cancelled, that Dr Singh was indisposed.

Late in the afternoon, Rajdeep Sardesai of CNN-IBN called me. He had heard from a 'reliable' source that Dr Singh had submitted his resignation, he said, and his channel was going to run with the story. Did I have any comments? I requested Rajdeep to hold on, assuring him that I would return with a comment. When I called Subbu, he suggested I call 3 RCR directly and ask to speak to the PM. I did so and Dr Singh came on the line. I told him what Rajdeep had said. Dr Singh kept quiet for a while and suggested I say nothing. I knew the deed had been done.

I did not call Rajdeep back and did not take his calls either. Obviously guessing something was wrong, he ran with the story, citing 'reliable sources'. However, he reported the resignation not as a certainty, but as a likely event. I switched my mobile off, knowing that I would be flooded with media inquiries.

Within a few minutes, I was summoned by the PM. When I met him at home, he looked unusually relaxed. Clearly, the burden was now off his shoulders. Yes, he told me, he had spoken to Sonia the previous day and told her that his position had become untenable. He also explained what had led to his offer to resign. The Indian side had been all set to go to the IAEA to negotiate an India–specific safeguards agreement but the Left wanted the draft agreement to be shown to them before they authorized the government to go to the international body. This was impossible, said the PM. As a secret document, the draft agreement could not be shown to those not in government until the negotiations with the IAEA had ended. Moreover, India would be placed in an embarrassing position if, at this stage, the government chose to stay away from the IAEA, on account of the Left's arm-twisting. The IAEA chief, Mohamed ElBaradei, had privately assured Indian officials that he would ensure a positive outcome for India. Thus Dr Singh had concluded that if the government did not go to the IAEA now, he had no option but to quit.

Dr Singh also saw little point in continuing the charade of negotiations by the UPA–Left committee. It was clear to him that the Left would never support the government. The choice before the government was, in his mind, obvious: ignore the Left and proceed, or agree with the Left and stay put. Explaining this to Sonia Gandhi, the PM had then told her that if the UPA chose the second option, it would have to find another prime minister to lead the coalition. Sonia requested Dr Singh to sleep on the issue. When, after meeting him the next morning, she realized he was serious, she summoned Pranab Mukherjee. That crucial meeting had been on as I had driven past RCR that morning.

Pranab Mukherjee had left RCR that morning to meet Karat and Yechury and tell them what had happened. The next morning, on 19 June, *The Hindu*'s lead headline was 'Congress-Left Near Break-Up on Nuclear Deal'. It reported, among other things, that a meeting of the UPA–Left committee scheduled for the 18th evening had been postponed because of the PM's threat to quit if he was not allowed to go ahead with the nuclear deal. Two days of hectic activity followed.

The following day, I learnt from a political reporter that Montek had gone to see Sonia. I assumed she had summoned him to get him to speak to the PM and soften him up. Just a few minutes after I had heard this, I spotted Montek in South Block and invited him into my room, and asked him what Sonia had told him. Surprised that I knew of this meeting, he immediately asked if I had heard about it from Dr Singh. That giveaway question confirmed my theory that Sonia had asked Montek to persuade Dr Singh to withdraw his resignation.

Montek admitted as much. Yes, Sonia did request him to convince the PM not to resign, he said. So what did the PM say, I asked. Not surprisingly, Montek ignored my question, but proffered the view that 'boss could wait' on the deal. He reasoned that Dr Singh would still be PM in 2009, after the US elections were over. He felt it would be easier for the Congress party to conclude the deal with a Democrat in the White House. I recalled Kerry's advice and told Montek that it had to be now or never. Clearly not keen to discuss the matter, he agreed with me too and laughed in his characteristically friendly manner. 'Tough call for boss,' he said and walked out of my room.

I sat there worried. If Sonia had summoned Montek to get him to advise the PM to back off, surely she would deploy others too. Many around Dr Singh were wont to be even more risk averse than him. They would in all likelihood counsel him to remain in office and complete his term rather than be heroic and risk a downfall. Would Dr Singh then have the courage to stand firm and call their bluff, I wondered.

My own view that Sonia simply would not allow the PM to step down was shared by Subrahmanyam. He urged me to persuade the PM to stand firm. 'Tell him that she cannot afford to see him go. She will have to back him, but he must be firm. Only you can tell him that,' said Subrahmanyam, when I went to seek his guidance.

I then called on Dr Singh at 3 RCR. Both he and Mrs Kaur were seated in the living room, each reading a book. That was such a familiar sight. I had seen them this way on innumerable occasions; just the two of them, reading together in companionable silence.

When I asked him about Sonia's message, sent through Montek, Dr Singh confirmed that she was trying to persuade him to wait and not force the pace of events. I warned him that if he did not act now, the rest of his term would be wasted. The Left would smell victory and might even press for a change of prime minister. I reminded him that the Left had a track record of doing just that. They had claimed credit for replacing the 'pro-business' Morarji Desai with the 'pro-farmer' Charan Singh in 1978; of forcing the exit of V.P. Singh and replacing him with the 'young turk' Chandra Shekhar in 1989; of helping 'leftist' I.K. Gujral replace 'pro-Narasimha Rao' Deve Gowda in 1997. Now they would claim credit, I warned him, for replacing 'neo-liberal' Manmohan Singh with 'secular' Arjun Singh, 'Bengali' Pranab—the CPI(M) was essentially a Bengal party—or 'leftist' Antony, who was an old ally of the comrades from Kerala.

Dr Singh laughed. 'I am ready to go. Anyone of them can be made PM. Why not?'

I agonized over what his record in office would be, if he were to go. After all, the party was busy claiming credit for all the good work done in his time. Between Sonia and the NAC, they would say they had done everything. 'It will be as if you did nothing,' I told the PM. 'If you don't get through this one initiative that everyone identifies with you, what can you claim as your own legacy?'

Dr Singh remained quiet but Mrs Kaur nodded her head in agreement. I then used an argument that I knew would appeal to her.

'Ma'am, he will just be another Gujral if he does not do this!' She laughed.

'Everyone knows Gujral was prime minister, but what did he achieve?' I continued. 'In fact, what did Deve Gowda achieve? What did V.P. Singh achieve? At least they have the excuse that they were in office for just about a year each. After four years, what can the PM claim he has done, when all the credit for everything, other than the deal is given to her?'

'*Haan*,' she said in agreement. He continued to remain silent.

I was not sure what Dr Singh thought of my outspokenness, but I was not too worried. I had already informed him of my plans to quit and move to Singapore for personal reasons. He knew why I had to do that. He also knew that I had no axe to grind in urging him to stand his ground.

————

Finding the Left adamant, and unable to let Dr Singh go, Sonia Gandhi finally took a call. The government would be allowed to go to the IAEA and complete negotiations on the safeguards agreement. She left it to Pranab Mukherjee to try and prevent the Left from withdrawing support. It remained to be seen whether he could swing that.

After all the hectic activity of the preceding days, Saturday, 21 June was a quiet day. I had lunch at home and was enjoying a siesta when my mobile phone rang. A friend of the Samajwadi Party leader Amar Singh was on the line.

'Mr Baru, I have a message for you,' he said. 'My friend Mr Amar Singh is in a hospital in Colorado. He wants you to tell the prime minister that American doctors are very good and they are taking good care of him. He is very happy there and he says Americans are such warm and friendly people, we should have good relations with them.'

I was not aware that Amar Singh had been hospitalized. So I politely inquired after his health and said I would inform the PM. 'It would be good if you can convey this message as soon as possible,' he added. 'Maybe the prime minister would want to wish Amar Singh a speedy recovery.'

Later that afternoon, I met Dr Singh and conveyed what was clearly a political signal from Amar Singh. He had hinted, through this intermediary, at the Samajwadi Party's willingness to support Dr Singh on the nuclear deal. I felt Amar Singh might want to speak directly to the PM and suggested Dr Singh call him. He had a perfect alibi for doing so, given that he was in hospital and in poor health. The two men were not distant acquaintances. Indeed, Dr Singh and Amar Singh, both members of the Rajya Sabha, got on well even though their personalities and reputations were poles apart. In fact, Amar Singh often demonstrated great regard and affection for the PM. It was in the nature of Parliament to facilitate such peculiar, and unlikely, friendships.

Months later Amar Singh would claim credit for getting the nuclear deal done. Calling me from his hospital bed in Singapore, he asked me to come and see him. So I paid him a visit, walking in after Amitabh Bachchan, his wife, Jaya, and their family had left the room. 'So who do you think are the architects of the nuclear deal?' he asked me. Before I could reply, he added, 'You will say George Bush and Manmohan Singh. Let me tell you, it was George Bush and Amar Singh.'

I have no idea what the PM did after that call from Amar Singh, but a couple of days later media reports appeared suggesting that Mulayam Singh Yadav was rethinking his opposition to the nuclear deal. Karat panicked and called on Yadav. On 25 June, a few hours before a meeting of the UPA–Left committee, Karat met Yadav at his son Akhilesh Yadav's home in Delhi to secure his support for the Left's unchanged opposition to the nuclear deal. Mulayam remained non-committal and said that he had convened a meeting of his party on 3 July where they would take a final decision. Karat met Yadav again on 1 July. After that meeting, Amar Singh, who had returned from the US by then, briefed the media and said the Samajwadi Party wanted all secular forces to remain united. 'A division in secular forces will be harmful for the country.'

The message to the UPA was reinforced. The Samajwadi Party was willing to part ways with the Left and support the Congress on the nuclear deal in the name of the 'unity of all secular forces'. The next day, on 2 July, Narayanan called on Yadav and Amar Singh and briefed them on the nuclear deal. On 3 July, the United National Progressive Alliance, an outfit headed by Yadav, met to take a final view and resolved to consult 'experts and scientists' before taking a decision. Yadav and Amar Singh went straight from this meeting to call on former President Abdul Kalam. Kalam promptly issued a statement in support of the nuclear deal and urged Yadav to support the government. Not only was Kalam a distinguished technocrat, a Bharat Ratna and a former Rashtrapati, he was also a Muslim. His support for the nuclear deal with the US was exactly the kind of political backing Mulayam needed to justify the switch to his own cadres. It was all preplanned and worked like clockwork.

That afternoon Narayanan met Amar Singh and Samajwadi Party MP Ramgopal Yadav, also someone who enjoyed good personal relations with Dr Singh, at an undisclosed location to avoid the media. The venue, many believed, was an IB safe house in Lutyens' Delhi. After their meeting, Narayanan handed me an elaborate statement to be issued to the media that contained several re-statements of government policy aimed at satisfying the Samajwadi Party. Mulayam and Amar Singh wanted the PMO to give public assurances that in going ahead with the nuclear deal, India would neither compromise its independent foreign policy and strategic autonomy nor disrupt its relations with Iran, and so on. The party wanted these assurances primarily because of its large Muslim support base.

Narayanan's activism on this front may well have been shaped by his desire, triggered by Dr Singh's poser, 'Who knows what you have done all your life as an intelligence officer?', to enter the history books. Equally, he may have been expected to deliver on his usual boast to one and all that he had 'a file' on them. Narayanan may well have had many on his interlocutors in this set of negotiations, and this time he would be making use of them in the best interest of the country and not just his government and its political masters.

On 8 July, Dr Singh flew to Japan to participate in the G-8 Outreach meeting. I stayed at home to wind up my affairs since I had already submitted my resignation and was scheduled to leave for Singapore by the end of July. On board his aircraft, Dr Singh met the accompanying media and told them that the government had decided to go to the IAEA to conclude the safeguards agreement 'very soon'. Many in Delhi were surprised. I called Jaideep Sarkar who was with Dr Singh. 'Yes, he has done it,' said Jaideep. In mid-flight, after leaving Delhi and with no one to stop him, Dr Singh took the final plunge.

With Mulayam and his twenty-nine MPs on his side, Dr Singh was confident that he would have the numbers in Parliament in case a vote of confidence had to be secured. A nervous Congress party did not know what to say. Journalists trying to get a reaction from the party found no one willing to comment.

The next day, on 9 July, the Left Front predictably announced the withdrawal of its support to the UPA government. Pranab Mukherjee then jumped the gun by issuing a statement to say that the government would seek a vote of confidence in Parliament and only then go to the IAEA. He was unaware of what was going on in Dr Singh's mind. Far away, in distant Sapporo in Japan, the PM was finally acting on his own. A day after Mukherjee's pledge that the government would not approach the IAEA until it had won the trust vote in Parliament, the government in fact chose to approach the IAEA, rubbishing Mukherjee's assurance.

Returning home on 10 July, Dr Singh informed President Pratibha Patil that he would seek a vote of confidence later that month. The media was full of reports and analyses, and statements from the BJP and the Left, both of whom had made common cause in their opposition to the deal. The Congress party was clearly confused and went silent. Dr Singh agreed to meet a few senior editors from the electronic media because TV was not only playing a larger role in influencing public opinion, but most news channels were broadly supportive of the PM. The print media was still dominated by an older generation of journalists who were either sceptical about relations with the US or had explicit pro-BJP or pro-Left sympathies. Television journalists, on the other hand, were younger, more open-minded and less politically biased. In fact, almost every TV channel was willing to be supportive of the PM with very little effort on my part.

With the date set for the vote of confidence, Dr Singh got down to gathering support. He spoke to all UPA leaders and met as many MPs as necessary. He asked for a list of MPs who had spoken in his support on various occasions and made sure that he called each one of them. The debate in Parliament was exhaustive and had several moments of great oratory, and well-informed and reasoned discourse as well as moments of high emotion, showmanship and drama. The argument that a strategic understanding with the United States would not go down well with India's Muslim community was rubbished by several Muslim MPs from across parties, including Asaduddin Owaisi of the All India Majlis-e-Ittehadul Muslimeen, Omar Abdullah of the National Conference and Mehbooba Mufti of the People's Democratic Party, all of whom spoke eloquently in Dr Singh's support. Whatever the outcome of the vote, whoever heard the debate was now well informed on the facts and the fears.

Returning home late on the first day of the debate, 21 July, I switched on the TV and tried to relax. One of the channels was playing a song from a yet-to-be-released film called *Singh is Kinng*. The song had great rhythm and beat. It was the kind of song that made you shake your shoulders and hips. As I went to bed I amused myself by imagining TV news channels playing this song the next day were Dr Singh to indeed win the vote of confidence.

Tuesday, 22 July was a tense day. Congress party leaders and Narayanan met the PM to assure him that the government had the numbers. Dr Singh looked pleased and confident, though a bit nervous. Everything seemed to be going well until after lunch. But trouble was lying in wait. At 4 p.m., some members of the BJP placed wads of rupee notes on the table of the Lok Sabha secretary general and alleged that they had been paid this money in exchange for support to the government. Senior BJP leaders then informed the media that a sting operation had also been conducted by a TV channel and proof of the bribing would be shown on TV. I was in South Block at the time and rushed to Parliament. Dr Singh was closeted with Sonia Gandhi, Pranab Mukherjee and other senior party leaders. Prithviraj Chavan came out of the room and called Rajdeep Sardesai of CNN-IBN, the TV channel that had filmed the alleged sting, and warned him of legal consequences if the channel televised the visuals.

When Sonia Gandhi and other leaders left the PM's room, I walked in. Dr Singh was ashen-faced; he looked pale and ill, almost as if he would collapse or break down crying. I had never seen him like this— silent, motionless, shell-shocked and grief-stricken. This was not the way he had imagined the day would end. This was not the way, either, that he had imagined the issue would play out. This was his most important political initiative, for which he had fought a hard political battle for three long years. He was on the cusp of victory. Despite the betrayal of the Left, he had managed to stitch together a coalition of the willing. He had never imagined that in the end his heroic enterprise would be so sullied by scandal.

Watching him in silence, I could read his mind. Only the previous evening, on the 21st, he had firmly denied allegations that he was securing support for his government by paying bribes. He had bravely asked the Opposition to produce evidence, confident that there would be no such evidence. Advani was on TV reminding the PM of this challenge. 'Yesterday he asked for evidence. Today we have brought it.'

But, at no point in the negotiations with Yadav or any other political party had the PM authorized offering cash in exchange for votes. The carrot he was willing to offer was ministerial berths in exchange for political support. That, indeed, was what he had offered Yadav. This was, after all, a legitimate bargaining chip in democratic politics. In all democracies around the world, coalition governments are built by political parties extending support in exchange for ministerial berths and other governmental perks. That is how coalitions had been built in India, too, in the past. He had done nothing illegitimate and Mulayam had extended support. So, how did this 'cash-for-votes' scandal happen?

Was this the initiative of an overenthusiastic wheeler-dealer in the party or a conspiracy to sully the PM's image and reputation? Was it the work of those angry with Dr Singh for forcing a split with the Left and a near collapse of the government? Were there elements that hoped he would resign and quit, opening up the possibility of a change of leadership and a return to business as usual with the Left? A variety of conspiracy theories swirled around in my mind as I sat in front of a man who looked defeated only hours before a victory.

———

When the Lok Sabha reconvened, Dr Singh hoped he would get a chance to speak. But that right and courtesy was denied to him by an Opposition that heckled and disrupted the session. He had spent considerable time over the previous week working on his speech. Montek, Narayanan and I worked on various parts of it with the PM himself adding sentences. Referring to the betrayal of the Left, which had originally agreed to support the initiative he had taken and then backed out, he wanted to say:

> All I had asked our Left colleagues was 'please allow us to go through the negotiating process and I will come to Parliament before operationalizing the nuclear agreement'. This simple courtesy, which is essential for the orderly functioning of any government worth the name, particularly with regard to the conduct of foreign policy, they were not willing to grant me. They wanted a veto over every single step of the negotiations, which is not acceptable. They wanted me to behave as their bonded slave.

He had agreed to conclude on an uncharacteristically personal note:

I have often said that I am a politician by accident. I have held many diverse responsibilities. I have been a teacher, I have been an official of the Government of India, I have been a member of this greatest of Parliaments, but I have never forgotten my life as a young boy in a distant village. Every day that I have been prime minister of India I have tried to remember that the first ten years of my life were spent in a village with no drinking water supply, no electricity, no hospital, no roads and nothing that we today associate with modern living. I had to walk miles to school, I had to study in the dim light of a kerosene oil lamp. This nation gave me the opportunity to ensure that such would not be the life of our children in the foreseeable future. Sir, my conscience is clear that on every day that I have occupied this high office, I have tried to fulfil the dream of that young boy from that distant village.

But the speech was never delivered, merely tabled and circulated to the media. That afternoon Lok Sabha Speaker Somnath Chatterjee, who belonged to the CPI(M), revealed in public what we all knew in private. He expressed his anger at the political games Prakash Karat had been playing and at the wrecking of a coalition that he [Somnath] had helped construct. A short while earlier, he had refused to accept the CPI(M)'s demand that he quit as Lok Sabha Speaker because his party had withdrawn support to the UPA. Chatterjee had been elected Speaker as part of the Left's understanding to support UPA. On 22 July he went on to chair a meeting of political parties in Parliament to resolve the crisis created by the so-called 'cash-for-votes' scandal and reconvened the Lok Sabha to put the confidence motion to vote. The next day, the CPI(M) politburo met and expelled Chatterjee from the party's membership. Chatterjee remained unfazed. He had not only disapproved of Karat's tactics, but had also openly supported the prime minister and his initiative.

Somnath had personal regard for Dr Singh. Their friendship was cemented by their years together in the Rajya Sabha. But Dr Singh would always recall the fact that Somnath's father, Nirmal Chandra Chatterjee, a lawyer and a public intellectual and once-president of the Akhil Bharatiya Hindu Mahasabha, had awarded him a scroll of honour for securing the first rank at Amritsar's Hindu College way back in 1950. It was the same Somnath who had held up a copy of the *Economic Times* on budget day in 1992 to charge the then finance minister with leaking budget secrets to the IMF. Now, more than fifteen years later, he presided over Dr Singh's toughest day in Parliament and declared his victory. At the end of a long day, made longer by the fact that several MPs had preferred to cast their vote on paper, rather than use the Lok Sabha's electronic voting system and those votes had to be physically counted, Somnath announced that 275 MPs had voted in support of the government, 256 had voted against it and ten had either abstained or were absent.

An uproar greeted the victory. I sent a text message from my mobile phone to several journalists with just three words on it: 'Singh is King'. Late that night, when I reached home and switched on the TV, every channel was running that jingle from that movie with visuals of a tired prime minister standing in front of TV cameras holding his hand up in a V-sign.

13

A Victory Denied

'There cannot be two centres of power. That creates confusion.
I have to accept that the party president is the centre of power.'

Manmohan Singh, 2009

It was early evening on Saturday, 6 September 2008. I was in Singapore travelling to the university campus where I taught, when my mobile phone rang. It was Jaideep Sarkar, the PM's private secretary.

'NSG waiver is done!' he said. The PM was thrilled and Narayanan was ecstatic, he added, describing the celebratory mood that had swept RCR after this important breakthrough in the India–US nuclear agreement.

At noon that day in Vienna, the NSG had finally voted to lift the embargo on nuclear trade with India. Dr Singh had made the history that we all hoped he would make. Its news had reached Dr Singh while he was drinking his afternoon tea in Delhi. I had been keeping close track of events from Singapore, with Jaideep keeping me informed. I knew much drama and hard bargaining by various NSG member countries had gone into the final outcome. President Bush had delivered on his promise by finally twisting China's arm to get it to vote in favour of India. I placed the mobile phone back in my pocket and looked out of the bus at Singapore's greenery. Tears welled up in my eyes.

My thoughts went back to all those battles in Parliament, the arguments within government, the negotiations with the US, my own negotiations with the media and arguments with colleagues and politicians. For three years, I was a part of it all. When the deed was done, I was far away on an alien university campus.

I called my friends, Jaishankar, who was now India's high commissioner in Singapore, and Raja Mohan, an important analyst and media commentator on the deal, who was, like me, a professor at a Singapore university. Jaishankar, the son of my guru K. Subrahmanyam, Raja and I had all been in Washington DC on 18 July 2005, the day when it all began to come together, with the US implicitly acknowledging India's status as a nuclear weapons power. We had been in the thick of it all for three years, each in his own way. Even after moving to Singapore Jaishankar was retained by the PM as a negotiator, Raja continued to write his columns and I had continued my speech-writing for Dr Singh, writing and emailing speeches between cooking at home and teaching at the university. We decided to meet the next day and raise a toast.

I alighted from the bus at Bukit Timah and went for a walk in the botanical gardens, with my mind in the buzz of New Delhi. I had asked Jaideep to convey my compliments to the PM and I knew he would. But I wanted to speak to him, hear his voice and get a sense of his excitement. I could have asked Jaideep to connect me to him, but I knew both he and the PM would be busy and that he would say he would do it later, in the evening. I decided to use my 'hotline'— Muralidharan, the PM's personal assistant—to get to the PM right away.

Murali was always somewhere close to Dr Singh and whenever I needed to get to the PM without delay, bypassing his two private secretaries, I would call on his mobile. Murali would just walk across to Dr Singh and hand his phone over to him. That is what I did as I walked through Singapore's beautiful botanical gardens and Murali did exactly what I had expected him to do. Dr Singh was on the line.

'Hello?' he said in his soft voice.

'Sir, congratulations! You have done it!' I said.

'We have done it!' he replied in a tone of rare excitement. When he asked if I was in Delhi, I told him I was calling from Singapore.

'So when are you coming back?' he asked.

'Sir, I am in the middle of a semester here. I will be in Delhi in December. I will see you then.'

'Okay,' he said and then, to my utter surprise, added, 'You come back now, whenever you can. I have not yet appointed anyone in your place.' I was nonplussed. Why was he asking me to return immediately? He knew I was teaching and as a former professor ought to have known that I would not be able to leave a teaching job mid-semester. More to the point, I wondered why he associated the successful conclusion of the nuclear deal with my return. Was it that he felt he was now politically stronger, perhaps even likely to not just last out his full term but even secure a second one? Why did he say 'come back now'?

It was true that the PM had not appointed a media adviser in my place, but had relied on resources within the government. When I left in August, Gopalakrishnan of the PMO had been given the additional charge of handling the media, and in December, Deepak Sandhu, the government's principal information officer, had replaced him. We had agreed that I would continue to help him with his speeches. He had anyway said to me, more than once, that all he needed was a speech-writer and he did not want any projection in the media. Was he now thinking differently, I wondered? With the nuclear deal done, was he now prepared to give me more freedom to function as a media adviser? Did he want to politically empower himself?

Despite these unresolved questions in my mind, I felt heartened by Dr Singh's invitation and agreed to accept it. I assured him that I would return as soon as I possibly could but, given my personal commitments, it was unlikely that I would be back before the elections. Returning to his victory in Vienna, I made bold to suggest that he was now free to do what he wanted on the policy front. I pointed out that the successful culmination of the negotiations on the nuclear deal had politically empowered him and that he should use the space he had gained to make his own decisions. This was the time, I stressed, to challenge his critics and assert his authority.

'Let me see,' he said in his plaintive tone, and the call ended.

When I called on him during a visit to Delhi in December, much was weighing on his mind. Grappling as he was with the aftermath of the Mumbai terror attack of 26 November and with the ongoing global economic crisis following the recent collapse of Lehmann Brothers, he appeared tired and preoccupied. I could see how both crises had impacted his health. He did not say much, made routine inquiries about my family and asked me more than once if I was happy in Singapore. He recalled his conversations with Lee Kuan Yew, Singapore's founder-statesman, and spoke of how he had learnt a lot about China and its leadership from those conversations.

I was not surprised when, within days of my return to Singapore, the news of his aggravated heart problem reached me. In late January, he had to be hospitalized for a major surgery. Murali kept me informed about his recovery. On learning that he had been discharged and was now resting at home, I decided to fly down to Delhi to look him up. Landing in Delhi on a February morning I called Jaideep and Indu. I was told Dr Singh was at 5 RCR, which had been turned into a mini-hospital, still under constant medical care, and no visitors had yet been allowed to see him. It turned out later that these restrictions had been put in place because of anxiety about his recovery, which had been slower than expected.

I decided I would call on Mrs Kaur, go back to Singapore, and return only when Dr Singh was able to receive visitors. I called Murali and sought time with her. Returning my call, Mrs Kaur asked me to come and see her. When I arrived at 3 RCR I was asked to go to 5 RCR where Mrs Kaur met me at the portico and took me in. A team of doctors was sitting in the visitors' room. I removed my shoes, washed my hands and went in. Dr Singh was asleep.

'Sanjay Baru is here,' Mrs Kaur whispered into his ear. His eyes opened and he smiled, and then shut them again. She asked him gently if he would like to have a cup of tea. He opened his eyes again and looked at me. She said, 'Yes, I will get him some tea. You also have some tea.'

Encouraged by the fact that he had not shut his eyes again, Mrs Kaur helped him to sit up in bed and tucked a pillow behind him. She then ordered tea. He asked for a biscuit and soon, his favourite

Marie biscuit arrived with his tea. He sat silently while she helped him sip his tea. He then asked how I was and inquired after Rama, Tanvika and my father. We spoke for a few minutes when Srinath Reddy, the leader of the PM's team of doctors, and a friend from my school and college days in Hyderabad, walked in. Srinath indicated that I should now leave the room and let Dr Singh rest.

As we walked out, Srinath whispered to me that apart from the PM's family, the NSA and a couple of others, no one had yet met Dr Singh after the operation. Murali, who was with us, said I should not let anyone know I had seen him because both President Pratibha Patil and Sonia Gandhi were waiting to meet him and had not yet been given time. They might take it amiss if it got about that I had jumped the queue. I reassured Murali that no one, apart from my immediate family, even knew I was in India, and I was now on my way to the airport to take a flight back to Singapore.

Srinath said, 'He is still very frail and weak. We were worried that he was not fighting back. He is not eating enough and needs to get up and walk. So when Mrs Kaur heard you were here, she wondered whether meeting you might help revive his spirits. I can see it has. He has not spoken for an entire day. Whatever he said to you were his first words today.'

As I drove back to the airport I rewound his words in my mind.

I remembered what Dr Singh said at a farewell lunch he had hosted for me at 7 RCR. I had been flattered to be told that he wanted a proper banquet organized for me. He had invited Montek, Rangarajan, all the senior PMO officials, including Prithviraj Chavan, Narayanan and Nair, the Cabinet secretary K.M. Chandrashekhar, the foreign secretary Shivshankar Menon, the finance secretary Duvvuri Subbarao and two guests from outside the government whom I had wanted there—my guru K. Subrahmanyam and the former governor of the Reserve Bank of India, Bimal Jalan.

The seating had been like at an official banquet, with the PM and myself facing each other, and others placed around us according to rank and protocol. At the end of a long meal, during which many of us recounted the ups and downs of our time in the PMO, Dr Singh thanked me for the work I had done and said that he would miss me.

Turning to those around the table he said, 'We have been partners.'

It was an emotionally charged afternoon, reflective of our complex relationship. When I had started out with him as his media adviser, I had been a professional journalist who knew him well, but was not intimate with him. Mani Dixit was unquestionably the man closest to him in his PMO. But after Mani's death, I had filled some of that vacuum. I had become the recipient of his confidences, asked to run confidential errands, and I had been by his side through the nuclear deal. My job had become a 24×7 obsession, somewhat to my wife's ire; the only domestic chore I recall performing during that time was dropping my daughter to the bus stop every morning. Though we rarely spoke of it, I knew Dr Singh had defended me time and again when others in the Congress party had called for my dismissal. He may have been disappointed by my decision to leave but never showed it. Rather, he was understanding of my personal compulsions, like a family elder would be. It was a bond cemented by the ups and downs of an eventful tenure. Yet, I was touched and surprised to hear him openly say that we had been 'partners'.

After lunch, when I sought his permission to leave, he stepped forward and hugged me with both arms.

'In Punjab it's called a *jhappi*,' said Montek as the two of us walked towards the car park.

I went back to Delhi in late March to meet him after the elections were announced. Both Dr Singh, with his illness now behind him, and Mrs Kaur looked more relaxed than the last time I had seen them. We were seated in the living room at 3 RCR and the table, as always, had a few books on it that they would have been reading. The conversation, as always, began with ritual inquiries about my family.

I suggested to him that now that elections had been called, he should contest a seat in the Lok Sabha. If the party returned to power, he would be PM again, but this time, I argued, he should be in the Lok

Sabha. Even if the party lost, he would at least have the satisfaction of ending his political career by winning a seat in the House of the People. Ever since his defeat in the South Delhi constituency in 1999, which his family and friends suspected had partly been caused by internal sabotage by Congressmen, this had been a touchy topic.

Dr Singh did not react. Mrs Kaur smiled and looked at him quizzically. I persisted, suggesting that he contest from Assam and from Amritsar. He owed it to the people of Assam, the state he had represented in the Rajya Sabha since 1991, to contest from there, and he owed it to himself to contest from Amritsar, Mrs Kaur's home town and the city closest to his heart. He would win in both places, I assured him, and he could then decide which seat to retain.

'My health will not permit campaigning,' he said, and added, 'anyway it is for the party to decide.'

I did not yield. I argued that he need not worry about campaigning. He could record a few DVDs and his campaign managers would take them around. If Mrs Kaur campaigned for him, that would be more than enough, I said to him. 'Ma'am will be a huge draw both in Assam and Amritsar. The crowds will come to see her and she can easily address them and seek their votes on your behalf.'

Both laughed. '*Haan!* Why not? I can address public meetings,' she said, exuding confidence, and clearly liking the idea.

I decided to strike while the iron was hot and went on. 'Do not agree to continue as PM if they expect you to remain in the Rajya Sabha. Why should you leave it for the party to decide? Make this a condition. Insist that you want to contest in the Lok Sabha elections. In 2004, you were the accidental PM. In 2009, you have every right to return to office on the basis of your record. You have given the party five years of power. You have managed the coalition, handled the nuclear deal crisis. The economy has done well despite all the problems with the Left. You have saved it from a crisis.'

I reminded Dr Singh that his party was asking for votes in his name and seeking a second term for him. 'Let me warn you, Sir,' I said, 'if the Congress loses they will put the blame on you. They will say your policies cost them the victory. So, in case they win you should be able to claim the victory for yourself. Please contest the Lok Sabha elections.'

With those words of unsolicited advice, I left and returned to Singapore. He did not contest the elections. I never asked him if he had indicated an interest in doing so and was advised against it, or if he was not even asked and had reconciled himself to remaining a member of the Rajya Sabha.

Back in Singapore I would get the occasional email or telephone call from a journalist who would bring me up to speed with election news and political gossip. Many believed that Dr Singh's face had been printed on the cover of the manifesto and on election posters so that the expected defeat in that election could be explained away as his defeat and Rahul Gandhi, whose picture was not printed on the party manifesto or posters, could then claim leadership as the agent of change. One senior political journalist who claimed he had spoken to Ahmed Patel told me that Rahul, in fact, looked forward to a tenure as the leader of the Opposition so as to burnish his own political credentials, differentiating himself, perhaps even distancing himself, from Dr Singh's legacy. Few expected the Congress to return to power until almost the very end of the campaign. They all underestimated Dr Singh's popularity and the lacklustre image of the BJP's prime ministerial candidate, L.K. Advani, among his own partymen.

When the results came in, not only had the UPA won a clear majority but the Congress improved its tally from 145 seats in UPA-1 to 206. While this represented only a modest shift in vote share—the Congress's vote share went up by 2.02 per cent—it represented wider urban support for the Congress. The UPA not only won almost all the seats in all metros, save Bengaluru, but also saw a 19 per cent increase in urban votes compared to a 14 per cent increase in the rural vote. In 2004 it was Sonia Gandhi who helped the Congress move up from the 114 of 1999 to 145 seats. In 2009, it was Dr Singh's tenure during UPA-1 that helped the party secure 206 seats—nine more than the 197 seats that Rajiv Gandhi managed to deliver in 1989, after five years in office. In Punjab, the Congress saw a massive 11 per cent increase in vote share, five times more than the national increase in the Congress's vote share. Had Dr Singh contested from Amritsar, he would have won easily. Dr Singh's five years of 9 per cent growth, his standing up to the Left on the nuclear deal in defence of the national interest, and the BJP voters' disappointment with Advani's lacklustre leadership had helped win the urban voter over.

The fear generated by Dr Singh's critics in the Congress party that the nuclear deal would alienate Muslim voters proved to be misplaced. The theory that the rural employment guarantee programme would be a vote winner was also disproved by the fact that the country's more backward states voted for the BJP and other parties, while it was western Uttar Pradesh, Andhra Pradesh and a clutch of urban centres that gave the Congress its additional seats. What rural and Muslim voters had said to Vidya Subrahmaniam of *The Hindu*, when asked who they would support, truly summed up the mood. '*Congress ko. Sardarji ko*,' they had said, calling the PM a '*neyk aadmi*' (good man).

This was also a historic verdict. For the first time after 1962, a sitting prime minister who had served a full five-year term was being re-elected with an improved majority. Indira Gandhi entered office in the middle of a term and got re-elected in 1971, after victory in a war with Pakistan, so she did not get two full terms in succession. After Nehru no PM has managed to get re-elected after a full five-year term. Vajpayee's re-election in 1999 followed a premature end to his first term. Dr Singh's victory was a game changer.

———

On the day of the victory, as results poured in, I was watching the news on CNN-IBN on my laptop at home. The panellists were discussing if the stunning results were because of Manmohan Singh. Then the channel's political reporter Pallavi Ghosh appeared on the screen, reporting from the Congress party office. She had Prithviraj Chavan with her.

'So who is the architect of this victory?' Pallavi asked Prithvi. 'Sonia Gandhi or Manmohan Singh?'

Prithvi, the man who was handpicked by Dr Singh to be his MoS in the PMO and kept there for a full five years despite a lacklustre record, said the politically correct thing, 'Both!' He then added a spin, 'This victory is a vote for Rahul Gandhi. Rahulji's good work helped us win.'

The chant became the official mantra. Rahul Gandhi, every party loyalist claimed, was the architect of the 2009 result. In the very hour of victory, its authorship was denied to the man who made it happen.

The way I saw it, if the Congress had lost, the blame for the defeat would have been placed squarely on the PM's shoulders. It would be said his obsession with the nuclear deal cost the party the support of the Left and the Muslims. His 'neo-liberal' economic policies would have been deemed to have alienated the poor. His attempt to befriend Musharraf would have been regarded as having alienated the Hindu vote. A hundred explanations would have been trotted out to pin the defeat on the PM. Now that the party was back in office, and that too with more numbers than anyone in the party had forecast, the credit would go to the party's 'first family'. To the scion and future leader. It was Rahul's victory, not Manmohan's.

After the elections, Dr Singh did try to be more assertive, taking a view on who would be in his Cabinet and who would not, and resisting the induction of the DMK's A. Raja and T.R. Baalu, for their unsavoury reputations. Watching from the sidelines, I had hoped he would not buckle under pressure. Dr Singh stood his ground for a day, managed to keep Baalu out, but had to yield ground on Raja under pressure from his own party. To me, it was a reiteration of the message that the victory was not his but the Family's.

On 2 June 2009, I flew down to Delhi and met Dr Singh. I was told he would see me at 7 RCR. When I reached 7 RCR I was told he was at 3 RCR and I should go there. I decided to walk and took the path that Dr Singh would take almost every day, along the spacious lawns of 7 and 5 RCR, through the wall that separated them, with an expanse of green and tall trees all around. Meanwhile, Dr Singh had been informed that I had arrived at 7 RCR and chose to walk towards it. We met at 5 RCR. It was past ten in the morning in early June. The temperature must have already been upwards of 38 degrees Celsius. It felt blazing hot. I asked him why he was walking in the hot sun.

'Oh, this is nothing,' he said, as he continued to walk briskly towards 7 RCR. 'I campaigned in this heat.'

I had read about it in Singapore. Everyone was amazed that after a major surgery in February, he was out campaigning in April–May. Dr Singh was a step ahead of me. Murali and I were walking behind him, with the SPG guards a step behind.

He half turned his head towards me. I could see the expression of great pride on his face when he said, 'I was willing to sacrifice my life for the victory.'

He asked me what my plans were. I told him that my contract required me to give two months' notice. If I gave in my resignation that very day, I would be able to join by 1 August. But, I clarified, I did not want to return as media adviser. Deepak Sandhu was doing a good job as his press secretary. I could help her and support her but it was best she continued. I could be called 'adviser to PM' and do whatever he wanted me to.

'You can be called secretary to PM. Dhar Saheb used to be called secretary to PM,' he said.

The reference to Professor P.N. Dhar, the Delhi School economist who was inducted into Indira Gandhi's PMO and worked alongside P.N. Haksar, left me surprised and flattered. I had enormous regard for Dhar, with whom I made friends during my days as editorial page editor of the *Times of India*, persuading him to publish his account of what transpired at Shimla in 1972 between Indira Gandhi and Zulfiqar Ali Bhutto, twenty-five years after the event. According to him, Bhutto had been ready to settle Kashmir at the summit, but Indira, showing statesmanship, did not force concessions that he would have found hard to defend at home. Dhar's column, when published, received a lot of attention in Pakistan and India, and we would discuss this often. In the process, I learnt about his special relationship with Indira, as an adviser with an academic rather than a bureaucratic background.

So I was excited by Dr Singh's reference to Dhar and his suggestion that I could play that kind of a role in the PMO. But I was not comfortable with the designation of secretary in the PMO, though that was the rank I had had as media adviser. If I was designated 'secretary' rather than 'adviser', I would have to report to the principal secretary. As media adviser, I reported directly to the PM, so I suggested he designate me 'adviser' rather than 'secretary'. He agreed, and I went back to Singapore.

On 3 June, I submitted my resignation to Kishore Mahbubani, the dean of the Lee Kuan Yew School of Public Policy, where I taught. I shared with Kishore my real reason for quitting but requested him to keep it confidential. A few days later, a government gossip website, www.whispersinthecorridors.com, reported that I would be returning to the PMO. I had no idea how the news had leaked out but I put it down to just intelligent guesswork or speculation. The 'whispers' website was normally fed by secretarial staff and reporters. Someone might have seen me at RCR and put two and two together.

The editor of *Business Standard* T.N. Ninan called me a few days later to say that his correspondent had filed a report that I was to return to the PMO and would be made responsible for monitoring implementation of the UPA's flagship programmes. I told him I was not aware of this. He assured me that the reporter had secured the story from Prithviraj Chavan and said *BS* would run it unless I denied it. I assumed Prithvi had briefed the reporter after having been told of the decision by the PM. So I did not deny it but asked Ninan to make sure the story was authenticated by the PMO. Little did I suspect that this leak might have been part of an effort to sabotage my return.

The day after the *BS* story appeared, Jaideep called me and said that the news report had created problems 'with the party' and that the PM had asked him to advise me to delay my return. I told him that I had already submitted my resignation and it would be embarrassing for me to tell the dean that I would just hang around till some uncertain date in the future without taking up any teaching work. I could either return on 1 August or on 1 January, after teaching for one more semester. Jaideep suggested I come to Delhi and meet the PM.

It was not convenient for me to make a trip to Delhi at that time. I was in the middle of teaching and other work. I was also angry and irritated by this turn of events. To tell the truth, I was dismayed by the PM's display of spinelessness, even after this handsome victory. If he was unable to make appointments in his own office, he was 'yielding space' too soon. That phrase—yielding space—was one that I had picked up from him when he advised me not to drop out of a tour with him because someone else would end up doing my job. Why, I wondered, was he yielding space now, succumbing to pressure to keep me out? Clearly, I had not yet understood the extent to which the party would go to defang the PM.

I told Jaideep that I could not afford to buy another ticket, having just gone to Delhi and returned at my own expense, so I would come in early July after a scheduled trip to Kathmandu for which the Asian Development Bank (ADB) was paying. I was doing a report on SAARC for the ADB. I flew into Delhi from Kathmandu on 11 July and met the PM the same day.

'Some problems have come up regarding your appointment, can you delay your return?' Dr Singh asked me. I explained my constraints.

'Okay, you come back in August. I will sort this out by then.'

After that brief exchange, the conversation moved on to the agenda for the new term. He wanted ideas on moving forward with Pakistan, since he was shortly to meet his new Pakistani counterpart Syed Yousaf Raza Gilani in Sharm el-Sheikh. We also talked about his priorities for the economy and the relationship with the US, under a new President. Barack Obama had not voted in favour of the nuclear deal. I also warned him that the BJP would be even more critical of the government in its second term, since the party would be fighting for survival, having performed even worse in 2009 than in 2004. The conversation went in various directions, and then it was time for me to leave.

I returned to Delhi on Saturday, 1 August and sought an appointment with the PM for the 3rd. When I did not hear from the PMO for the next four days I knew something had gone seriously wrong. Finally,

I was asked to see Dr Singh on Saturday, 8 August at 5 p.m. in the evening at 3 RCR. This was exactly one year, to the day, since I had quit the PMO.

When I arrived Nair was with him and I was asked to wait in an anteroom. I could hear their voices and then there was silence. The door opened and Murali invited me in. Nair had left, walking out of a side door, and Dr Singh was alone, seated on a sofa and looking pale and anxious. The last time I had seen him like this was on the night of the terror attack in Srinagar, when he had to make up his mind whether he should go to Kashmir the next day against the advice of his officials and launch the Srinagar–Muzaffarabad bus service.

I sat down and waited for him to speak. I avoided the usual pleasantries and the pointless 'how are you'. He remained motionless. Even the peacocks had gone quiet. He finally broke that deafening silence.

'I cannot take you back into the PMO. Why don't you become a member of the Planning Commission for now? I will see later how to bring you back here.'

I had expected to hear something like this. I did not want to embarrass him by asking what had gone wrong. I guessed this was part of the party's effort to limit his degree of freedom. One more blow. Or, it might have been the work of the people around him, who had perhaps been happy to see me go and were not keen on my return. After all, I had been seen as the PM's troubleshooter and troublemaker in UPA-1. I had been unwilling to kowtow to the party High Command or yield space to my senior colleagues. I had encouraged the PM to stand his ground on the nuclear deal, I had projected the PM rather than Sonia or Rahul, and so on. I then said what I had come prepared to say.

'Sir, I joined you in 2004 because you wanted me to. I worked for you, not for the government. I have never fancied a government job. If you are having problems now, I will find something for myself outside government.'

I then told him I already had an offer from T.N. Ninan to succeed him as the editor of *Business Standard*. I would take that up. Dr Singh sat back and relaxed.

'Oh good. That is even better than the Planning Commission.'

I took his permission to leave and stepped out, walking all the way, a good half kilometre, to the car park.

———

Several weeks later, after I joined *Business Standard*, I was invited for a function at 7 RCR. As he circulated among the guests Dr Singh walked up to me and asked why I had not come to see him for a long time. The next day, I sought an appointment and called on him. We talked about many things. Finally, he turned to the subject weighing on both our minds.

He said, 'I am sorry about what happened. You see, you must understand one thing. I have come to terms with this. There cannot be two centres of power. That creates confusion. I have to accept that the party president *is* the centre of power. The government is answerable to the party.'

I saw no point in disagreeing with him or contesting his thesis. But, of course, I did disagree with it. The prime minister was answerable to the Parliament and the government was governed by the Constitution. The party president was only the leader of her party. The prime minister was the leader of the country as a whole and the head of government. One could go on and on, discussing these things threadbare. But this was neither the time, nor the place. Each one of us finds our own rationale for what we do and do not do. He had found his.

Epilogue

Manmohan's Legacy

'Am I in trouble?'

Manmohan Singh
October 2010

I have an indelible image in my mind of the way Dr Singh sat, on that summer morning of 2 June 2009, shortly after he had declared to me, in a moment of rare emotion, that he would have sacrificed his life 'for the victory'. His normal posture was restrained and formal: he sat straight, with his hands resting on the arm of a chair or on his lap, much as he might do in a conversation with a visiting dignitary. But now, as we spoke of the election result, and much else, he was supremely at ease, reclining with his right leg on his outstretched left, the right ankle resting on the knee of the left. It was a posture that exuded confidence, and suggested that he felt, at this moment, the master of all he surveyed. The one other time I recall seeing him sit like that was after the 123 Agreement was done in 2007.

The nuclear deal was the crowning glory of Manmohan Singh's first term. As Narasimha Rao's finance minister, he had made history by opening up the economy. Now, he had made history once again, by giving India a new status as a world power. Having conceded the greater part of the prime minister's turf to Sonia and his senior colleagues, foreign policy was one area where he zealously guarded the space he

271

had secured for himself. True, he retained his influence over economic policy through Chidambaram and Montek. But foreign affairs was his sole preserve and he made sure it stayed that way in UPA-1. It was the area where he could articulate his vision for India in a changing world, and project his personality, without coming into conflict with the priorities and the profile of the Congress president.

Had there been no opposition to the nuclear deal, it would have neither gained the prime minister notoriety among his critics, nor would it have imparted a statesman-like sheen to his image, at home and abroad. Had the BJP claimed credit for starting it all, or the Left claimed credit for shaping the final outcome, as some of its 'moderates' would have liked to do, the deal would have had many fathers. Had Sonia fully backed Dr Singh, the Congress would have claimed credit, reminding the country that it was Nehru who began India's nuclear programme, Indira who first tested a bomb and Rajiv who authorized weaponization.

But none of this happened. Dr Singh was left to his own devices and he made sure he had his way. He cajoled the nuclear establishment into falling in line. He pushed Narayanan to seal the deal. He ignored the doubters in the external affairs ministry and empowered the believers. He convinced President Bush that backing the deal, at home and abroad, was in America's interest too. He went to Trombay and addressed scientists. He went to Washington DC and addressed Congress. He reached out to China and Pakistan, softening their resistance. He spoke repeatedly in Parliament, at length and emphatically, and courted public opinion.

In standing firm in the face of Sonia's wavering commitment to the deal, Dr Singh underscored his own political relevance. Faced with the threat of his resignation, Sonia chose to support him rather than change the prime minister, as his critics in the party and the Left Front assumed she would. There was no one else in the party who had his qualities of competence and compliance. She was certainly not prepared to name Pranab Mukherjee as prime minister or even as deputy prime minister.

Finally, Manmohan Singh exhibited political skills that no one thought he had. He befriended the likes of Amar Singh and Mulayam

Singh Yadav to bolster the UPA government after the Left withdrew support. His act of self-assertion against an ideologically motivated cabal dictating foreign policy to the government paid off. His reputation soared. The urban middle class that had deserted the Congress and voted for Atal Bihari Vajpayee in 1999 and 2004 returned to its fold in 2009.

With that electoral victory, he had now made a different kind of history, becoming the first prime minister after Jawaharlal Nehru to have returned to office after a full five-year term and with an improved majority to boot. Nehru managed that only in 1957, not in 1962. Dr Singh did not contest Lok Sabha elections in 2009 but became the indisputable candidate to head the new government. No one, not even Sonia, could deny him the prime ministership. In democratic politics, electoral victory is the ultimate test of performance and the prize every politician cherishes. Dr Singh believed he had delivered on that score in the summer of 2009 and that is why he exuded the confidence he did, on that day. But then, he made the cardinal mistake of imagining the victory was his.

Reflecting later on the conversation during which he asked me to return from Singapore and rejoin the PMO as his adviser, I felt that rather than thinking of me as his P.N. Dhar, he had been imagining himself to be the victorious Indira of 1971. This time round, he may have convinced himself, his performance and destiny had made him PM. Not Sonia.

Bit by bit, in the space of a few weeks, he was defanged. He thought he could induct the ministers he wanted into his team. Sonia nipped that hope in the bud by offering the finance portfolio to Pranab, without even consulting him. The PM had been toying with the idea of appointing his principal economic adviser C. Rangarajan, the comrade with whom he had battled the balance of payments crisis of 1991–92. He tried to put his foot down on the induction of A. Raja of the DMK (though the 2G scam became public knowledge only in 2010, he may well have known of Raja's role in it), but after asserting himself for a full twenty-four hours, caved in to pressure from both his own party and the DMK.

Then Sharm el-Sheikh happened. The BJP, nursing electoral wounds, used the opportunity provided by a controversial joint statement by the Indian and Pakistani prime ministers to tear into Dr Singh. That was to be expected. But surprisingly, even shockingly, the Congress criticized its own head of government, refusing to back him even after he had defended himself in Parliament.

Dismayed, he chose to surrender. When he told me he could not take me back into the PMO because he had come to accept that there could not be two centres of power, the subtext was that my return would signal his desire to project himself as PM. He chose to yield space. This was not the Manmohan Singh of the nuclear deal or the victorious PM of the summer of 2009. I was struck later by how much the monsoon months had dampened his spirit.

Dr Singh never really recovered from that initial deflation of his authority and it came to affect multiple areas of governance. Even though the economy performed well in the early part of UPA-2, by 2011 it was showing signs of a slowdown combined with inflation and rising deficits. Having yielded space to Pranab in North Block, Dr Singh had little control over fiscal policy. His chosen domain, foreign policy, had little joy to offer him in UPA-2. With Barack Obama in Washington DC, the bonhomie of the Bush years was gone. Not only was Obama preoccupied with his own domestic economic problems, but America's dependence on China to help it deal with the global economic crisis increased Beijing's leverage and reduced New Delhi's salience. Moreover, Obama and his secretary of state Hillary Clinton had not voted in favour of the nuclear deal. Obama's decision to withdraw from Afghanistan increased Pakistan's importance for the Pentagon and, thus, negatively impacted the US approach to India and South Asia.

Matters were made worse by UPA-2's incompetent handling of the civil nuclear liability bill. In its original draft, the bill would have enabled India to resume nuclear energy commerce with supplier nations and help Indian nuclear power companies enter the global market. However, inept political handling resulted in the BJP joining hands with the Left to demand changes to the government draft. These changes did not satisfy international suppliers, nor indeed India's own companies.

Dr Singh's crowning achievement of UPA-1, the nuclear deal, lay in tatters. Yet he soldiered on as a loyal member of his party.

Waning India–US relations inevitably affected the postures of regional players. China became assertive, risking a border confrontation with India after years. The military regime in Pakistan disowned the Musharraf–Manmohan formula on Kashmir and the prime minister never managed to travel to Pakistan, even to visit his place of birth at Gah. The only silver lining to this dark cloud was the new relationship with Japan.

Things were even worse on the home front. When charges of corruption were levelled against his Cabinet colleagues, Dr Singh could not put up a convincing defence of his own role in decision-making. In UPA-1, the Opposition had tried to sully his reputation for integrity, but with no success. In UPA-2, it managed to make a dent and stabbed away until there was a bleeding wound.

In UPA-1, Sonia and the Congress party did not really have a Plan B; Rahul was not fit to become prime minister and Sonia did not trust anyone else apart from Dr Singh. In UPA-2, a Plan B began to emerge as Rahul started getting ready to take charge. The poor showing of the Congress in the Uttar Pradesh and Bihar assembly elections prevented him from rising fast enough. But that did not deter his supporters and Dr Singh's critics from constantly calling for a change of leadership. I wondered, as many in the country did, how the relationship of trust that I had witnessed between Sonia Gandhi and Manmohan Singh during UPA-1 had weathered these strains in UPA-2.

Speculation was rife that all was not well. When a family friend of Rahul, working as an analyst with a foreign consulting firm, put out a paper suggesting that Dr Singh had become a liability for the government the Delhi durbar was agog with speculation. Was this a message from the family itself? After a series of other humiliations many wondered why Dr Singh was not calling it a day. Was it the case that Dr Singh was adamant about completing his tenure, which he did believe was something he had earned through hard work? For his part, Dr Singh let it be known to anyone who asked him that he was ready to go, if asked to. So, was he insisting that he be dismissed, or just giving Sonia time to help her prepare Rahul for the transition? Was he overstaying her invitation or holding the fort? No convincing answers were available but the political and media speculation that went on weakened his authority further and damaged his reputation.

In UPA-1, the media came to view Dr Singh as the man who could throw his resignation letter on the table and leave. In UPA-2, the same media came to see him as clinging on to power in the face of humiliation. In UPA-1, Dr Singh was willing to secure and defend some policy space for himself. In UPA-2, he seemed to surrender to his own party leader and the allies. In UPA-2, as at times in UPA-1, Dr Singh sought an alibi in 'coalition compulsions' but this time the media and the public were unwilling to buy that. Many came to believe that in not asserting the authority inherent in his office he had devalued it. He had failed to live up to the trust that voters had reposed in him, personally, when they had re-elected the UPA.

The compromises Dr Singh had made in UPA-1 were less visible to the public. Critically, they did not involve charges of corruption and did not occur against the backdrop of economic gloom. Moreover, the stand he took on the nuclear deal erased any memory of his submissiveness to Sonia in the public imagination. In the end, Singh was King. In UPA-2, his long public silences, his reduced visibility, the corruption exposes, the 'policy paralysis', as the media dubbed it, and, above all, his willingness to be pushed around by his party and coalition partners, and, as it turned out later, to have his decisions publicly challenged by Rahul Gandhi, irretrievably damaged his image.

Returning from a successful visit to China in October 2013, Dr Singh said he would now leave it to history to judge his record in office. He invoked the judgement of history once again at his last national press conference on 3 January 2014, saying:

I honestly believe that history will be kinder to me than the contemporary media, or for that matter, the Opposition parties in Parliament. I cannot divulge all things that take place in the Cabinet system of government. I think, taking into account the circumstances, and the compulsions of a coalition polity, I have done as best as I could under the circumstances.

Historians will undoubtedly note that in UPA-1 the economy logged the highest rates of growth for any plan period since Independence, generating revenues that the government could deploy in rural development, infrastructure, education and defence. India's global profile was better than ever before and India had finally been recognized as a nuclear weapons power. To top it all, the incumbent prime minister won an impressive election victory and secured a second term in office. But, historians will also record that UPA-2 was a tale of missed opportunities, of weak and unfocused leadership, and a confused foreign policy.

In UPA-1, Dr Singh proved to the people of India and to his own party that he was fit to be prime minister and historians will surely laud him for performing that feat despite a circumscribed role. The next elections will show whether UPA-2 can convince public opinion that it has been worthy of the mandate given to it. If it fails to do so, it remains to be seen whether history will be generous enough to accept Dr Singh's stoic detachment from the moral failures of UPA-2 and allow him to be remembered mainly by his achievements in UPA-1.

It was against the backdrop of his declining external and domestic performance and profile that Pranab Mukherjee made that remark to me in 2011, that the image of the government and the country is inextricably linked to the image of the prime minister. He was right. With the emasculating of the prime minister, not just Manmohan Singh himself, but his government and, ultimately, the country, became the losers.

In October 2010, Shobhana Bhartia invited Dr Singh to address the annual Hindustan Times Summit, as she had done every year since 2004. However, this time there was no reply from the PMO. She called me and asked if I thought the PM was shying away from a media event because of the controversy surrounding the telecom licences issue, popularly called the 2G scam. Would he feel reassured if he were told that I would chair the session, she asked. I was amused and said I had no objection to chairing the session even though this was a *Hindustan Times* event and I was the editor of another newspaper. A couple of days later she called to say that Dr Singh had accepted her invitation and that she did tell him I would chair the session.

I then called Indu Chaturvedi at 7 RCR and told him that in case someone were to ask the PM a question on the 2G issue I would have to allow it. I was now back in the media and could not behave like a media adviser and protect him from public questioning. Indu clarified that the PM was prepared to reply to all questions and would also read out a written statement.

On the appointed day, Shobhana and I received Dr Singh at Taj Palace Hotel and walked him to the dais. While Shobhana was welcoming the audience, Dr Singh turned to me, smiled and asked, 'Am I in trouble?' He asked me to come and see him the next day.

The expected question on 2G licences was asked. Dr Singh had a prepared reply and read from a typed sheet:

> As far as allocation of 2G spectrum is concerned, Parliament is in session. I would not like, therefore, to make any detailed statement. But there should not be any doubt in anybody's mind that if any wrong thing has been done by anybody, he or she will be brought to book. For all this to happen, in a democracy, we have to allow Parliament to function. We are ready to discuss all issues in Parliament. We are not afraid of a discussion.

I went across to 7 RCR the next day.

Inevitably, we discussed 2G. My advice to him was that he should defend the policy itself and have the charges against Raja investigated. The Comptroller and Auditor General (CAG) of India, it could be credibly argued, was taking an 'accountant's' view on policy. Several analysts had already said so and that was also the editorial line I had taken at *Business Standard*. The government's policy had enabled it to offer cheaper telecom services and made it possible for millions of Indians to become connected. The economic and social benefits of the policy far outweighed the revenue loss to the exchequer, which the CAG had focused on.

However, if some firms had been unduly favoured, those responsible should be punished. Why should he defend his corrupt ministers, I asked. He was not responsible for their corruption, since they had been foisted on him; he was responsible for formulating government policy. The policy itself was not flawed, even if some in government had disagreed with it. He shared my views that day. However, the government persisted with its ill-advised 'zero loss' argument (that the deal had caused no revenue loss to the exchequer), revealing how little control the prime minister had over the political narrative.

The telecom issue came on the back of public criticism of the government's handling of the 2010 Commonwealth Games. The games fiasco was waiting to happen. The first minister for sports in UPA-1, the late Sunil Dutt, could never focus on the essentials and much time was wasted in turf battles between his ministry and the Indian Olympic Association headed by Suresh Kalmadi. Dr Singh would come away exasperated from those meetings. Dutt's successor, Mani Shankar Aiyar, was openly opposed to hosting the games and wanted India to withdraw its invitation. Dr Singh, who was never too happy with Dutt's stewardship, disagreed with Aiyar's cavalier approach, but did little to either take charge or place a competent person in charge. At one point, he tried to get Rahul Gandhi interested, suggesting to him that just as his father, Rajiv, had acquired both administrative experience and a reputation for good organization when he took charge of the 1982 Asian Games, the younger Gandhi could also make good use of this opportunity. Rahul showed no interest. Five years of UPA-1 were largely wasted and work on the October 2010 games began in right earnest only in mid-2009.

While the new sports minister M.S. Gill and the efficient new secretary Sindhushree Khullar worked hard to stage the games, the media's negative perception about the games' organization and charges of corruption levelled against Kalmadi and Delhi chief minister Sheila Dikshit damaged the government's reputation. It had become all too obvious that the games were being threatened by poor organization and weak coordination between different agencies. The PMO stepped in and decided to take charge. But it was too late. While the games went off well, the damage to the government's image was severe and became etched on the public mind. UPA-2 was beginning to be seen as bumbling and corrupt.

The scandal relating to the allocation of coal blocks during the period when Dr Singh handled the coal portfolio further tarnished the prime minister's image. Here too, he was charged, not with corruption, but with turning a blind eye to the corruption of others. Public opinion was no longer willing to excuse him for choosing not to claim and exercise the authority that was his due as prime minister.

Watching this debacle unfold, I was convinced, even more than before, that the prime minister's decision not to return to office via the Lok Sabha was his biggest political mistake. The political authority and legitimacy that a second term in office offers a head of government was denied to him by his remaining a member of the Upper House and not securing for himself the imprimatur of a popular mandate.

He could easily have said to Sonia that he would prefer to retire as PM than to once again return to the job from the Rajya Sabha. If she had refused him a safe Lok Sabha seat he could have gone into retirement on health grounds. He would not only have been hailed for being the first PM to voluntarily retire but he may well have become a global statesman, invited to chair UN commissions and lecture around the world, like so many distinguished former heads of government. If, on the other hand, he had returned to the job from the Lok Sabha he would have had a much better chance of asserting his authority and running his government his way.

Initially, I saw his subservience as an aspect of his shy and self-effacing personality, but over time I felt, like many, that this might be his strategy for political survival. Was it just unquestioned loyalty to the leader or a survival instinct that prompted him to remain silent? Whatever the motive, his image took a fatal blow. One consequence of this was the demand that the PM and his office be brought under the purview of Lok Pal, the anti-corruption ombudsman, whose creation became a cause célèbre for civil society activists. Several prime ministers had successfully resisted this demand over the years, citing national interest and political stability. Dr Singh succumbed.

No one, bar the odd Opposition party politician or irresponsible social activist, accused Dr Singh of questionable acts of commission. However, a great many charged him with one act of omission—of not acting like a prime minister, when he was, in fact, the prime minister. His decision to turn introvert, reduce his travels within India, not address a press conference till he finally did so to announce his retirement, and not be more communicative, all at a time when the social media was flooded with sarcasm and ridicule, only wounded him more.

As these crises unfolded, all the inherent weaknesses of the political arrangement were revealed, among them poor administrative leadership in the PMO and an unimaginative political and media strategy in response to the challenges. Irritated with what he regarded as a short-sighted and unimaginative response of the Hurriyat leaders to his Kashmir initiative, and their unwillingness to participate in the J&K round-table he hosted in Srinagar in May 2006, Dr Singh had called them 'small men in big chairs', on the flight back from Srinagar. By the end of 2013, editorial writers, civil society activists and political analysts were all beginning to ask if Dr Singh was also not a 'small man in a big chair'. Some even accused him of diminishing the chair to feel more comfortable in it.

Should he have resigned at the first whiff of scandal, owning moral responsibility for the corruption of others, instead of defending the government? Perhaps. Could he have resigned? Maybe not. The party would have hounded him for 'letting it down'. It would have then accused him of trying to occupy the high moral ground and quitting on principle to avoid being sacked for not 'delivering the goods'. When the horse you are riding becomes a tiger it is difficult to dismount.

Along with the corruption controversies, the economic slowdown after 2012 and persistent inflation turned Dr Singh's own political base, the urban middle class, hostile. As the government's popularity declined, the Congress party began to switch gears and focus on succession, hoping Rahul Gandhi would rise to the occasion and take charge. Planted stories began to appear in the media about Dr Singh's imminent retirement. However, Rahul's repeated inability to deliver results for the party in a series of state elections meant that Dr Singh could not be 'retired' and created a vacuum at the top.

Probably to bolster his image, Rahul chose defiance to authority as his strategy for political relevance. He had already declared in 2009 that his route to power would be as a 'rebel' rather than as a successor to Dr Singh's legacy. He had said to a gathering of students at JNU in 2009, 'The hierarchical system exists [in the Congress]. It is a reality. But what is the option before me? I can either propagate the system or change it. I am not the one to propagate it so I am trying to change it. You do not like the system; even I do not like it. We have to work together to change it.' How could the vice president of a party, that too the son of the party president, be the 'agent of change' without positioning himself in opposition to the incumbent PM?

Aware of this strategy on Rahul's part, I was not surprised when he chose to go public, in late September 2013, and criticize an ordinance that the Union Cabinet had cleared aimed at amending the Representation of Peoples' Act, 1951, to remove constraints on lawbreakers becoming lawmakers, so to speak. In response to a Supreme Court ruling of 2012, that a member of Parliament or state assembly would be immediately disqualified if convicted by a court in a criminal offence and given a jail sentence of two years or more, the government sought to amend the existing law so that such convicted legislators could continue as elected representatives if they appealed before a higher court within three months. The original bill for this purpose could not be passed in Parliament and the government chose to amend the act through an executive fiat. A public outcry against the ordinance placed the government on the defensive.

Rahul could have urged the government to respond to public

opinion and let the PM handle the matter on his return to India from an official visit to the US. Instead, he decided to demand the ordinance's withdrawal, calling it 'nonsense' in front of TV cameras, hours before Dr Singh was to call on President Obama. This public display of disrespect to Dr Singh and disregard for the dignity of the office of the prime minister on a day like this was, I felt, reason enough for Dr Singh to call it quits. He chose not to.

It should have been clear to Dr Singh and his advisers that the Congress party would not go out of its way to defend him against this Opposition onslaught on the ordinance. During UPA-1, it had been forced to defend the PM even when it did not agree with his actions, to ensure the stability of its first-ever experiment in running a coalition government. That compulsion was no longer there. This time round Rahul Gandhi was waiting in the wings.

I had begun my association with Dr Singh as a critic of many of his policies. As I got to know him and then work for him, I became truly impressed by his intellect, his humane persona, his gentle and civil conduct, his political instinct and his deep patriotism. I shared his vision for India in the twenty-first century: a liberal, plural, secular India, an open society and an open economy, pursuing inclusive growth and at peace with its neighbours. He was not a popular leader like Vajpayee, nor an experienced politician like Narasimha Rao. Yet, he showed the country that an ordinary, honest Indian, an *aam aadmi*, to use the current buzzword in politics, could become prime minister through sheer hard work and professional commitment.

So I, like millions of his middle-class supporters, feel tragically cheated that he has allowed himself to become an object of such ridicule in his second term in office, in the process devaluing the office of the prime minister. This book is an effort to offer a balanced view of Dr Singh's personality and of his record as head of government.

It is a testimony to the eternal nature of the great Hindu epic the Mahabharata that so many of India's movies and television soaps continue to portray their characters as modern-day versions of the various protagonists of that power play. The characterization of today's personalities in terms of the Mahabharata's has, quite naturally, extended to the world of politics. As I have mentioned, early in Dr Singh's tenure Yashwant Sinha, a long-standing critic of the PM, derogatorily called him Shikhandi, the man–woman character in the Mahabharata, a theme that was later taken up by some members of the Aam Aadmi Party. Knowing that Bheeshma, the Mahabharata's grand strategist and great warrior, would never raise his arrow against a woman, Arjuna hid behind Shikhandi while attacking Bheeshma. Was Yashwant Sinha implying that the Arjunas of the Congress were hiding behind a Shikhandi PM to battle the Bheeshmas of the BJP? Did he mean that Sonia and the Congress would have found it difficult to stitch an anti-BJP alliance without the protection offered by Dr Singh's personality? Or, was he disingenuously suggesting that he was not a real man and a real leader?

As UPA-2 began to unravel, another Mahabharata comparison came to suggest itself to some of Dr Singh's critics. They likened him to the blind king Dhritharashtra, unhappily presiding over a strife-torn kingdom. I never accepted this view of a man who had earned himself the slogan 'Singh is King'. Rather than call him blind, I would say that he sometimes chose to close his eyes to ensure the longevity of his coalition. He shied away from keeping himself briefed every day about the faults and foibles of his ministerial colleagues, something that monarchs have done from time immemorial. He averted his eyes from corruption.

To my mind, he was rather like a Bheeshma. The name Bheeshma, given to Devavrata, means 'the one who takes a terrible vow and fulfils it'. A good, wise and brave man but on the wrong side, defending a disreputable lot, Bheeshma was a tragic hero rather than an object of pity. Bheeshma was also the king who had to lie on a bed of arrows— condemned to an unsure mandate, an uncomfortable existence and an inelegant exit.

For all his wisdom and strategic brilliance, and despite the enormous respect he commanded from both sides of a family at war, Bheeshma faced his most embarrassing moment when the hapless Draupadi asked him why he could not protect her when she was being disrobed. She mocks Bheeshma for seeking refuge in the finer points of dharma.

An angry and troubled Bheeshma remains silent. Dr Singh's silences in UPA-2, for which the media mocked him, made me wonder whether he too was consumed by impotent rage like Bheeshma.

Like Greek epics and Shakespearean plays, Indian epics too have no untainted heroes. Leave alone mortals, even the gods have flaws; Lord Rama's treatment of Sita raises a question that has never gone away. There are questions that will probably haunt Dr Singh too, most of all: why did he not quit when he realized he had lost all vestiges of control over his own government? If his failure to do so arose from loyalty to the Congress or a promise to Sonia, it was misplaced—and unrewarded—loyalty. Except it enabled him to remain in office, even if not in power. His apparent commitment to ensuring Rahul's succession, perpetuating the Congress party's control by one family, was even more misplaced. That was Bheeshma's failure too: he should have put his foot down on the Kaurava succession. Moreover, promising loyalty to hereditary succession is a monarchical attribute, not a democratic one. That was Dr Singh's fatal error of judgement.

Acknowledgements

This book would not have been written but for the persistent encouragement of Chiki Sarkar and Kamini Mahadevan. Their former colleague Ranjana Sengupta was, in fact, the first to seek to persuade me to write the book. Once I began writing, several friends encouraged me to be honest in my rendering and I thank them for the courage they gave me. This final version is the product of the editorial guidance and help I received from Chiki, Kamini and two eagle-eyed and critical reviewers of earlier drafts, namely my father, B.P.R. Vithal, and my editor, Anjali Puri.

My gratitude is also due to several friends in the media who, over the years, urged me to write this book and helped me jog my memory about events and issues.

Thanks are due to my friend Shirish Kumar for the English translation of Muzaffar Razmi's Urdu couplet and to former colleagues in government who helped me get some of my facts right.

I owe a debt of gratitude to John Chipman at the International Institute for Strategic Studies for allowing me to take time off from my institutional responsibilities to write this book and to K.C. Sivaramakrishnan and Pratap Bhanu Mehta for their hospitality at the Centre for Policy Research.

Finally, and most importantly, thank you Rama and Tanvika for putting up with me, and the odd hours I kept during the weeks I stayed home to write this book. Hopefully that time I spent at home has made up for all the time they said they missed not having me around during my PMO days. Needless to add, I am grateful to Dr Manmohan Singh for giving me the opportunity to work for him and with him.

Index